TILLIE LEWIS

The Tomato Queen

KYLE ELIZABETH WOOD

ISBN: 153737267X
ISBN 13: 9781537372679
Library of Congress Control Number: 2016914652
CreateSpace Independent Publishing Platform
North Charleston, South Carolina

TILLIE LEWIS

With love to:

Richard Glass Williams
My late husband, father of my daughters, the man whose philosophy
included the sage advice for most things in life: "Say more *yes!*"
Tillie was all your wonderful idea; thank you.

Dr. Clair "Doc" Weast
Your charming arm-twisting, stories, and the creation
of the Tasti-Diet made this tale possible.
Neither Tillie Lewis nor I could have done
this without you.

Wayne Charles Wood
My husband, the enormously talented artist whose
love, patience, and belief in me made this book,
and all else, worth doing right.
You make my life a joyful adventure.

VOLUME XXIII   JOLIET, ILLINOIS, U.S.A., APRIL, 1952   NUMBER ONE

PACKOMATIC SALUTES TILLIE WEISBERG LEWIS

OUTSTANDING BUSINESSWOMAN OF THE NATION FOR 1951

as Selected by the Women Newspaper Editors of America

From a grocery clerk to the president of one of the "big five" canning concerns of the world, a business that has an annual value of more than $20,000,000 — that is the success story of Tillie Weisberg Lewis, president of Flotill Products and hailed as queen of the pear-shaped tomato.

Tribute was paid to Mrs. Lewis and she was crowned "The Tomato Queen of the World" by Lieutenant Governor Goodwin J. Knight at a testimonial dinner given in her honor by the City of Stockton, California, on March 3. Seldom is a woman honored by a whole city and seldom does a woman head up a $20,000,000-a-year business.

Guests of honor at the testimonial dinner were editors, presidents of many large factories, presidents and managers of banks. presidents of colleges, judges of Superior courts, QMC colonels and commanders, state senators, mayors, assemblymen, school superintendents, chamber of commerce executives, district attorneys, suppliers, friends and neighbors — more than nine hundred of them.

Tillie started her career at the age of fifteen, in Brooklyn, New York, where she worked for a wholesale grocer who imported the pear-shaped Italian toma-

Tillie Lewis, founder and president of Flotill Products, Inc., Stockton, California, was honored on March 3 at a testimonial dinner given by the City of Stockton and attended by almost a thousand of her Stockton friends and neighbors. Above, she is being congratulated by Lieutenant Governor Goodwin J. Knight, of California, who crowned her "Tomato Queen of the World."

Queen of the World

CONTENTS

INTRODUCTION

She didn't sew ladies' hats or whip up facial creams or cosmetics. She didn't bake cookies or candies, enter beauty contests, or march for women's rights. She was a dynamo who always knew she had all the rights she needed. Other people just needed to kindly get out of her way.

The Tomato Queen was America's first female captain of industry. With neither family money nor a wealthy husband, she created a megafortune in the "no girls allowed" business world. She was a successful, savvy leader of men who personally developed and manufactured many products. Her contributions to the economy of California—in terms of jobs and innovations in the food industry, human and women's rights, racial and religious tolerance, combatting global hunger, and union/management advancement in the workplace—were unprecedented.

Folks had strong opinions about Tillie Lewis. She was dynamic and demanding, self-centered and generous. She was either loved or loathed; there was little middle ground. She was a feminine force to be reckoned with as she built a food-industry empire in the midst of the Great Depression with tenacity, passion, and focus—a feat that she deemed time and again to be simple common sense.

Tillie had more awards and titles than a heavyweight boxing champ. She was known to the world as the Tomato Queen, the Duchess of Diet, the First Lady of Larder, and Tillie of the Valley to name but a few.

Innovation in products, processes, and policies were second nature to the fiery little redhead. Man, woman, black, white, Christian, or Jew—all were offered opportunities to grow right along with her company. Tillie Lewis put her employees first, and they returned the favor. Most worshipped her.

In 1935, her cannery was one of the places that folk like those from *The Grapes of Wrath* were desperate to reach. Imagine their surprise when they limped into California's agricultural land on foot, or on fumes, and found that "the boss" of this agricultural empire was a welcoming and beautiful young Jewish divorcée straight out of Brooklyn, clad in a silk dress and high-heeled peep-toe shoes.

The journey of Tillie Lewis sets sail through historical events, times, and places as a participant upon several great stages. She stood with the superfamous and with humble workers of the fields alike. To Tillie, each person was as rich in value as the next.

She was arrested by law enforcement for allegedly spying on behalf of Fascist dictator Mussolini. She was accused and investigated by the FBI, under the direction of J. Edgar Hoover at the time, for being a "debaucher of youth" in one incident and for international piracy during another. The deepest cut of all was when she was sued as a war profiteer during World War II.

Between arrests and accusations, she was rewarded by the United States for her patriotism, ideas, and innovations in products. These ideas expanded from canned food to medicine, politics, and combatting world hunger.

The story of Tillie Lewis is based upon solid research and historical "best guesses" in a few instances. There are gaps of time in her story, such as during the Ziegfeld Follies chapters. The Ziegfeld photography studio, White Studios, did not snap pictures of just anybody in 1911, yet Tillie kept her photo as a memento of a more risqué past than she was willing to share with the public. From 1911–1914, plausible events have been compiled based on hints from her family, hard artifacts, and the research of other people from the same time period. We have no idea what Miss Tillie was actually doing during these years. The evidence she left behind suggests that this theory of events is more than likely but less than definite.

Due to the inhospitable, unaccepting, and judgmental times toward her gender and faith during her lifetime (1896–1977), Tillie could not tell the whole truth of her beginnings from Brooklyn tenement poverty to fabulous prosperity. A woman's moral reputation was a far more important commodity then than it is today. She should not be judged in hindsight for choosing to dodge insurmountable prejudice with a few bent truths. She should be applauded for having the courage to swim against the tsunami of her time.

Many historical sources were from people who were eighty-plus years old with memories that might have been fragile. The truth is nigh on impossible to ascertain in the best of circumstances, but these tales were recalled by people who'd had no contact with one another in many years, yet they shared the same vision of this extraordinary woman who had inspired them so deeply.

The author was invited into their homes and into their memories. They themselves were examples of pluck and determination. Some were inventors, scientists, or genuine heroes—or regular, lovely middle-class folks—of varied races and faiths who were lifted into their happy positions by Tillie Lewis. They were all loyal, hardworking Americans who personified the title of the "Greatest Generation."

A few subjects' relatives refused to allow their stories to be told. Some names have been deleted and a few names have been changed to appease. The story of Tillie Lewis is in no way diminished by these revisions. The fact that some people still vehemently despise her nearly forty years after her death demonstrates the power that Tillie Lewis held. For good or naught, nary a soul who personally knew her was indifferent to the late, great Tillie Lewis.

Chapter 1

FANNY BRICE, ZIEGFELD, THE DEL GAIZOS, AND TOMATOES

A half-truth is a whole lie—Yiddish proverb

Fanny Brice had a dirty mouth. There were no two ways about that.[i] On a brief respite from her troubles, Tillie was doing her best to enjoy the sunshine and to ignore her hostess's more uncouth antics. Fanny knew that extreme vulgarity would get Tillie's goat eventually. While Tillie could swear with the best of them, she wasn't one for gratuitous profanity.

The ladies had been friendly acquaintances for more than twenty years. They met while performing at the Ziegfeld Follies in 1911. In those days, Fanny Brice was a meteoric new star and Tillie just a teenaged temporary bit of Ziegfeld fluff. Twenty-seven years later, Fanny was one of the highest-paid comediennes in show business, while Tillie was the first female industrialist in America.

Fanny was hamming it up in a comedic rendition of the tango around the pool with her perennial houseguest, the professional dancer/choreographer of stage and screen, Harry Pilcer. Tillie's seventeen-year-old nephew, Albert, was leaning his bony elbows on the pool edge watching the famous pair dance. Albert dangled his gangly body in the water while enjoying the impromptu routine.

Fanny teased young Albert, "Howz about a dirty ditty, kid?" This sat Tillie straight up in the chaise lounge, salad bowl–size Panama hat fluttering to the decking and pouty lips forming an objection as Fanny began belting out,

> Lovie Joe, that ever lovin' man
> From 'way home in Birmingham
> He can do some lovin' an' some lovin' sho'
> An when he starts to love me I jes' hollers "Mo"!
> —"Lovie Joe," from the 1910 Ziegfeld Follies[ii]

To Albert's delight, Fanny's encore featured a string of obscenities that left him breathless from laughter and left Tillie horrified. When Tillie shushed Fanny "because of the boy," Fanny just got louder and dirtier. Albert was thrilled to have won a private performance from Fanny Brice and Harry Pilcer.[iii]

It was early November 1937. The women were commiserating over their business and men problems. Fanny's "rat" of a husband, Billy Rose, had dumped her for the newest movie mermaid[iv] starring in Billy's latest film, *Aquacade*. The girl wasn't all that pretty, but she was young and an Olympic swimmer. As far as Fanny was concerned, Billy Rose was all wet, too, and their marriage had definitely dried up.

Tillie's man, Florindo Del Gaizo, had died not three months before. Florindo was Tillie's first love, business partner, and personal financier. Tillie was in a true state of loss. To add to her woes, from Florindo's funeral on, Tillie's friendly moneylenders were no longer friendly.

Tillie hailed from New York's deplorable tenement poverty at a time when most women were without voice and without choice. Tillie refused to surrender to fate. She elected to defy virtually all common dictates of decorum and society and do as she darn well pleased. Fanny, however, was a Jew born into a fair- to upper-middlin' Irish neighborhood in New York and was always pretty free to do whatever she chose to do. Tillie's sickly mother died young. Fanny's mother was the hearty breadwinner of the family: a real go-getter.[v]

Compared to Tillie's situation, Fanny began life downright rich. Tillie's people were strict Orthodox Jews, while Fanny's were strictly not very religious, "Jewishly" speaking.

Both women shared passions for success, home decorating, high-end fashion, and plastic surgery.[1]

Fanny was a woman who boldly said whatever was on her mind, while Tillie simply *did* whatever was on hers. Fanny enjoyed cheating at cards, while Tillie didn't mind cheating with married men.

Fanny was forty-six and happy to admit her age. Her showbiz career had one foot in the movies with MGM[2] making a few "yawners," but she was about to blast off via the national radio waves from Hollywood with her beloved character, Baby Snooks.[vi]

Tillie rarely told the same age twice. She didn't forget her age; she simply dismissed it. To Tillie, aging was an idea she refused to accept. She knew how to adjust her birth year to suit the occasion and did so with regularity.

Fanny was renting the Beverly Hills estate of Countess Dorothy di Frasso, complete with the aforementioned pool, the countess's furnishings and fine art, and even her silver place settings.[vii] The property epitomized all that meant splendor in Hollywood in 1930.

The Countess di Frasso, infamous for her madcap adventures, was a woman of diverse taste in both men and mansions. It was she who nurtured, then introduced, the young Gary Cooper to all the right people at her other mansion in Italy, the "Villa Madama,"[3] designed by the Renaissance painter and architect Raphael for the Medici Pope Clement VIII in 1518. Compared to these nouveau-riche Hollywood types, the countess had serious money. After the romance with "Coop" ended, the countess dried her tears on the shoulders of "Murder, Incorporated"[4] gangster Bugsy Siegel.[viii] The rich and famous often found having an infamous lover or two to be all the rage.

In any event, Fanny had dibs on the Hollywood "House d'Countess" until her own house in swanky Holmby Hills was completed. Fanny drolly dubbed her mansion "Pelican Park."

---

1   Fanny Brice had a nose job that led columnist Dorothy Parker to quip, "She cut off her nose to spite her race." Tillie had facial peels and lifts throughout her life to remain youthful.

2   The Metro-Goldwyn-Mayer movie studios.

3   The "Villa Madama" was purchased from the countess in 1941 by Benito Mussolini as his personal residence.

4   Infamously cruel arm of organized crime.

Tillie was the first female industrialist—boss and owner—in a field comprised of only men. With Del Gaizo dead, she was financially on her own for the first time in her life. In order to obtain funding for the future, because she was a woman, her Ziegfeld past had to get lost, buried, finished, -kaput.

Hoping the notoriously honest Fanny Brice could help alleviate her dilemma with a well-turned lie was a foolish idea. Fanny was an entertainer. Fanny Brice told folks who didn't like what she was selling "to drop every part of dead," and she'd get a laugh. Fanny wasn't buying the need for Tillie's biographical revisions. Fanny Brice could not tolerate a phony. Comic stars didn't live in the real world, where decorum was essential.

Tillie's tomato-canning business required a spin on Tillie's past. She was going to have to peddle backward on that past to save her future. Tillie needed to invent a more "acceptable" history that contained smidgens of the truth; half- or three-quarter truths would be nice. Tillie never wanted to tell a whole lie. Nonetheless, she couldn't admit that she'd spent her teen years dressed in nothing but feathers and a smile, or that she'd been gallivanting around the world with a married man while her own husband, Louis Weisberg, stocked the shelves in New York alongside her brother-in-law and her sister, Beatrice.

Tillie knew that to obtain the loans to save her company, Flotill, "phony" would have to become her new religion. This was 1937, and bankers didn't loan small fortunes to women with tarnished pasts. Heck, they didn't loan twenty dollars to most women, period. If she had been a man, people would have laughed, slapped her on the back, winked, and bought her a beer.

Fanny Brice and the other show-biz folk cracked jokes and sang songs, and—ta-da—won applause and admiration. Tillie developed a like-dislike attitude toward entertainers. She didn't really admire them. Tillie admired people who, like herself, came from nothing and forced the world to bend by labor, sweat, not ever giving up, and serious willpower.

She believed show-biz fortunes were won by luck, not hard work. Entertainers provided the public a few moments of distraction. Entertainment was a luxury. The public, the regular Janes and Joes, often had to do without luxuries to put food on the table: the very food Tillie intended to continue providing for them.

Tillie's company, Flotill, canned Italian tomato products using the specialty pear-shaped variety of tomato she'd personally introduced to the United States from Naples, Italy. Tillie wanted not only to continue in business but to grow into an agricultural superpower. With her partner dead, now she had to find the capital to do it.

The grim reaper had come in August and taken her partner. She had no intention of sitting back and letting her business die as well, even if it meant she was going to have to tell a whopper of a fib (or two). The work—and Flotill Products itself—was no fib. Needing the money was a desperate truth.

This snippet of a holiday allowed Tillie time to think. She could see and hear Fanny goosing up her funny-girl routines to prepare for her new radio career, and Fanny was in rare form. Tillie would have to do her own version of the same thing.

Tillie righted herself from her lounging position, called Albert out of the pool, and said that she was going back to work: back to Stockton to rally her financial clout. Tillie Weisberg determined that nonbusiness-related frivolity was time that she could not afford. Time-consuming friendships with Fanny Brice and everyone else were the first casualties of Tillie's climb to gain a reputation as a woman who was serious about success.[ix]

TILLIE

Women have a future in big business, but it takes a lot of courage, fortitude, and stick-to-it-iveness—Tillie Lewis

When she officially moved to Stockton, California in 1934, she did so as the first female captain of industry in the United States. Stockton's leaders saw her as an ineffectual infant in a business meant only for strong men. They expected her to go broke, quickly, and the sooner the better. The farmers, bankers, and businessmen were certain the dumb broad was building a flimsy tomato-packing shed that would fail before the end of the first season, sending the little lady back to wherever she'd come from. For goodness sake, she was a beautiful woman who dressed like a movie star: a Brooklynite, a divorcée, a Jew. From farmers to society ladies, the Stocktonian elite despised her on sight.[x]

These were times when women were rarely in charge of their own household budgets, yet Tillie was forging a creative, forward-thinking, buy-and-sell-only-the-best-product business model that she'd learned in Italy from the food and finance empire of the powerful but all-male Del Gaizo family. She added her own pyramidal system of leadership that allowed the (normally misogynistic) men who worked for her to maintain their dignity without sacrificing her absolute, perfectly manicured, and iron-fisted control over every aspect of her empire.

This was the Depression, a time when John Steinbeck was writing *The Grapes of Wrath* about the suffering of poor families (including whites) who were making their last-gasp effort toward survival to make it to the agricultural fields and canneries of California.

Many companies applied Jim Crow laws[5] at this time: the discriminatory laws refusing Mexicans, blacks, Asians, and Oakies into their workforces. In stark contrast, Tillie hired people based completely upon loyalty and merit, without bias toward anything other than their ability and character. Giving good, hardworking folks a leg up and not a handout began Tillie's unique managerial methodology that would create lifelong support from her employees and their families. Tillie understood discrimination: no matter her accolades, riches, or success, the cream of the crop in Stockton would always consider her the "Jew broad."

THE POMODORO

Tillie's agri-empire began rather humbly. She planted a very special tomato in America: a thing that men of science—learned botanists—said could not be done.

It was the pear-shaped San Marzano tomato from Naples. Rich, meaty, tangy—it was a solid fruit that made thick, red sauces for the pastas so loved by Italians. Little, round New World tomatoes made the former Romans want to weep, since, to their palates, measly American tomatoes were all water and

---

5 Jim Crow–related racial, religious, economic, and gender discrimination was not just a Southern problem: discrimination was rampant across the country.

no flavor. Americans said "tomato"; Italians said "pomodoro"[6]—San Marzano pomodoro, to be precise. Tillie smugly corrected people who called her special import the "pomodoro tomato" with, "I'm afraid you just said the tomato-tomato, dear."

THE DEL GAIZOS

Vincenzo Del Gaizo was as restless as Mount Vesuvius, the volcano that defined his world. While his land holdings held him to Naples, more than four million other Italians emigrated between 1880 and 1924. Most headed to America. Italian emigration was fueled by dire poverty. Life in Southern Italy, including the islands of Sicily and Sardinia, offered landless peasants hardship, exploitation, and violence during the struggles for Italian independence.[xi]

Difficulties and distance aside, Italians in America were tied to the rich earth, the fire of the great volcano. Thousands of Italian migrants left their mother Italy for the promise of a better, richer life in foreign lands.

In their letters home, their complaints were often of missing the taste of Italia, with nothing but bland canned food on the shelves of the local American grocery markets. Vincenzo Del Gaizo got their message. He understood that this fertile soil of Vesuvius fed homesickness along with bellies. Del Gaizo's remedy for his compatriots' taste buds, and his own pocketbook, was to can the rich fruits and vegetables of Naples with recipes from his Italian mother's kitchen and ship them to America.

By 1880, Vincenzo Del Gaizo had built a company in Naples with a customer base in New York who were starving for more Del Gaizo products. The demand was greater than he could produce and ship to them. He decided to meet that hunger for Del Gaizo products through expansion and excellence: quality in quantity. His mama would be proud.

Both a visionary and a perfectionist, Vincenzo structured his success on a forward-thinking and creative business model in which he would buy and sell only the best products.[7]

---

6 *Pomodoro* is the Italian word for tomato.

7 His son would one day teach this number one key to success to Tillie Weisberg of America.

Vincenzo traveled the world buying the best canning equipment available, along with the latest techniques, to improve and increase production. Twenty years later, as the 1900s rolled in, the Del Gaizo family celebrated both a new century and the opening of their state-of-the-art canning factory. It was the first such company in Naples. Vincenzo was driven to do more, to grow bigger. He left his wife and five sons behind to run the Naples operation while he opened an office in New York to further expand and serve the North American market, including in Canada.

Vincenzo strove to infect his sons with his love affair, his passion, for the rich fruits of Naples that had lifted his family from penury to prosperity. Wealth spoiled the elder sons, who found the temptations of the nuevo-riche difficult to resist, especially the swashbuckling ladies' man, Florindo.

Florindo married young and well at the age of twenty-seven. His wife was a faithful woman, a good Catholic who was ripe for motherhood. Florindo Del Gaizo loved his family, but it was pleasure, not business, that inflamed his passion. He lived for yachting, racing, fencing, gambling, fine wine, and finer women. Mama mia, what to do about Florindo?

Vincenzo's youngest, his eighteen-year-old son, Luigi, would prove to be capable of managing the Naples canneries and associated businesses. Luigi was the most astute of his sons, emulating—then besting—his father's vision. While his father was busy conquering Canada and the United States for the Del Gaizo company, Luigi was steadfast at the helm of Del Gaizo in Italy.

In 1905, while at his main office at 141 Broadway in Manhattan, Vincenzo Del Gaizo suddenly died. He was sixty-one years old. He had invested a large portion of Del Gaizo capital in the United States.

He bequeathed more than material wealth to his sons: he left his blueprint for the future. Vincenzo's vision included a simple but powerful business plan.

* Listen to the market and to trends. What do people *say* they want, versus what are they *actually* buying? Take heed, because filling this need is true opportunity.

* Constantly focus on one central idea, and expand your business to fit that path. For the Del Gaizos, the focus was food. Everyone had to eat.
* Money and real estate were central to making the whole business grow. Having control in the banking system and owning property were key.

Before his death, Vincenzo began investing in real estate, into which Luigi was expanding under his father's supervision. Luigi capitalized on the family name, and success, with the banks of Italy, using bank money to buy more land. Luigi thrived on the wisdom that his father extolled and added a few more tenets toward triumph.

* Having all your eggs in one basket is risky, but having a monopoly on food, funds, and land is like owning the farm: all the poultry and every basket. You are going to sell a lot of eggs and be able to carry the money to the bank in those baskets.
* Use bank loans to invest in the highest quality, most technologically advanced equipment so that you can then sell superior products. This should expand your customer base.
* Own the real property, and no landlord can take it from you. You have control.
* Make all decisions based on sound personal research and investigation.
* Never outright gamble.[8]

With his father dead, Luigi Del Gaizo, at twenty-three years of age, was now the undisputed head of the family and the business. To avoid losing the stronghold of business in America, Luigi ordered his big brother, Florindo, to take over their father's US market.

In an attempt to curtail Florindo's philandering and to keep Florindo's mind on this important American market, Luigi sent Florindo's wife, Elvira, and his two young children along with him to New York to their late father's office at 141 Broadway. The idea was twofold: halt the womanizing and

---

8 These are Tillie's keys to success that she learned from the Del Gaizo family.

establish a Del Gaizo family home in New York and perhaps even produce a few American-citizen Del Gaizos in the process.[xii]

Elvira didn't care for New York. She loved the Del Gaizo villa[9] more than any other place on earth. Elvira was seldom in America for long periods of time, which allowed her to save face during those times when Florindo simply didn't come home. Florindo was well known, and probably admired, for his prowess with the ladies, performed with full Italian machismo. Elvira was comforted by the knowledge that her husband might stray from her bed but never from his church. Florindo wasn't about to leave their marriage and spend eternity in hell. His extramarital flings had always been a part of her life: *nussun problema* (no worries) that she would ignore. Florindo always returned with his rakish smile and a gift to make amends, Italian style.

Florindo imported Del Gaizo products into New York and into the new Chicago office, as he was instructed. He kept Elvira happy by fathering five more children with her, all the while courting the ladies of the Broadway stage and the Ziegfeld Follies, until one fifteen-year-old Ziegfeld chorus girl, Miss Tillie Ehrlich, stole his heart.

Fifteen-year-old Tillie posing for the Ziegfeld Follies in 1911 for White Studios, wearing a coquettish smile and more makeup than clothing.

---

9 Via Tasso 256, Napoli (Naples), Italy, 80122.

ZIEGFELD

A pretty face is the best resume—Fanny Brice

Florenz "Flo" Ziegfeld's talents lay in selecting lovely young women and displaying their best assets advantageously on stage. Tillie Ehrlich was a Germanic-looking girl with enormous eyes that glistened with adventurous luminescence. Ziegfeld capitalized on those eyes.

Ziegfeld transformed the Jewish teen from Brooklyn bumpkin into a Follies version of the smoky-eyed French actress and sensual sensation named Polaire.[10] To complete the look, Ziegfeld bobbed Tillie's Victorian-style long hair to chin length and disheveled it to further emulate the Parisian actress's avant-garde style. Tillie was nearly naked in a lacy chemise and a long, single-strand pearl necklace, wearing more makeup than clothing. The teenaged Tillie's peeking eyes twinkled up from under wavy, bobbed bangs with a come-hither, invitational smile. This short bob was all the rage in Paris.[xiii] Ziegfeld stressed class, not trash. His audiences were high-rollers: people of style and means. A display of temptation was his goal. The girls were groomed to convey not lust but desire.[xiv] Adorable teenaged Tillie fit that standard.

Posing for the professional photographer of White Studios thrilled Tillie, even if she was standing in a room full of strangers in her underwear.[xv] While the camera lens briefly focused on Tillie's winsome gaze, Tillie was drinking in the details of her surroundings. Tillie first spied Fanny Brice during the photo shoot for the Follies. Only twenty, Fanny was one of the lead performers.

Fanny Brice was laden with silks, satins, and furs, and her long hair was brushed to gleaming. The White Studios photographers took their time with Miss Brice.[xvi] It was clear that being the star, the center of attention, was the place to be if you wanted to be fussed and fawned over. The distinction between the star treatment and the nobody-chorus girls' dismissal made a

---

10 Polaire was a French singer, actress, and dancer with a fourteen- to sixteen-inch cinched waistline who modeled for Henri Toulouse-Lautrec at least once. Polaire sang the French version of the song "Ta-ra-ra Boom-de-ay" (Henry J. Sayers, 1891).

lasting impression on Tillie Ehrlich. To be dripping in jewels, furs, and extravagant props was Tillie's goal. Henceforth, she would strive to make herself the glittering centerpiece whenever possible.

The Follies of 1911 opened on Broadway at the Jardin de Paris on June 26 of that year and ended on September 2. In addition to Fanny Brice, another highlight was the black American comedic sensation, Bert Williams. Tillie's encounters with Williams, and other artists of color, solidified the idea, to her sensibilities, that within every race there were hard-working, talented people in addition to bums. Being a decent person was all a matter of personal character, not skin color.

Tillie's tenure with the Follies was brief, likely only from 1911 to 1913. Nonetheless, she made the most of her time on stage as decorative fluff, enjoying the clothes, glamour, and attention heaped upon the Ziegfeld stable of beauties. She'd acquired the taste and freedom associated with women of the stage, and there was no going back.

Tillie Ehrlich was a bright, ambitious girl from a strict Jewish home who was throwing tradition out the tenement window like ticker tape during a parade. Tillie had the stuff to make a name for herself, just not on Broadway. Tillie had beauty and spunk but not much else as far as the theater was concerned. Tillie was well aware of her talents, but song and dance were not among them. She was smart, quick, and fiercely determined to avoid entrapment into a lifetime of servitude and poverty, no matter what. She enjoyed the attention of men. Like many of the other nonperforming showgirls, Tillie would accept the title of "gold digger" as long as it was for solid gold. Tillie was no floozy. Her hopes were to place at least a ring of that gold on the third finger of her left hand.

Encounters with "stagedoor Johnnies" were commonplace. They'd stalk a gal with roses, jewelry, and furs, often waiting for hours to win a moment with a chorine. Wealthy swells married some of the Follies girls and made proper upper-class wives and mothers out of them. These gents enticed Ziegfeld girls into stepping out of their knickers and straight into prestige as society ladies who would quickly forget, ignore, and deny their humble beginnings. Tillie was on the lookout for her Diamond Jim Brady,[11] her Prince Charming to bewitch, bejewel, and betroth her. With any luck, he'd also be Jewish.

At an after-party one night, the thirty-six-year-old Florindo Del Gaizo spied the fifteen-year-old Tillie Ehrlich.[12] Next to the other ladies, Tillie was more a cutie than a beauty, but "Flo" Del Gaizo liked younger girls who still had their innocence rather than seasoned eighteen- or nineteen-year-olds who had been around. The Follies drew girls who wanted nothing to do with their Victorian-corseted peers. Tillie was new, and she was bright. She had just entered the field and had not yet been picked over by various men. She was, to Florindo Del Gaizo, a sweet fruit still on the vine.

To Tillie, Florindo Del Gaizo stood out, even though he wore the same type of black tuxedo that all the other men wore. They looked like a colony of penguins.[xvii] There were brash men like Diamond Jim, who was flashy and fleshy, tucking hundred-dollar bills under everyone's dessert plates, wine glasses, and who knows where else. Florindo Del Gaizo posed in regal elegance. He looked and moved like royalty.

Florindo Del Gaizo was the king of Italian products in America and Canada. He had business cards and the Broadway office to prove it.[xviii] Italian newspaper ads in the Italian neighborhoods of major American cities proclaimed Florindo Del Gaizo as sole agent for the US and Canadian Italian customers who wanted the best foodstuffs from Naples. There was but one man to buy from in North America when you wanted Italian quality on your table. Tillie was smart. She was aware. She could see what the ladies who succeeded in snaring a ring had done versus the fools who were now drowning in gin and sin. Tillie spent every girlish moment she could going gaga over Del Gaizo. She focused her attention on the singular Del Gaizo and nary another penguin in the tuxedoed flock.

---

11 Diamond Jim Brady went from hotel bellhop to megamillionaire. Brady wore ten-karat-diamond buttons on his underwear and gave hundred-dollar bills to nearly everyone he knew. His habit of spreading his wealth in gems as gifts to Ziegfeld girls was what made his name synonymous with "generous to a fault."

12 There is no record of her name nor idea of what stage name she might have chosen. Tillie was in the land of taboo.

Due to her youth, she was certainly overlooking her strict upbringing at the moment, but she couldn't ignore it entirely. Her father's disapproval had to have been sitting heavily on her shoulders, shouting in her ear in Yiddish.

Many of the girls drank and smoke excessively and would vie for attention by every means possible.[xix] Tillie drew the line at one man and remained in control of her actions in public. Tillie had two sides, and one of them was quite prudish and proper. Self-destructive was never a term to describe Tillie Ehrlich. She expected her Flo Del Gaizo to leave his wife and marry her.

He didn't.

1900: Turn of the century for the Ehrlichs. Left to right: Beatrice, Jacob, and Rachel ("Rose"); four-year-old Myrtle ("Tillie") stands in front.

Chapter 2

BIRTH, DEATH, SPANISH FLU, AND MARRIAGE

Jacob and Rachel "Rose" Ehrlich married in Austria in 1887. In 1891, their eldest daughter, Beatrice, was born in Bobrka, now in Ukraine.

Intending to make a home for his wife and daughter, Jacob Ehrlich emigrated to New York in 1893, knowing full well that the streets there were paved in ghettos, not gold. Jacob had come too late to enjoy the easier transition to American life enjoyed by the German Jews, who had trickled into American society in smaller, less conspicuous numbers starting around 1859.[13]

Just after the American civil war, German Jews in the United States held fast to their core beliefs but relaxed their strict dietary laws and other customs, which led them to found the more palatable Reformed Judaism. This allowed them to blend into America's mainstream with relative ease. These German Jews had pride in themselves for their religious and cultural flexibility in regard to assimilation within American culture. They held Jewish newcomers in disdain for refusing to "go Yankee." These Reformed German Jews were the business owners and managers, while their more Orthodox brethren flooding into America from 1891 on would be their workers—their lower class.

Immigration manuals at the time promised opportunity through focused hard work:

---

13 Rabbi Morris Jacob Raphall became the first Jewish clergyman to deliver a prayer at the opening of a session of the House of Representatives in 1860.

Hold fast, this is necessary in America. Forget your past, your customs, and your ideal. Select a goal and pursue it with all your might. No matter what happens to you, hold on. You will experience a bad time, but sooner or later you will achieve your goal.[14]

Jacob didn't like America, but America was going to have to do. There was no place else to go. He'd saved every penny to purchase passage for his wife, Rachel (known as Rose), and their daughter, Beatrice, to join him as soon as possible. This required Jacob to forget about the luxury of a private room or even a bed at all. As did many others, he shared whatever spot was available on the floor as a place to sleep with bachelor men. It was common for men and women to have no bed to sleep on; they lay shoulder to shoulder with other bargain borders. The tenement owners cruelly packed every square inch with rent-paying bodies.

Jacob sewed night and day at a coat factory. Finally, he sent for his family to join him in 1895.

New York's ethnic diversity was color coded on district and street maps. Jacob Riis, author of *How the Other Half Lives*, stated that the "maps of 1890 showed more stripes than the skin of a zebra and more colors than the rainbow." Neighborhoods, streets, and most apartment buildings were regulated not only by race, religion, and income but also by regions of immigrants' mother countries. Jews from Galicia-Austria, Russia, Romania, Hungary, Poland, and Syria were separated into subghettos by housing, synagogues, and neighborhood stores. With the exception of the Syrian Jews, most spoke Yiddish and could communicate with one another, but the newcomers preferred the comfort and security of segregation.[xx]

The Ehrlichs lived with Galacian-Yiddish speaking Jews. They, like most of their neighbors, spoke no English. They depended upon their children if they needed any translation to be done. Jacob was a tailor, as were most of their neighbors. Rose sewed piecework from home and cared for Beatrice while she was expecting their new baby. To help with the cost of a roof with a bed, the family took in a single, male boarder.

---

14 Conlin, Joseph R. *The American Past: A Survey of American History*, 7th ed., vol. 2. Boston: Wadsworth/Cengage Learning, 2003, p. 490.

MYRTLE "TILLIE" EHRLICH

On July 13, 1896, during a massive heat wave coupled with a tuberculosis epidemic, "Tillie," whose birth name was Myrtle, was born. She was the first American-born child of Jacob and Rose Ehrlich. Tillie was born in the tenement room without the benefit of a hospital or a birth certificate. This lack of birth certificate would serve Tillie well throughout her life.

In the tenements, children lived in fear of abandonment by the outright desertion (or the death) of their parents. Street orphans, who often lived in gangs, were common playmates in Tillie's world, living in the shadows of the Lower East Side.

Tillie had no recollection of her mother as a healthy woman. Rose had contracted tuberculosis from the stale, airless environment of the tenements soon after Tillie's birth. The girls watched their mother being consumed from within, coughing up blood and wasting away.

Tillie was bright and observant. The abandoned street waifs told their somber stories. Tillie could see that her own mama had the same look of death that had landed the street urchins alone in the shadows of the tenements. Tillie's fragile, fading mother forced little Tillie to begin to build an emotional shell to protect herself from a world that might leave her to fend for herself, too.

In the early 1900s, the best tuberculosis cure centers were thought to be in the thermal springs of Czechoslovakia. The thirteen main and three hundred smaller spas served everyone from princes to paupers in separate, and decidedly segregated, levels of prestige and comfort.

With her two daughters, Beatrice (thirteen) and Tillie (eight) at her side, Rose voyaged to Czechoslovakia to pray for relief in the healing waters of the sulfur springs found there. Those prayers would not be answered.

Rose died early in the year 1904 and was buried in the Jewish cemetery of the Czechoslovakian spa town of Karlovy Vary, also known as Karlsbad. The motherless girls traveled in steerage home to their now-widowed father.

Upon their arrival in New York, the girls were greeted by their "new" mother. Jacob had married a thirty-year-old woman named Bilha on January

30, 1904. There would be no time for grieving their beloved mother. This perceived indifference to the death of her mother hardened Tillie. Bilha never liked either of the girls, and the feeling was more than mutual.

LIFE GOES ON

Another killer heat wave began in late June of 1905, raising the death rates in the tenements to record highs. Twenty-three thousand of New York's poorest died of a dual epidemic of tuberculosis and pneumonia. The broiling temperatures lasted until July 10 of that year, when a torrential cloudburst suddenly quenched the suffering but inconveniently flooded Lower Manhattan. The sudden deluge dropped the temperature thirteen degrees within a half hour. Terrifying lightning struck in Brooklyn and twice at Ellis Island, leaving two thousand immigrants first prostate from the heat and then abruptly fearing for their lives during the unprecedented storm.[xxi]

Yet life went on. Benjamin Ehrlich was born to Bilha and Jacob. Jacob now had the son he so wanted to carry on his name and masculine traditions. Beatrice and Tillie dearly loved their baby brother. The family nicknamed him Bernie.[xxii]

According to the 1910 census, ten households lived in the rented tenement building with the Ehrlichs, including six German street musicians. English and Italian were the primary languages spoken in buildings 214 through 216. Yiddish was the language of the Ehrlichs. Jacob was still a tailor at the coat factory. He could read and write in English, though he was not known to speak English, although being totally forthcoming to any government agency was contrary to the thinking of many emigrants, many of whom had escaped from countries bent upon displacing or dispatching them.

The census stated that Bilha (or Bessie) was illiterate in English. Thirteen-year-old Tillie was the only admitted English speaker in this Yiddish household. Also occupying the apartment was a Russian-Jewish boarder named Isaac Cohen, who also worked at the coat factory.[xxiii] Fifteen-year-old Beatrice was not mentioned. "Bea" was likely at work at the local kimono factory. Beatrice still lived there, as well, but since Isaac

Cohen was a divorced bachelor, to admit this might have appeared unseemly, though taking in lodgers to make ends meet was the norm in poor families. Tillie's nephew Arthur Heiser (discussed later in this book) later reflected,

> It must be clear that Jacob Ehrlich was no slouch. He made a living. He did not make a good living or a great living. His wife and children had a set of everyday clothes, a set of clothes for temple, a good pair of shoes, a roof over their heads, and two meals a day on the table. That was living. In the early 1900s, this was an honorable thing, since many families had much less.[xxiv]

Due to his deep religious convictions, Jacob Ehrlich was voted president of his temple, Odessa Hevra Schule, on McKibbon Street. In this important role, Jacob advised young Jewish men, including his son. Jacob taught with the good books and with the proverbs of his people to strengthen the spirit; some teachings were that to be a true Jewish man, one must:

> Find the discipline to never say "Poor me."
> Turn suffering into resilience and determination.
> How can I turn this misfortune into something of value?
> Get up on your feet every time you are knocked down.[xxv]

While these messages were not intended for her, since she was female, Tillie was an astute listener who clung to these words for strength and direction while enduring the poverty of affection within the Ehrlich home and throughout her lifetime.

BOOK LEARNING

Eastern District High School, located at 227 Marcy Avenue, served the Jewish immigrant children of the Williamsburg ghetto. The space was designed to seat two thousand students. The student body totaled close to three thousand.

Unnamed former students said that "the whole scene in Brooklyn was kids were poor, but they'd use their intellects like knives to cut their way to college." One Jewish kid in 1908 Brooklyn felt "revulsion against the low socio-economic and cultural level of their parents."[xxvi]

The Ehrlich girls' "general courses" consisted of physics, chemistry, advanced mathematics, and three foreign languages. The school focused on the development of strong spoken English skills, since most students spoke Yiddish at home; Beatrice and Tillie were no exception. [xxvii]

In 1853, only Massachusetts and New York had passed compulsory laws requiring all children ages eight through fourteen to attend school. All forty-eight states had finally adopted compulsory elementary school laws by 1918.[xxviii] The fact that Beatrice and Tillie regularly attended "normal school" and then attended Eastern District High for at least one year was a testament to their father's desire to see his daughters get a good academic start in life.

Beatrice recounted stories of what seemed to her to be sumptuous school lunches prepared by Bilha for their half-brother, while a thin, boiling broth, too hot to eat quickly, was offered to the girls. According to Bea's stories, Bilha sent the two girls off with either empty stomachs or scalded mouths, and punishment for repeated tardiness from unsympathetic teachers awaited them at school.[xxix] That aside, it would be two precious baby dolls—unexpected gifts from Jacob—that Bilha returned to the store before admonishing the girls for their selfishness by accepting them that would forever taint the feelings Bea and Tillie held for their "evil stepmother." [xxx]

In Bilha Ehrlich's defense, second cousin Jerry Hochheiser still remembers his aunt Bessie, Tanta Bilha, with fondness. On visits as a young child, he'd ask, "Tanta Bilha, can I have one of your special cookies and a glass of wine?" His mother would shriek, "Tanta, a little boy shouldn't have wine!" Tanta Bilha would then respond, "Sha, my wine is little more than grape juice." According to Hockheiser, Bessie was a "sweet and loving woman," and it was Tillie who shamed the family with her "frequent trips between the USA and Italy, while willingly accepting the amorous approaches of Florindo Del Gaizo."[xxxi] In many cultures, male offspring are valued, while girls are not. Boys may drink wine, and girls must mind their manners.

Tillie quit Eastern District High School during her first semester there. She claimed she went to work folding Japanese robes, earning a few dollars a week at a kimono factory near the phonograph shop where her father worked.[xxxii] The actual kimono folder, and seamstress, was probably Tillie's sister Beatrice. The evidence indicates that sweathouse labor was not for Tillie, ever.

Unhappy as her home life was, Tillie was born and raised in Brooklyn—one of the most exciting places on the planet, then and now—but in 1910, when Tillie was fourteen years old, the earth really did revolve around New York.

Everything exciting was happening in Brooklyn and Manhattan. The cities were joined by the Brooklyn Bridge and the Williamsburg Bridge and by subways, trolley cars, and ferries. Anyone could cheaply and easily get around.

The more likely scenario of events that would form the woman she later became was that a month shy of fifteen years old, Tillie auditioned on Broadway. She took the subway to the building at 1514–1516 Broadway (at Forty-Fourth Street), known as the Jardin de Paris, during a casting call. Other folks knew the place as the Ziegfeld Follies.

TILLIE'S FOLLIES

Tillie got the job. The *New York Times* proclaimed, "Mr. Ziegfeld has come close to outdoing himself. Of course, the show was mostly girls and glitter, music and rapid action, but the crowd liked it...Fanny Brice, Lillian Lorraine, Harry Watson, Bert Williams...there seemed almost too many of them. They got in one another's way...The 'Follies of 1911' contains no more plot than any other Follies, but it does seem to have more fun."[xxxiii] In the article "'Follies of 1912' Is a Beauty Show," the paper reported that "Flo Ziegfeld contributions will be chiefly recalled as a picker of feminine loveliness, some fifty-seven or more varieties of girls which are on exhibit."[xxxiv]

The real talent, the true performers, referred to the gals whose entire skill set was walking across the lavish stage dressed in the often-massive headpieces and flowing gowns as "clotheshorses." Tillie was a clotheshorse. She was sturdy enough to carry both the weight of the ensemble and the verbal slights by the dancers, singers, and comics. Heck, she was a cast member of a glamorous stage show. She was meeting people who were famous or no doubt would be famous soon. She was attending parties that the rich, renowned, and even royalty attended.

Her boss was Flo Ziegfeld. Flo had a wife and plenty of willing Follies girlfriends, plus a few to spare.

Florindo Del Gaizo was Tillie's "Flo." Del Gaizo had a wife and kids. Tillie was, at least as far as she knew, the only girlfriend.[15] He kept her dimpled knees deep in furs, pearls, and flattery while whispering love everlasting to her in Italian. He was sorry to tell her that, as a Catholic, he would never divorce his wife. His faith and his extended family in Naples would never allow a divorce. Going to hell via excommunication from the church was probably not as disturbing to Del Gaizo as going to the poorhouse, courtesy of excommunication from the family Del Gaizo. Tillie needed to understand that she would be the respected mistress, the second wife, and the love of his life. He would give her all the diamond rings she wanted, except the one that mattered.

With the clout of her wedding ring, Mrs. Elvira Del Gaizo suddenly summoned her husband home to Italy.

Home he went.

THE GREAT WAR: PROFIT AND HONOR TO SOME
Flo probably intended only a brief visit to Italy—to report directly to Luigi, his baby-brother boss, and to kiss the wife and kids while enjoying Naples for a respite from all that is New York—when Archduke Ferdinand of Austria and his wife were assassinated in Sarajevo, on June 28, 1914, and with that, war!

Within weeks, most nations of the world had taken sides. The major combatants were Germany and the Austrian-Hungarian Empire versus the Allies: the British Empire, Russia, and France. Italy was promised to Germany and

---

15 Florindo Del Gaizo was deeply in love with Tillie (and only Tillie) from their first meeting, according to her great-niece Barbara Heiser.

Austria, but Italy held back. The Italians eventually joined the Allies, as did Japan and the United States, late in the war.

As Napoleon Bonaparte said, "An army fights on its stomach."

This quote and truism astronomically increased the production, and profits, for Del Gaizo-Santarsiero's business. Hungry troops needed to eat, and canned goods were the safest, most expeditious way to feed them. The Del Gaizos became exponentially richer as a result of the First World War.

Germany surrendered symbolically on the eleventh hour of the eleventh day of the eleventh month of 1918. In the four-plus years of battle (from June 28, 1914 to November 11, 1918), seventeen million people had lost their lives, and twenty million had been wounded.[16]

Italy knighted Luigi Del Gaizo for transforming a small canning company into one of the major industries in the country. The Del Gaizo firm fed the Allied troops throughout the war. This won Luigi Del Gaizo, and the Del Gaizo Company, the economic weight and social prestige to help revive the Bank of Southern Italy.[xxxv] The major winners in the war seemed to be the merchants.

The Del Gaizos, including Florindo, were now rich beyond their dreams and were connected intimately to both the Italian government and the Italian banks.

IMPATIENTLY WAITING

The romance of Tillie and Florindo was on hold for the duration of the war. The lovers wrote a lot of letters.[17] They stayed in touch romantically as well as on a business level. Tillie was bored and lonely. Del Gaizo suggested that she hone her skills in the Italian and French languages and take accounting classes to keep busy and to improve herself.

---

16 The Treaty of Versailles was signed on June 28, 1919, in the Palace of Versailles, officially ending the Great War.

17 Tillie's family stated that they threw away Tillie's huge collection of love letters after she passed away.

Living in Brooklyn, attending tenement schools with Irish-accented teachers, then going home to a Yiddish-speaking family made Tillie's accent about as Lower East Side/Brooklyn as a gal can get.

Since Tillie shared a nearly identical philosophy of self-improvement that Dale Carnegie was teaching at the local YMCA just down the street from Tillie's place in Brooklyn, it is highly likely that Tillie at least obtained a copy of his 1913 publication *Public Speaking and Influencing Men in Business*.

Influencing men in business and treating customers and employees like the most important people in the room were some of most important things Tillie did on her way to making her own fortune. Carnegie's book was, and is, a no-frills, to-the-point primer that combines "public speaking, salesman-ship, human relationships, personality development, applied psychology,"[xxxvi] elocution, voice lessons, correct word usage, and pronunciation, thus enhancing memory and much more.[18] Tillie Ehrlich used, at least, a Carnegie-type system to lose her Brooklyn-Yiddish accent completely.

TO BEA OR NOT TO BEA

Tillie's big sister, Beatrice, was a traditional Jewish girl with few aspirations to become anything more than a good wife and mother. Needing a trade until she could find a husband, Bea learned to sew from her father. In 1909, she created a cape for $1.25, earning a profit of eighty-seven cents. She was overjoyed about her good fortune.

By 1911, while her little sister was prancing about at Ziegfeld's in fashionable ladies' undergarments, Beatrice had been stitching those unmentionables for more than two years in a factory, twelve hours a day, six days a week. Bea earned four cents per hour, three dollars per week, and contributed most of those wages to her father.

Bea's only splurging was on books and music. She traveled alone to the Metropolitan Opera House to revel in the classics. She could only afford standing-room-only tickets with her fifty-cent limit for the ticket plus a

---

18 Dale Carnegie's book was everything Tillie would have needed to appear highly educated and to lose her Brooklyn accent.

program. She collected stacks of programs as reminders of the sweet sounds that seemed to come from heaven above.

When Bea turned twenty-one, the Bloomingdales department store offered an upright piano, with delivery, on credit to Beatrice for five dollars a month: a total of $250. The piano didn't take up much precious space thus was approved by her father. But her stepmother could think of better ways for Bea to spend her money rather than making noise. Bilha forbade Bea from wasting the gas lamps on lighting so that she could practice.[19][xxxvii] This was the final straw. Bea had to get out of this house.

Twenty-two-year-old Beatrice Ehrlich soon met a young and eligible grocery store manager named Samuel Hochheiser, who was twenty-three. After a respectable courtship, they married on February 8, 1914, at the Odessa Hevra Schule. The reception was held at the Capitol Hall on Manhattan Avenue in Manhattan. The party ended at two in the morning.[xxxviii] Tillie was miserable.

Tillie didn't want to lose Beatrice. Yes, there was Benjamin, her darling half-brother, but Tillie knew she would now be the only girl—the only target for the wrath of Bilha at the house. Please, war, be over, she prayed, and send Florindo Del Gaizo soon.

LIBERALLY THINKING

Everyone was witness to the suffragettes occasionally marching the grand avenues, carrying banners and passing out leaflets calling for freedom from the tyranny of "wifery."

Women, as a rule, loved their husbands and children. And many wished to have a vote in matters from the bedroom to the boardroom and from the apartment house to the White House—just not enough to make a fuss about it. Most women were comfortable rocking the cradle, not the boat.

Female-created business magazines were in their fledgling stages at this time, but they were available. Women writing for women was simply amazing. Ladies, with and without husbands, were publishing near blasphemy: women did not need to make marriage and motherhood their chief goals in life. It was

---

19 Accounts from several Heiser family members.

a whole new idea, and it was in writing. Helen Ruttenber wrote in *Business Woman's Magazine* (December 1914, volume 1, number 3) in "She That Hath a Trade":

> Should not all women be business women? That is, should not all women prepare themselves against the exigencies of a future which may make self-support necessary? Matrimony as a career is now a thing of the past…"Preparation" sounds the keynote of activity for the girl of to-day who is the woman of to-morrow…If [a woman] does not marry and she is prepared she is self-supporting [and] had the satisfaction of knowing she is a "live wire" and is allied with the real issues of the day…Benjamin Franklin's axiom now applies to both sexes, he that hath a trade hath an estate and he that hath a calling hath an office of profit and honor.

Tillie Ehrlich was every inch her family's "live wire."

UNTIL DEATH US DO PART (OR SOMETHING BETTER COMES ALONG)
Tillie attended schools at night while working at her brother-in-law's little neighborhood store during the day. New York University's School of Commerce offered business training to the sons and daughters of immigrants. Tillie reveled in the opportunity to learn practical subjects like business math, accounting, and the foreign languages that were spoken by the actual clientele.

Tillie later told the public, time and again, "I married at fifteen, a much older man, and worked in my husband's grocery store until I found that amazing can of pear-shaped tomatoes." We know this is not so. Tillie was eighteen years old now, not fifteen. Her grocery-store career began when she was working for her brother-in-law, not her husband. As Arthur Heiser later recalled,

> She had a photographic memory. She never forgot a face, a name, or a number. Book keeping, inventory control, and payroll came easily

to her. She picked up languages just as easily. The customers were our neighbors, who spoke mostly Yiddish, or Italian, with English sprinkled in. Tillie was fluent reading, writing, and speaking in all three languages, which set the store apart from the other mom-and-pops, since the successful little shops were social-gathering gossip joints as much as a place to buy eggs and bread.[xxxix]

Sam added a partner named Louis Weisberg. The store was doing fine for a little mom-and-pop joint.

The war dragged on.

Did the love letters stop coming from Italy? Did Florindo Del Gaizo lose interest in Tillie? Was Tillie bored? Did Tillie just want to get out from under Bilha's roof by any means necessary?

What occurred between the time Tillie met Del Gaizo and his departure early in 1914, before the Great War broke out?

Tillie, clearly embarrassed by her Ziegfeld-era teenaged behavior, ignored this period of her life, from 1911 to 1914, leaving only the documented friendships with Fanny Brice, Harry Pilcer, Eddie Cantor, Jimmy Durante, Milton Berle, the Marx Brothers, and numerous other stars of Ziegfeld and early Hollywood from the time period—along with the White Studios photograph of teen Tillie clad only in her scanties—as evidence.

It is unknown what events led up to Louis Weisberg and Tillie Ehrlich tying the knot on November 12, 1916, but evidently they did. There is no documentation of a ceremony, party, or any other to-dos associated with a wedding. There is one photo of a solemn, weary-looking Tillie, alone, wearing a modest sack dress with a slender gold band on her ring finger. She was now Mrs. Tillie Weisberg.

Louis Weisberg was a sweet, gentle man. Everyone liked Louis, including Tillie. Every photograph depicts kindness in his face. Tillie referred to theirs as a "loveless marriage" in multiple articles describing her early life. It was a marriage of convenience between two good friends. Louis Weisberg shared an address and his last name with Tillie. It is likely the couple shared no more than that.

THE SPANISH FLU AND A FLIP OF GOOD FORTUNE
America entered the war on April 6, 1917. The assistance of the United States brought the war to a close on November 11, 1918. The boys came home and brought death with them.

> I had a little bird
> Its name was Enza
> I opened the window
> And in-flew-Enza
> —1918 child's jump-rope singsong

The Spanish flu hit. Tillie and Sam Hockheiser, Bea's husband, caught that flu, along with much of the world's population. The exact numbers of those made ill are unclear, but the death toll was enormous. Up to fifty million people, globally, perished from this flu spread by several means including the returning soldiers of the Great War.

Tillie and Sam survived, but their grocery store at 469 Greenwich did not. Louis Weisberg simply couldn't run the whole operation alone while the rest of the staff recovered.

From her sickbed, Tillie read every book, paper, and article available about successful grocery businesses. She designed a plan to open a wholesale grocery business rather than another mom-and-pop shop. Tillie suggested that they should import both Jewish and Italian products. She bet Sam Hockheiser that her idea would work. Tillie won the bet. On the toss of a coin, they began to trade right out of the house.[xl]

Soon, dried and canned goods were stacked about every available space in the residence. They delivered and sold nonperishable items of all kinds. Tillie kept the books, and the men carried the goods to the local stores. Bea cared for the household and the sons she and Sam Hockheiser were joyfully producing. The business was growing to the point where the neighbors began to complain.

MOSALINA PRODUCTS

> *Find a need. Fill it to the best of your ability and to the*
> *highest of standards. Expect that need to change and be*
> *three steps ahead of the competition*—Tillie Lewis

It was time to expand outside the neighborhood into a real warehouse. Louis Weisberg's brother, Joseph, now joined the business. Sam Hockheiser and Louis Weisberg rented a large warehouse space in the Bush Terminal Building. The location is just what Tillie insisted upon. Tillie's sickbed studies indicated that they'd found the right spot.

Tillie thought of a catchy name for marketing. Since they were Jews selling to Italians, she cleverly combined the name of the Hebrew prophet Moses and the Italian painting the *Mona Lisa*. She christened their new enterprise Mosalina Products, a moniker that would appeal to their Italian customer base and give a nod to their kosher food aisle. Mosalina Products opened at 24 East Thirty-Third and Thirty-Fifth Street in Brooklyn.[xli] Mosalina Products was effectively located just off the Hudson River and its waterfront channels, with easy access to railroads and roadways.[xlii] Arthur Heiser later said,

> It wasn't a store. Regular people didn't stop in to buy groceries. This was a real import business. A pretty big outfit. They were selling orders to grocery stores and restaurants. They imported products from Italy: a rainbow assortment of olive oils and vinegars, dried pastas, cheeses, and tomato products, with emphasis on the pear-shaped tomatoes that the Italians craved. That pear-shaped tangy, meaty tomato [the San Marzano pomodoro] was the staple of all Italian sauces.
>
> The pungent aromas of those cured salamis, fat links of sausages, the culatello ham, the dried cod fish called *baccala*, and cheeses

like mozzarellas, Sicilian caciocavallo, and parmesans hanging from hooks above their heads, dripped flavors and scents that reeked with the flavors of Italy.[20]

The special treat of a favorite cheese and a familiar table wine soothed many a homesick Italian soul.[xliii] Mosalina Products was a big success.[xliv]

Now with a little money in the bank, Tillie and Louis Weisberg moved out of Tillie's sister's home. It was high time, too, since Sam and Bea had been blessed with the last of three beautiful boys. Saul, born in 1916; Arthur, born in 1917; and brand-new baby Albert, who arrived five days before Tillie's birthday, on July 7, 1920. Beatrice was a wonderful, doting mother who made classical music, literature, and good manners an intricate part of her sons' lives. Auntie Tillie adored her nephews. They were the greatest gift her sister could have shared with her.

Tillie and Lou rented a home nearby, where they rented out a room to Louis's elder brother.[xlv] That was fine, since Tillie wouldn't be staying for long.

Once the 1920s lived up to their name and got roaring, so did Tillie. Florindo Del Gaizo wrote to say that he was coming for her. The life of the simple housewife would be no life for Tillie.

IN THE CHIPS

Florindo Del Gaizo sailed to New York now that the Great War and the last vestiges of the influenza outbreak were over. After depositing his wife and children at his New York home, Flo headed straight for Mosalina Products to formally rekindle his romance with Tillie Ehrlich, now Mrs. Weisberg. Florindo was enchanted anew by the delightful Tillie, who had added financial accounting and fluent Italian and French to her growing repertoire of skills.

Tillie was now twenty-four years old. Florindo was forty-five.

---

20 The recollection of a similar experience in her own family's import business was recalled by the author, artist, and heirloom tomato expert Dr. Amy Goldman.

Women won the vote.[21] While her suffragette peers were celebrating across the nation with horns, banners, and flags, Tillie was nearly oblivious to the commotion. Tillie appreciated that American women had won the right to vote, but she also knew that women were not welcome to much of anything else. Tillie never waited around for anyone to give her the right to do anything. She just showed up and did it.

It seemed to Tillie's sister Bea that Tillie personified lady luck herself. No matter what, Tillie always seemed to get her way. Beatrice nicknamed Tillie "Chips," since she was often "in the chips." Just as in the game of poker, the bigger your pile of chips, the richer you were. "Chips" loved her nickname. Her family and closest friends would call her Chips from this point forward in private.

According to her nephews, she was never involved in the suffrage movement. Her nephew Albert said, "No, I don't think 'Chips' gave liberation much thought. I don't think there was a time when she didn't have the upper hand in most situations. I think she was born liberated, and the words 'can't' and 'no' did not exist in her vocabulary."

As many American women cried with joy over gaining some control over their destinies, Tillie was busy at the Del Gaizo office at 141 Broadway in Manhattan selling stocks and bonds and making three to four times as much money as the average American man at that time.[xlvi] Tillie always had a head for figures, as well as a figure that turned heads.

Flo and Till opened an office at 99 Hudson Street in Manhattan in 1924. They dubbed the business Flotill, combining the pet names they had for each other. Flotill imported the Del Gaizo family's Italian products and doubled as a stock brokerage.

Del Gaizo continued to clarify to her that divorcing his wife to marry Tillie was not an option. Tillie's people were less than thrilled that she was fooling around with a married, Catholic man with a herd of children. Everyone was puzzled with Tillie's husband, Louis Weisberg, who did not seem to mind his wife's flagrant infidelity in the least.

---

21 On August 26, 1920, the Nineteenth Amendment to the US Constitution became law: American women could now vote.

To Jacob Ehrlich's horror, his daughter Tillie broke every religious, societal, and social convention by trading her moral reputation for an applied education in high finance and immersion in an agricultural empire as the mistress of a married Italian playboy. Jacob and Bilha felt riddled with shame. Decent Jewish women did not behave like this for any reason.

Whenever Florindo's wife was in town, Tillie popped home to her husband at the Ocean Avenue house that Tillie still used as her legal address. The rest of the time, Tillie lived with Flo in the finest hotel suites money could buy from New York to Naples and Paris to Hong Kong.

For Tillie, the world was an oyster that was never out of season.

Tillie crowned in a diamond tiara and silver lamé gown.
Dinners on luxury liners were formal.

DODGING A DICTATOR

From their home base in Naples, the Del Gaizo family were now the wealthiest canners of tomato products in both Italy and France. When Mussolini became dictator of Italy in 1922, the Del Gaizos added investments in Italian banks to their portfolio. The Del Gaizos paid whatever tributes they needed to pay to keep Il Duce content and out of their family businesses.

Nonpolitical capitalists in their private thinking, the family Del Gaizo wisely kept their opinions, and profits, to themselves. They all donned the required black-shirt uniforms only for affairs of state, saluted like genuine Fascists, and quietly went about creating a fortune for themselves in relative capitalistic peace.[xlvii]

Just as his late father had done, Luigi Del Gaizo was projecting ahead. So far, Mussolini seemed blind to the Del Gaizo family's successes, but Luigi wanted to expand: bigger was better. Luigi merged Del Gaizo Inc. with a smaller canning outfit, Santarsiero & Co., creating multiple canneries that would be outside the dictator's grasp.

Larger companies with greater profits might inspire a power-hungry dictator to grab these Italian industries if the mood so struck; having them based out of the country, beyond the Italian borders, was a safer bet. Del Gaizo-Santarsiero was the dominant provider of canned Italian food in Paris, London, Liverpool, and Brussels, as well as in North America.

With Luigi's measured leadership, the Del Gaizo riches were growing in both Europe and in America. In March of 1923, capital for growth doubled. True to his nature, money was burning a hole in Flo's pocket, so he decided it was time to celebrate. Flo wouldn't marry Tillie, but he would spoil her with fashion and finery of all kinds. She would look like a queen, if not a wife. Tillie was given carte blanche to Florindo's credit to purchase whatever she wanted so that she could dress herself just as well as—if not better than—the ladies of the Broadway stage and Hollywood films on their travels. She gleefully took him up on the offer.

As Arthur Heiser said, "Tillie was not a loose woman, but she did have a flexible morality where wealthy, powerful men were concerned."

On May 28, 1924, sailing on the *Aquitania*, Flo showed Tillie the world on a month-long tour to Italy and France. He introduced her to numerous wealthy, important people—people with power. They were, naturally, mostly men. These were contacts she intended to keep for life. Del Gaizo taught Tillie that positive social contacts were a commodity as good as gold: sometimes as good as gold *and* diamonds.

On Del Gaizo's nickel, Tillie traveled first class both with and without him. On a cruise, back from another European holiday when Florindo needed to stay in Naples, Tillie traveled back to New York alone. Tillie met the British Lord Harry Clifton. Lord Harry was sole heir to the eight-hundred-year-old lands and estates of Clifton, Nottingham, England. The Clifton family owned the manor house, called Clifton Hall (the seat of the Clifton family), along with Saint Mary's Church.[xlviii]

The young and dashingly handsome Lord Harry and Tillie enjoyed each other's company on the voyage home. So much so that Harry sent Tillie a note, on his family-crest stationery, thanking her for the lovely time, along with a fourteen-plus-karat,[22] cushion-cut, canary-yellow diamond ring. Tillie discovered that business and pleasure sometimes mixed quite nicely.[xlix]

The bigger the pile of "chips" Tillie piled up, the greater the shame for Jacob Ehrlich. He and Bilha barely spoke to Tillie, and extended family weighed in on the tsking.

For many years, Jacob Ehrlich worked as a paid-by-the-piece tailor. He then worked in a phonograph store selling Victrola phonographs. Material objects were of little interest to Jacob. Faith in the word of God was Jacob Ehrlich's gold.

It is probable that Tillie, from her Wall Street earnings, and Beatrice, from her husband's Mosalina Products profits, shared their wealth with their father, since Jacob Ehrlich suddenly owned a sweet shop of his own: a little candy-and egg-cream-soda affair. He had that wonderful little bit of a store until he and Bilha moved to Israel, in 1931. To Beatrice's sons, Chips having a lot of money was fine, but Grandfather having a candy shop made Saul, Arthur, and Albert very popular with the other kids.[l]

THE GRAND TOUR

In March of 1926, Luigi Del Gaizo summoned Florindo to an in-person, sit-down meeting in Naples. Tillie proved herself a valuable asset to the company, since she was outselling Florindo in the stock world, keeping impeccable accounting books, and communicating with customers and to Luigi fluently in

---

22   The exact size of this diamond is unknown. From photographs, paintings, and eyewitness accounts, the diamond was *big*. Guesses were that it was from fourteen to twenty-five karats.

Italian, English, and French. It seemed to Luigi that this little Chips could do many things. Tillie was officially invited in as part of Del Gaizo Inc.[li]

Forever one for frivolity, Florindo made this Del Gaizo business trip a full ten-month grand tour of Europe and Asia. Tillie certainly wasn't going to turn down this opportunity. She had no idea if she'd ever have such a chance to see the world again, being just the girlfriend.

Tillie's husband bid her a smiling farewell as she prepared to board the Italian luxury liner the SS *Conte Rosso* with Florindo Del Gaizo.[23] The *Conte Rosso* was designed specifically for a warm Mediterranean ocean voyage. Its lavish Italian interiors outclassed many ships. The *Conte Rosso* featured beautifully designed outdoor dining areas. Formal outdoor dining was new to the industry. The *Conte Rosso's* fresh-air gourmet service became the standard for excellence in sea crossings. Tillie mailed her husband photos of herself and Del Gaizo, dressed nautically, signed, "To Lou, with love. Chips & Flo."

The capitalist, not Fascist, Florindo Del Gaizo, dons a government-ordered black shirt and medals for doing absolutely nothing. This was required of his status within the business community of 1926 Italy.

---

23 Louis Weisberg is pictured with Tillie's sister Beatrice and sons waving bon voyage to Tillie, who took the photos and signed the back.

The first city the couple enjoyed was Florence, Italy, where Flo and Tillie played Fascist dress-up on their hotel balcony. Florindo donned his formal-medaled Fascist black-shirt uniform, spats included, then snapped into the straight-raised-armed salute to a giggling Tillie. She was his conquistatore. She had conquered his heart.

An expert swordsman, Florindo fought several friendly duels to amuse his fair lady. Even Tillie challenged him. She put on protective padding, while Flo remained sweat- and stain-free in his white tennis sweater and crisp white slacks. Tillie playfully crossed blades with him. She lost promptly and decisively.[lii]

Next came multiple stops at the Del Gaizo farms, offices, and villa. Tillie watched and learned while playing in the orchards of seemingly endless fruits and vegetables. She hung in the fruit trees and rode in the car with Flo and a number of unnamed Del Gaizo children and family members: male and female, young and old. Photographs featured a great many smiles and lots of hugging; Tillie appeared to have been generously welcomed by the family Del Gaizo.[liii]

Tillie in the Del Gaizo orchards of Naples, enjoying the
learning process of agribusiness, Italian-style.

In the evenings, Flo and Till dressed formally for dinner and dancing. Florindo bought Tillie a black chiffon gown with matching elbow-length opera gloves. Petite pearls, in a triplicate pattern, embellished the gloves and gown. She was such a vision that Flo swept her off to Naples for a professional photograph. In the photo, the auburn-haired beauty's gloved fingers extend to caress a white long-stemmed floral bouquet. Tillie's smile captures her pleasure in the moment.[24]

The following morning, mingling with armed Fascist troops out in force, Flo and Till gathered in the Piazza Venetia in Rome with the crowd to hear Mussolini speak. Mussolini was making his first public appearance since the assassination attempt by Gino Lucetti on September 11, 1926.[25] Mussolini was letting the people know it would take more than a madman with two bombs, a gun loaded with poison bullets, and a dagger to kill him.[liv]

After the speech, Florindo and Tillie met with Fascist officers and Italian businessmen for lunch. Later, Tillie and Florindo grinned broadly in their chauffeured car, enjoying the sites.

On December 5, 1926, Tillie was front and center, dressed in winter-white haute couture, traveling to see the fairy-tale buildings of the spa town of Karlovy Vary with a group of other well-heeled vacationers. Tillie traveled unaccompanied this time, without Del Gaizo. She was going to visit the place where her mother had died and to see her tombstone in the Jewish cemetery for the first time. Finding the stone, Tillie posed somberly, wistful and near tears, her elbow resting on the large stone carved in Hebrew under which her dear mama lay.

---

24 Photo in tortoise-and-ebony frame engraved "NAPOLI": a gift from Barbara Heiser to the author, and the cover photo of this biography.

25 In Tillie's 1926 photo-album photo, Tillie wrote "Mussolini piazza after assassination attempt."

Tillie with an armed Italian soldier sitting at a café in an Italian piazza with the Del Gaizo crew, discussing business.

Flo and Till were summoned to the Del Gaizo offices. With Mussolini's redefining, national-socialist programs threatening personal wealth in Italy, Luigi Del Gaizo discussed building an entirely new Del Gaizo plant in America with Florindo and Tillie.

The Del Gaizo boss wondered, was there a place in America to grow the Del Gaizo pomodoro, the San Marzano tomato?

Tillie often stated through the years that Florindo Del Gaizo was the only person who believed in her. It may be at this moment that Florindo suggested Tillie's direct involvement in the tomato project in America. Florindo absolutely believed in her. He was astounded by Tillie's business abilities, which appeared second nature to her. Since history has proven that the project went ahead, Luigi must have agreed.

Tillie was challenged to investigate the possibility of growing and canning the pomodoro in the United States. Tillie relished the task, and knew just where to do her research. After the voyage, she would go back home to Brooklyn and the libraries of the Brooklyn Botanical Garden (BBG), where she would find the perfect place.

First, Flo and Till traveled all over Europe, even taking that proverbial slow boat to China. Tillie wore elegant Chinese quilted-silk pajamas and carried a matching China doll she picked up in the orient. Tillie was Flo's living dress-up doll.

Tillie and Florindo enjoy a slow boat to China. Tillie and her China doll wear matching outfits. Tillie's stepmother will never take another doll away from Tillie.

Unlike a doll, she was anything but empty-headed. Her mind was on impressing the Del Gaizo family with her intellect and determination. If it was at all possible, she'd find that Mediterranean weather and soil content at home in the United States if such a place existed.

THE BROOKLYN BOTANICAL GARDEN GOES BANANAS AND TOMATOES

The BBG was a stone's throw from her old tenement. The BBG and its library were the source for Tillie's numerous accounts, in newspapers and magazines, of "struggling through night school, eating nothing but bananas and crackers."[lv]

From 1916 through 1934, the BBG held hands-on classes for ladies and children in the cultivation of fruit and vegetable gardens. Students learned to sow the seed in the earth and in greenhouses. A favorite plant for experimentation for the classes just happened to be the tomato.[lvi]

The BBG experimented with agricultural diseases, pests, and temperature preferences of various food crops, specifically the tomato. The Del Gaizo Italian pomodoro project gave Tillie a reason to dig deeply into a knowledge of agriculture, with emphasis on the tomato, from the roots buried in the soil up. In addition, experiments with great bunches of bananas were staples of the Economic House of the BBG,[lvii] which students and researchers like Tillie Weisberg often enjoyed as a snack.

She researched and "read every book I could lay my hands on about raising and canning tomatoes. I've read and I can quote [the sources]."[lviii] Tillie had become a walking tomato encyclopedia.

The BBG scientists told her that they did *not* think the San Marzano pomodoro would grow in America. Tillie argued that if red round tomatoes and French wine grapes grew prolifically in California's vast Central Valley, why wouldn't her tomato? A tomato is pretty much a tomato. Tillie reasoned, if specialty wine grapes (specifically French) didn't appear to care what country they were in, as long as the correct combination of sun, rain, temperature, and nutrients in the soil were present, any crop should be successful.

Tillie circled the upper Central Valley on her research maps to present to the brothers Del Gaizo as the American version of Naples. Chips knew she was right. The Del Gaizos thought so as well, but the stock market was booming.

The Flotill stock brokerage in New York was making a mint. Everyone agreed to ride the Wall Street gravy train. Tomatoes in America could wait.

Another voyage to Naples, this time to discuss the findings from the BBG research, produced a small miracle. According to the ship's manifest, Tillie claimed she was thirty-two years old when she departed for Italy, and she was twenty-eight years old upon her arrival back in New York. Tillie had lost four years. Probably noticing men in Italy—including Florindo—admiring younger women, she changed her age mid-Atlantic for the first verifiable time in her life. No one, not even her sister Bea, discussed her multitude of age revisions—ever!

THE CRASHES OF OCTOBER 1929

When the stock market crashed on October 29, 1929, Tillie and Florindo lost a great deal of money, just as much of the country did. Luckily, having some assets in Naples, and the backing of the Del Gaizo family, she brushed herself off, accepted her losses, and the plan B, the tomato project, became her single-minded focus. Like Luigi Del Gaizo, Tillie wisely reasoned that in good times or bad, people needed to eat.

Prior to the crash of Wall Street's stocks, the highlight of 1929 was a happy wedding. Beatrice and Tillie's half-brother, twenty-five-year-old Benjamin "Bernie" Ehrlich, fell in love with twenty-two-year-old Molly Zucher. They were married on July 7, 1929.

Four months later, *one* day after the stock market crash, Molly died of causes unknown. The date was October 30, 1929.

To both grieving families, the loss of the young bride was greater than any riches wiped out on Wall Street. To add to Benjamin's pain, Molly's parents buried their daughter, Molly Zucher-Ehrlich, in the Zucher family plot.[lix] Bernie never recovered from the loss of his sweet bride. It was a tragedy of Shakespearean proportions.

Benjamin "Bernie" Ehrlich joined his wife in death a year later, on December 28, 1930. He was buried alone.[lx]

Although his death certificate states the cause of his death as carcinoma of the lung with metastasis to the spinal cord, the family remained steadfast in their belief that the grieving newlywed had died of a broken heart.[lxi]

In that terrible year, the whole world mourned the swift end of gluttonous prosperity and the beginning of international destitution of a duration that would earn the title of the Great Depression. Things were going to get a lot worse for America and for the rest of the globe.

Jacob and Bilha suffered through the year 1930–1931 following Benjamin's death to perform the unveiling of the tombstone, known as *matzevah*, with the ceremonies of prayers and lighting of the *yahrtzeit*, a traditional candle for the anniversary of a death. Traditionally, it was officially time for them to move on with their own lives.

If Jacob and Bilha hadn't lost their beloved only son and daughter-in-law, perhaps they would have stayed in America to enjoy the blessings the couple would have brought. But Benjamin was gone. He was the son. He was the hope. Two daughters—whom his wife could not tolerate—were not enough to keep Jacob in New York when he had a chance to seek peace in the Holy Land.

Many Jews were immigrating to Palestine at that time. Bilha and Jacob joined the Zionist[26] movement and left the United States for good. Jacob found great comfort on the soil of what would become Israel. Jacob Ehrlich garnered even greater esteem as a man true to his faith in the land of his people.[lxii]

Before he left, Jacob Ehrlich posed for two photos. In one, he appears in a modest suit and a simple derby hat; in another, he wore the same suit, but covering his head was his yarmulke. Jacob stood next to his sons-in-law, Louis Weisberg and Sam Hockheiser, and his grandsons, Saul and Arthur. Tillie wrote on the back of the photograph, "Bring these back to me." Did Jacob and Bilha take something to be blessed in the holy land? Or was Tillie just hoping that her father would return?[lxiii]

Whatever her musings, with her father and Bilha out of America seeking solace in the promise of a Jewish state, she'd have no more clucks of

---

26 Zionism was a movement for the return of the Jewish people to their biblical homeland and the resumption of Jewish sovereignty in the land of Israel.

shame—none that held any importance to her, at any rate—to hold her back from seeking her fortune.

This parting was bittersweet: she did love her father and wished for his understanding of her drive for success, if not his approval of her methods. But she wasn't born a boy. There was nothing she could do about that.

Tillie loved her brother. He'd been desperately ill with cancer and grief before his tragic death. Losing him was barely tolerable. She carried her grief, as she had the death of her mother, in her heart, while her mind and body hurried ahead.

Chapter 3

CALIFORNIA: BANKRUPTCY, A FLOP IN MERCED, AND THE *DAISY GRAY*

The Wall Street crash, to say the very least, was both a personal and a global financial nightmare. Fortunately, Flotill was still importing canned foods from Italy. Considering the enormity of the disaster, all was relatively well with Flotill. The Del Gaizos' plan now was to get the Italian tomato, the San Marzano, in American soil as soon as possible before anything else went wrong in the world.

As the Great Depression deepened, American colloquialisms brought presidential insults into the English language to indicate desperate poverty. Herbert Hoover was the butt of dark expressions in darkening times. Shantytowns on the side of a dirt road were Hoovervilles. Hoover blankets were old newspapers collected and used as covers to shield the poor from the cold. Hoover wagons were old cars pulled by horse, mule, or the owners themselves when the money for gasoline ran out. While much of the country was wearing Hoover flags—pants pockets turned inside out, symbolizing that their pockets held no money at all—Tillie was wearing lacy Lily of France underthings. Her skivvies were divine, but her future was as tenuous as everyone else's. Today she could feel the comfortable restriction of fine lace and boning against skin that she could still afford to perfume, but tomorrow? Who knew?[27]

---

27 Tillie's early collection of Lily of France undergarments were a gift to the author from Harley and Bridgette Smith of Stockton.

The best Tillie could do was to go West and pray she would succeed with the California agriculture plan by providing jobs for the good people who were moving West, too. She and thousands of other Americans were on journeys of hope for a brighter future.

Tillie's earlier research suggested that California's middle-northern Central Valley was the right place to grow the Italian pomodoro.

California's Central Valley is 450 miles long and forty to sixty miles wide. The two areas that appeared the most promising to Tillie were Stanislaus and San Joaquin Counties. The enormity of the area was startling. San Joaquin County alone was greater in area than ten states in our United States.[lxiv] This was a huge area to search for the future Del Gaizo tomato home. But search she did.

Flo and Tillie were in constant contact by phone and by telegram with Naples. Seven copper cookers, all of superior quality, plus other equipment and seed were standing by, ready to ship to America to start growing as soon as they had the "go" from Luigi. Several experienced men from the Del Gaizo crew were at the ready to come to California.

Then, something else did go wrong. The US Congress approved and enacted the Smoot-Hawley Tariff. The Del Gaizo pomodoro plan came to a grinding halt.

SMOOT-HAWLEY TARIFF CRIPPLES FOREIGN IMPORTERS

On June 30, 1930, the Smoot-Hawley Tariff was enacted. Tillie become the Flotill company president of record to sidestep the 50 percent Smoot-Hawley foreign tariff that the United States placed on imported agricultural products in 1930.

The tariff was intended to protect profits for American agricultural products from the deluge of imported foreign products. Raising the tariff (i.e., a tax) to an exorbitant 50 percent would stop everyday foreign commodities, meaning that American farmers would make gains both in the United States and globally, at least in theory. Soon, most American special-interest groups wanted this tariff protection, too. The Smoot-Hawley Tariff raised taxes to 50 percent on most imports.

Other countries were enraged and promptly retaliated with their own import taxes. The world was thrust into economic and product isolationism. World trade declined by approximately 66 percent from 1929 to 1934.[lxv] Things had gone from bad to worse.

For Tillie Weisberg, her good luck was still holding out, this tarrif positively changed her life. Smoot-Hawley prevented foreigners from importing foreign products. As an Italian citizen, Florindo Del Gaizo could not inexpensively import the pomodoro to America himself. His American sweetheart, Tillie Weisberg, could. The Del Gaizos could legally finance the operation, but the official head of the company needed to be all-American Tillie.

Tillie Weisberg could import products from Italy—if she were named president of Flotill. She could bring all the equipment and seed in from anywhere she wanted and plant it as an American product, for American consumers.

It was done. Tillie had risen from the desperate tenements of Brooklyn to a luxurious lifestyle throughout the 1920s. Then, in the worst conditions of the Great Depression, she became the graceful, stylish, and multilingual first female president of an agricultural empire in the country.

Florindo and the family Del Gaizo owned 75 percent of the company, Tillie 15 percent, and other investors the balance. Tillie was the hands-on, on-site president, running Flotill.

She'd prepared for this since she was eight years old, all while at the mercy of a cruel stepmother and a society that planned to sentence her to a life of servitude that she would not abide.

She'd taught herself usable skills in accounting, marketing, research, and salesmanship, and even professional showmanship through the Ziegfeld Follies. She was prepared for whatever opportunity might come along. It just happened to be tomatoes. Tillie Weisberg and her new company would begin growing only the San Marzano pomodoro in the Central Valley, backed by—not run by—the fabulously successful Del Gaizo-Santarsiero food company of Italy. Time was of the essence: she had to move quickly and find her land.

THE MERCED MISTAKE

Tillie and Florindo originally chose Merced, California, as the place to build Flotill. Merced's climate was Mediterranean-like, but not right enough for the fussy San Marzano pomodoros. The soil is a wonderful spot to grow fruit and nut trees, dairy, and poultry products. But San Marzano tomatoes needed something more.

As a newspaper account put it at the time, Tillie complained that she "lasted only ten weeks in her Merced office as large as a wastebasket. The steam from the cannery poured over her while she worked and gave her a bad case of skin swelling."[lxvi] The Merced plant failed.[lxvii]

Tillie alone, under the direction of the Del Gaizo Company, filed for bankruptcy on May 11, 1932, listing $57,716 in liabilities, with zero assets. The bankruptcy was discharged six months later, in November. Mrs. Weisberg's bankruptcy did not affect her husband's business, Mosalina Products in New York. Louis Weisberg had never been involved, nor held any financial interest in, the business affairs of his wife.[lxviii] Tillie was financially free and clear to do as she pleased.

First order of business was to use her research notes to determine a new spot for Flotill and the pomodoros. A bit more toward Sacramento, California seemed to be the best bet.

STOCKTON: SOMEPLACE SPECIAL

Driving a rented Model A Ford, cloaked in a mink coat, wearing high-heels, and accompanied by two swarthy Italian men sent by the Del Gaizos to help, Tillie Weisberg toured the Central Valley for the *actual* perfect spot for the pomodoros.

Meanwhile, the local newspapers announced the arrival of another lady to Stockton, California, to great fanfare. The ruckus caught Tillie's attention. The trio motored along with throngs of locals, Depression-era hopeful job seekers, and the merely curious to witness the grand entrance of the lady. Her name was *Daisy Gray*. The date was February 2, 1933.

The *Daisy Gray* was the first seagoing vessel to enter Stockton's brand-new deepwater seaport. While most of the country was at a Depression-inflicted standstill, Stockton had already secured the go-ahead funding for this amazing dredging of the San Joaquin River: a direct sea canal snaking inland from the San Francisco Bay, deep into the Central Valley. The canal was a resounding success.

The *Stockton Record* crowed at the time, "The 1930–33 dredging of the Deep-Water Channel to a depth of 26 feet was Stockton's Panama Canal, its greatest engineering feat, a bid for municipal greatness…All vessels entering under the Golden Gate may [now] dock at the [Stockton] port." The paper further gloated that "a sign at the channel head informed sidewalk superintendents the channel deepening was 'the greatest municipal undertaking now in progress.'"

When the *Daisy Gray* poked through the fog in 1933, whistles, horns, and huzzahs sounded citywide. Stated the Stockton Record, "Within 15 minutes several hundred people were on the city docks. The noise, reflected the heartfelt satisfaction of local observers."[lxix]

Tillie smiled and mouthed, "Huzzah, indeed!"

WILL IT GROW, WILL IT GROW, WILL IT GROW?

Stockton shares Naples's Mediterranean climate.[lxx] Both regions' soils are comprised of rich, fertile loams. Stockton had three transcontinental railroad lines, several major highways, and now direct access to the sea. Stockton was just what Tillie and Flotill were looking for. Tillie stated in numerous publications, "San Joaquin County is one of the richest agricultural areas in the world, with a growing season of 287 days of the year."[lxxi]

Shipping is the most cost-effective method of transport. The Port of Stockton, only a few miles from the proposed site of Flotill, would carry the bulk of the production to the East Coast and to foreign markets hungry for pomodoros.

After establishing that Stockton was the right place to grow pomodoros, Tillie struck a deal with a local packer and a "truck farmer"[28] (who normally planted potatoes, asparagus, and onions) to plant the San Marzano pear-shaped tomato seed. The farmer was given enough seed to produce a hundred thousand cases of whole tomatoes and a hundred thousand cases of tomato paste. Tillie had to advance the packer the $10,000 Del Gaizo nest egg and reach into her own savings to pay a "bonus" to the truck farmer to plant the seed.

To more than meet the Smoot-Hawley requirements and maintain control as president of the company, Tillie wanted only American citizens as salespeople who were experts on the San Marzano pomodoro. That meant she was the *only* salesperson. She intended to sell all two hundred thousand cases as quickly as possible, crossing her fingers that she was right that the tomatoes would grow in the hearty soil of Stockton.

The Stockton farmer had no faith in this Italian seed sprouting or in the New York lady selling that much product of an unknown commodity. But the San Marzano pomodoros thrived beyond anyone's expectations. Tillie sold every single case in record time. What the farmer did not know was that Tillie already had contacts in Chicago and New York through the Del Gaizo product lines. She was certain she was a shoo-in for sales success.

She returned to Stockton to find that the farmer had only planted seed to produce fifty thousand cases instead of two hundred thousand. The farmer explained that he was certain the darn things wouldn't grow and that the fancy lady wouldn't be able to sell them if they did grow. Stockton rumors indicated that this truck farmer had sold the extra seed to others for a profit. Tillie was furious.

Tillie hauled one of the cases to Pacific Can Company in Stockton. She begged the company president to sample the new tomato. Pacific Can was impressed. Tillie told Pacific Can she was going into big production and would buy all her cans from them if they built her new company a plant she could lease with an option to buy with the backing of the Del Gaizo Corporation. Pacific Can agreed.

---

28 Small-scale agricultural farmer who sometimes sold products on side of the road off a truck-bed.

Tillie took a break, rested in her room at the Stockton Hotel, then made haste back East with portions of the promised orders, an apology that melted the hearts of red-blooded men, and a written guarantee to a bargain price for the following "pack."[29] Once again, misfortune was Tillie's ally. Her new customers were pleased by her honesty, charm, and an impressive discount so deep into the Great Depression.

She took the train back to New York and had a photograph of herself taken for Florindo, wearing a diamond hairpin and bracelet with a black cashmere dress. She was loosely draped in a white cap-shouldered ermine fur stole, looking every inch the movie star. Tillie signed the stunning portrait: "To my friend Florindo Del Gaizo. Feb. 10, 1934."[30] No matter the romantic relationship prior to becoming American president of Flotill, Tillie intended, from now on, to keep private matters private.

"To My Dear friend Flo": 1934 proves Tillie was no simple housewife, as she consistantly claimed. She was a glittering star—a bejeweled beauty— ahead of her time. Photo courtesy of the Bank of Stockton archives.

---

29 Pack refers to all the product grown and put up into canning production for the season.

30 Tillie made a point of calling her long-time lover "her dear friend" for the sake of her reputation.

Chapter 4

FLOTILL OF STOCKTON AND PEAR-SHAPED PROSPERITY

Mussolini was not an enemy of the United States in 1935; this would not occur until late in 1939. Americans were welcome guests of the ill-fated Il Duce. Tillie Weisberg boasted constantly of the power of the Del Gaizos in the Fascist regime at the beginning of Flotill's existence in Stockton.

In Philip V. Cannistraro's 1982 work, the *Historical Dictionary of Fascist Italy*, the author catalogued multiple aspects of the Fascist Italian government, including lists of key figures in Mussolini's world. Not one Del Gaizo or Santarsiero is mentioned. The common claim that the Del Gaizos were close chums of the dictator was false. It is true that every company (and its functionaries) had to pay tribute and publicly applaud; wear the uniform, the ribbons, and the medals; and tow the Fascist line to stay in business. The Del Gaizo family was in the business of selling canned food for profit. The Del Gaizos never sold Fascism.[lxxii]

However, Tillie's bragging that she was directly connected to Mussolini convinced her new, and seriously conservative, home of Stockton that she was likely up to no all-American good. From the beginning, as far as Stockton was concerned, Tillie Weisberg and her Fascists (real or not) were suspect.

Western Canner and Packer magazine printed the first article and photograph[31] of Tillie Weisberg and her Italian start-up crew in September of 1935. This was the first time that Tillie tried out her fibs—her three-quarter truths—about how Flotill came to be to the public.

In February of 1935, when Tillie Weisberg, surrounded by a mob of macho Italian men, turned over the first spade of earth to build Flotill, she was thirty-eight years old.

Tillie did not correct the writer when he stated that Miss Weisberg was "twenty-something in age, and one of the Italians [*sic*]." Tillie knew it was not a good idea to be an older Jewish divorcée in Stockton in the 1930s if one could avoid it. *Western Canner and Packer* wrote:

> The Italian race have long been enthusiastic canners and consumers of tomatoes and tomato products...Italian packers processed in their own country, in their own individual style and sold not only to their own people but to consumers all over Europe and to new immigrants to America.
>
> When the June 18, 1930...American duty of 50% went into effect...most Italian producers were compelled to [lose at least 50 percent in business] swallow this bitter pill without doing anything about it. However, one firm has done something very definite about the matter, though it took an American to show how it could be done...
>
> Mrs. Tillie Weisberg, a young business-woman of New York City, was interested in the importing business...Mrs. Weisberg set sail for...the land of Mussolini, and had the good fortune to make the acquaintance of Senatore Luigi Del Gaizo. The Senatore was and is— and this is more to the point—president of Del Gaizo-Scentarsiero, SA, largest canning company in Italy. Still further, he was and is the

---

31 The photo shows Tillie seated, with her Naples crew standing. With their menacing stares, the photo appears more like a group mug shot for the mob, which they certainly were not, than a welcoming grand opening.

head of the Italian Corporate State, one of the most influential and important divisions of Il Duce's government...

With five factories in Italy and one in France, with sales outlets all over the World—Mrs. Weisberg's proposition to let her establish a plant in America interested [Luigi Del Gaizo].

Mrs. Weisberg, who is still in her twenties...selected Stockton, California aided by Italian consul Harry Mazzera...

Flotill Products, Inc. was selected as the name—" Flo" for Florindo Del Gaizo, son of the Senatore[32] and active head of Del Gaizo Distributing Company...and "till" for Tillie Weisberg.

...From the outside the building appears no different from any other American packing structure...Inside, however, much of the equipment is of foreign manufacture...It was intended to use only pear-shaped Italian tomatoes planted from imported seed, but in mid-August the crop was so poor that it was not profitable to handle them...the pack is made of mostly domestic varieties.

...Also taking part in the affairs of the company [is] Vincent Del Gaizo, 28, eldest son of Florindo Del Gaizo. Vincent was educated in America as well as in Europe and speaks English fluently. Guido Alberti, married to one of the Del Gaizo girls and Cav. Antonio Alloca, who attended school with Florindo Del Gaizo..."[lxxiii]

Tillie evidently didn't like the way that read. She was still looking for the most appropriate story to reach the average homemaker whom she hoped would buy her high-quality, nutritious, and morally superior tomato products.

---

32 Luigi and Florindo Del Gaizo were brothers.

Tillie's first office at Flotill of Stockton. The photograph of a balding
Florindo Del Gaizo on the left wall will cause Tillie some trouble.

SLIGHTLY LESS THAN HALF THE TRUTH: THE OFFICIAL TILLIE TALE

From her age to her story about meeting the Del Gaizos, most of the
personal information she shared with the public was stylized into the self-
proclaimed Cinderella version she felt compelled to spin, with a few revisions, as she went along. The biggest whoppers were: (1) she was a young,
innocent housewife from Brooklyn, and not a businesswoman; (2) she was
on that voyage to Italy simply on a determined search for the pear-shaped
tomato; (3) she "accidentally" met Florindo Del Gaizo on the boat in
1934; and (4) Florindo, not Luigi Del Gaizo, was the bigwig Italian owner
of the Naples company and was the head of banking under Mussolini.
The fifth and final whopper was that, with no strings attached, Florindo
Del Gaizo, out of the kindest of his heart, gave the little homemaker Tillie
Weisberg $10,000, all the necessary equipment she needed, and three to
four bags of seeds to grow her dream tomatoes in Stockton—which, by a

miracle, she did. With only the experience of a Brooklyn housewife, she was now a successful president of a new tomato-processing plant that was up and running in less than a year.

This was the tale no one ever challenged. It became the truth according to Tillie.

THE HELP

Tillie had three Italian experts on hand for the company's start-up. They'd signed on for the entire season to teach the system and machinery protocol in addition to working full-time. They were Florindo's eldest son, Vincent Del Gaizo; Guido Alberti, a brother-in-law married to Florindo's sister, and Antonio Alloca, one of Florindo's oldest friends.

The Del Gaizo family did not have any problem with helping Florindo's lady friend, since it all helped the Del Gaizo bottom line thrive. Vincent, Guido, and Antonio were of enormous help and brought loads of Italian winking, pinching, and playful joviality to the mix.

Another man who joined the company was Lloyd Dunivan, a young man from the Midwest who was unafraid of work and challenges. He was an all-around handy fellow and an accomplished western-style horseman. Lloyd was welcomed to California by his elder brother Floyd and his wife, Esther. Both Dunivan brothers were good with their hands. Floyd was a master mechanic and electrician at Colberg Boat Works on Fremont Street. Both brothers Dunivan had been taught by life experience and a genuine love of automobile engines how to make machines run.[lxxiv]

Twenty-nine-year-old Lloyd landed the job as cannery superintendent at the new Flotill. Miss Weisberg took a shine to the blond, hazel-eyed, good-looking Lloyd. Was he technically the best man qualified to be her superintendent? Probably not at first, but Lloyd was willing to glean everything he could from Miss Weisberg and the Del Gaizo team. He had no intention of letting Miss Weisberg down or of losing this job. To everyone else, Tillie was Mrs. Weisberg. She was *Miss* Weisberg—heavy emphasis on the *Miss*—to the unattached, totally available Mr. Dunivan.

Harry and Elizabeth Turnbull were hired on as office staff. If something was done in the office that first year, they handled it. At one point, somebody suggested a picnic break in the forest at Twain Hart, a two-hour drive northeast from Stockton. Photographed in a crisp white blouse and a light sweater indicate that Tillie Weisberg was not a dirt-savvy kind of gal. The photo, processed on May 4, 1936, shows a picnic table stranded in the trees, along with an eye-rolling scowl from Tillie and the equally unhappy faces of Liz Turnbill and two unidentified others, indicating that camping would be crossed off the to-do list.

Leo Landuci, Joe Mariani, and E. Mariani were multitalented Stockton men whose positions were whatever they were needed to be, from supervisors to grease monkeys. They were ready to make the plant a strong force in the industry from day one.

Tillie Weisberg was boss, saleswoman, problem solver, buyer, and student, learning this business from the Del Gaizo boys. She worked night and day, seven days a week. From front office to the tomato-processing tables, Tillie Weisberg was an inspiration to everyone.

Meanwhile, Serafino "Ralph" Garcia was tamping down railroad ties with a shovel for the Santa Fe Railroad at Boggs Tract and Navy Drive in Stockton when he first spied Miss Weisberg late in 1934. She was watching the progress of the new railroad side spur with a small contingent of fancy-suited men. It seemed to Ralph that the little lady was the engineer explaining the tamping process to the men. It occurred to Ralph that these folks might mean direct access to a job at the new tomato-processing plant everyone was talking about.

Ralph asked his boss, C. C. Spence, if he could set down his shovel and take a short break. Covered in dirt and sweat, Ralph stepped a polite distance up to the business group and asked if he might apply for a job. The woman said with a smile as bright as the Stockton sun, "I am Miss Weisberg. Yes, of course. When we open, you may apply for a job."

Upon finishing the Flotill spur, as usual, Ralph migrated to general manual labor, this time for the Southern Pacific Railroad in San Francisco. He didn't like working as a migrant railroad laborer, but he was far happier "workin' on the railroad" than working as a migrant farm picker, like most Mexicans he knew.

A few weeks later, Ralph was on the San Francisco railroad tracks, filthy with muck, when he received a message from his mother that "Miss Weisberg's Flotill plant was looking for workers."

Ralph was on top of the world. His first job had been earning five cents an hour in the harsh fields picking crops. Now he was earning a respectable eight cents an hour with the railroad. If he got the job working at Miss Weisberg's Flotill, he'd be walking distance to home and be pushing the nearly middle-class wage of fifteen cents an hour.

Ralph silently prayed when he stood in front of Miss Weisberg, dressed in his Sunday best shirt and slacks. He presented Miss Weisberg a seven-line, hand-scrawled note from his boss:

> To whom it may concern,
> This is to certify S. Garcia has
> worked in my gang on the
> S. F. R for some time. I am
> glad to recommend him as a good
> hard working man always willing.
> —C. C. Spence.
> Section Foreman[lxxv]

S. Ralph Garcia showed the moxie, dedication, and loyalty that Miss Weisberg was looking for in her employees. Ralph, and others of his character, would accept and learn multiple job skills and responsibilities, simply by never saying no to any type of work.

Ralph was a floater. He filled in as a daytime general handyman sweeping up, changing light bulbs, and whatever else was needed. He switched, without complaint, to conveyor-line mechanic or night-security watchman if Miss Weisberg or Lloyd Dunivan, Ralph's direct supervisor, asked him to.[lxxvi]

This was the hiring policy of those first years at Flotill. Miss Weisberg met with you. She'd size you up in minutes and not in a negative way. She had already shaken your hand and smiled. It was as though she was looking within a person for all the terrific things they could do. She'd say, "I'm hiring you to do this. Would you be willing to learn to also try this or that? I have no idea what my little baby, Flotill, might need next." She had a gift about her that made employees feel as though she were very happy that you were thinking of coming to work to help her out.[lxxvii]

After she had her first-year help in place, with all the complications of a new industrial enterprise that Flotill entailed, Tillie made the time for a promotional photo shoot with *Vanity Fair* magazine's famed photographer Lusha Nelson.[33] Tillie intended to look every part the Queen of Tomatoes.[lxxviii]

1935–1936: BABY STEPS

Unofficially, Flotill had been in business since early 1935, preparing for the pomodoro crop harvest, acquiring cans, and hiring and training staff.[34] Officially, Flotill opened on July 13, 1935: Tillie's birthday. Tillie fudged nearly every major event in her life to fall upon her birthday. She decided she would be a legend one day, and she'd have serendipity surrounding her day of birth, no matter what day things actually occurred.

The first season-end-party photographs depict Tillie wearing a dark, long-sleeved, silk blouse standing in the center of her skeleton crew of Italians and Stocktonians in the Flotill yard. The Italians secretly hold unopened bottles of champagne; a few photos later, a grinning Guido is dousing the unhappily surprised Mrs. Weisberg with his sparkling bottle of French libation. Those Italians!

Soaked, sticky, and tired described both the champagne shower and that first difficult year. Flotill packed ninety-one thousand cases of tomatoes[lxxix]

---

33   Lusha Nelson (died 1938) photographed for *Vogue*, *Vanity Fair*, and various Hollywood studios, specializing in the rich and famous of the arts, sports, music, comedy, and business worlds.

34   The San Marzano pomodoros did not thrive in 1935 and were supplemented with tried-and-true round tomatoes; the next year the pomodoro flourished.

and nearly broke even. Tillie planned a huge fiesta for her people to enjoy while she cut out early. As Ralph Garcia laughingly said,

> From that first year, 1935, Tillie held an after-the-season dinner party. In the beginning, we had music and a huge BBQ right at the plant in Stockton. A whole steer and a couple of pigs were roasted with tables full of side-dishes, salads, and desserts. The booze was unbelievable! There were no limits on how much we could drink. Many folks drank way past their limit.
>
> Mrs. Weisberg was learning the business, even regarding social events. She was still learning about managing people. The first few years of Flotill, spouses were not allowed at parties. Mrs. Weisberg thought we should all mingle as the Flotill family without the stuffiness of wives, husbands, and kids.
>
> Mrs. Weisberg stayed long enough to enjoy a plate of food and a bite of a dessert, then she'd leave. That's when the parties started.
>
> Well, some of us mingled, all right. Those were some good times. People got dirty, real dirty. Dirty talk, dirty dancing, and railroad-car lovin' right there on those spurs I helped hammer in 1934–1935.

As Tillie matured, so did her company parties. A few illegitimate Flotill babies later, social events became genuine—with wives and husbands in attendance—family affairs.

After leaving the party, Tillie sailed back to Naples to discuss strategy with the Del Gaizos. She was reviewing the 1900s patriarch Vincenzo Del Gaizo's original business model under the tutelage of Luigi Del Gaizo, Florindo's brother and head of the Del Gaizo Company. She reinvestigated the Naples plant's current canning operation from top to bottom, both inside the plants and outside in the fields. This time she took copious notes. This time she was the American boss. What had she done wrong? How could she improve?

She learned that trying to do everything herself with a minimal staff was costing money, not saving it. She needed to hire more good people and delegate duties. She was needed most as the natural quick-thinking planner and problem solver of the company.

Tillie was ready for season two.

Back row, left to right: Lloyd Dunivan, Bill Puliston, Ronald Meyers, Pat Stanco, Howard Kurtz, Walter Foa, Arthur Heiser, Bob French, and Harry Turnbull. Front row, left to right: Unknown, Liz Turnbull, Tillie Weisberg, Lucy Heiser [Arthur's wife], and Mary French.

Flotill's second year began with a wonderfully abundant crop. Tillie often climbed up on a box to survey production and watch tomatoes roll past. Even in the one-hundred-plus-degree heat, she could be found on her perch. Then, smack in the middle of the packing season on a blistering August day, with tons of tomatoes sitting in the hot sun, the main boilers—those glistening copper kettles—failed.

A man ran up to her in a panic shouting, "The boilers are down!" Repair would be days away. The crop and the profits would rot. This was bad. Really bad. This could cost the entire year's profit if not repaired posthaste. Tillie climbed down from her roost and silently walked away in what she called "a think walk." As usual, she was wearing high heels and had to maneuver carefully over the railroad track when the idea stuck her: "Our boilers are really just steam pots. We have steam-engine trains sitting at our front door! If we can hook the train's steam engine up to our equipment... "[lxxx] Tillie hurried back to her office and asked the head mechanic if her "loco-crazy" locomotive-steam idea might work. He responded, "I don't see why it wouldn't."

Tillie called the Santa Fe railroad, whose engines were often on the spur directly in front of Tillie's office.

Tillie asked the railroad if they could hook up one of their steam-train engines with pipes, or something, to her factory's steam cookers. Santa Fe thought that they could. They called the process "shunting." Tillie asked how much this would cost. The answer was seven dollars. Tillie said, "Good, I'll take two." The 1936 tomato pack was saved.[lxxxi]

"I pick myself up, dust myself off, and start all over again"[35] became Tillie's theme. The year 1936 ended in the black: an excellent beginning for "Steam-Train Fame" Tillie Weisberg. She had a legitimate legend starting to grow along with her fields of tomatoes; 1937 should be fantastic.

THE SPINACH RIOT: ONE DEAD AND FIFTY INJURED

Spinach is usually the first crop of the year in San Joaquin County. On April 23, 1937, the local Agriculture Workers Union called a strike for higher pay that involved five canneries, all in production canning spinach.

Flotill was not directly a party to this strike, since Flotill canned only tomatoes, and tomatoes were not yet in, but many Flotill workers felt it necessary to join their cannery worker brothers and sisters in a strike that quickly turned violent.

Sheriff Harvey Odell deputized seven hundred regular Stockton citizens, arming them with pickaxes by the truckload, "with shaved-down handles for easy swinging." According to the local papers, "Stockton citizens believed this was Stockton's first Communist red scare." According to

---

35 From "Pick Yourself Up" (1936): lyrics by Dorothy Fields; music by Jerome Kern.

Wikipedia, a large group of 850 cannery and union picketers surrounded a truckful of nonunion workers (known as scabs) and a police escort with sirens blaring. The picketers stopped the truck and threw the spinach to the earth; Sheriff Odell's men fired tear gas into the crowd, and people on all sides threw rocks. The union mob pulled the deputy sheriffs from their cars and beat them with clubs; the deputies opened fire with shotguns at point-blank range. One man died in the riot, and the three-hour siege resulted in more than fifty serious injuries.[lxxxii]

This was a terrible time for Stockton. Tillie was aware that such tragedy could have fallen on her doorstep had this been a tomato strike. She vowed to stay personally even more active in increasing job satisfaction at Flotill to nip any strikes in the bud. The employees really were the caretakers of her precious baby, Flotill. Her gratitude for them was genuine. Tillie often stated, "Appreciate your employees" as a cornerstone to success.

NEPOTISM: IT'S A FAMILY AFFAIR
Tillie noticed that her employees, seasonal and nonseasonal alike, often lobbied to hire members of their immediate families to work for her. Tillie took this as a compliment and a dandy way to help avoid strikes. Tillie reasoned that the loyalty factor rose when household budgets depended entirely upon her. Rather than take advantage of this, she rewarded nepotism.

As was typical of Flotill employees, Ralph Garcia brought his father, his brothers Manuel and Frank, and his wife, Mildred, on board to work at Flotill. Tillie liked the elder patriarch of the Garcia family so much that she kept him on full-time as her gardener and handyman at her personal residence to maintain his full-time status. Tillie loved flowers. Her roses, in particular, seemed to love Mr. Garcia. Her flora responded to the Garcia touch with blooms in abundance.

Having the head of this proud Mexican family as an ally was an honor and, strategically, a smart move on Tillie's part in her quest for loyalty to avoid unwanted scenarios, like strikes. The Garcias made Flotill a second home and Mrs. Weisberg an honorary member of their family. Ralph Garcia said,

Mildred worked in the Flotill cannery until our babies began to arrive, in 1938. Tillie Weisberg never forgot an employee's special events or a family member's name.

Mrs. Weisberg often came out on to the plant floor, or cafeteria, to chat with all the workers. She always called everyone by name and asked about our families. She wanted to know friendly gossip. She'd want to know who was getting married, having a baby, and if anyone was unwell—you know, sick. She'd send a card, at least.

Everybody would gladly tell her because she sincerely seemed to care.

Mildred and I had five children nineteen months apart. The next paycheck, after each baby came, I would find an extra envelope with a savings bond and a hand-written note from Mrs. Weisberg asking us to contribute to our newborn's college fund.

She did the same for everyone in her Flotill family. She thanked us every chance she could.

The Munoz, Vargas, Bejerano, Weast and Espinoza families are but a few where most of the family worked for Tillie Weisberg. All they needed to do was to have a family member apply for a position they were capable of doing. A current worker's recommendation of character was usually good enough for Tillie Weisberg, [but] not because she was too lazy to check. No. No. No. The least lazy worker at Flotill was Mrs. Weisberg. She didn't question her employees' recommendations because she absolutely trusted us all.[lxxxiii]

JIM CROW AND REAL ESTATE

Now that Stockton appeared to be a winner as a full-time home for Flotill, Tillie looked for a permanent residence for herself. The same real estate/property exclusionary laws in most cities and states applied in Stockton as they did across the nation. As a Jew, Tillie could not buy a home in most brand-new neighborhood subdivisions due to the declaration of conditions, covenants, and restrictions (CC&Rs), which often forbade sales to persons of color, different nationalities, and certain faiths.[lxxxiv]

To argue the ruling would bring unwanted attention to the fact that she was Jewish, which could have resulted in a loss of business at Flotill. Tillie decided to ignore this battle and buy a house directly from an Italian medical doctor. She bought a lovely home at 1581 North San Joaquin Street, for sale by owner, by negotiating directly with the owner, Dr. John Vincent Craviotto, completely in Italian.

As a result, Dr. Craviotto and the neighbors believed that Tillie was Italian and had simply divorced some Jewish man named Weisberg. Tillie didn't exactly fib—she just didn't correct them.[lxxxv]

TILLIE WANTS HER BABY TO GROW

On June 28, 1937, Florindo Del Gaizo and Tillie Weisberg, as the financier and president, respectively, of Flotill Products Incorporated, hosted a dinner and motion-picture event in Chicago at the Monte Cristo Italian Restaurant. Invited were all their customers who carried Flotill tomato products under the Delsa Brand label. Delsa (*Del* for Del Gaizo; *Sa* for Santarsiero) was sold on the East Coast of both the United States and Canada.

The dinner featured tomato-based fare prepared with Delsa/Flotill products: Italian minestrone, spaghetti, and ravioli; filet mignon; and wine and spumoni.[lxxxvi] A photograph from Chicago depicts Tillie as the lone woman, festooned in a sequined gown and sumptuous fur, contentedly drowning in a sea of tuxedoes.

Flo and Till hosted similar gala events in California and New York for the Flotill customers in those markets. Talking Florindo into throwing a party was easy; convincing him to invest in anything other than a good time was another thing entirely. The leopard that was Flo Del Gaizo was a good-time-all-the-time, gent. Changing his spots into a growth-theory investor was going to be a battle.

After saving the pack with the steam trains, Tillie was officially in love with her little company. She referred to Flotill as her baby, and she meant it. Tillie had no biological offspring. She would defend Flotill to the death, like any good mother.

Florindo's plan for the future was to grow only the pomodoro in Stockton and spend the profits on other projects. Tillie was certain that *big* profits were ripe by expanding Flotill in California, canning all the fruits of that great valley.

TOO MUCH OF A GOOD THING

The 1937 tomato pack was so abundant that demand for more product was reduced by the 1938 season's end in November. No matter—Tillie and Flotill still increased their staff by two thirds and came in as the second top canner in California—employing 550 workers and packing only tomatoes—next to Richmond-Chase, which packed asparagus and peaches with a larger staff.[lxxxvii] Tillie took this as a win and a clear message that it was time to add more products.

Tillie came from poverty and lack. Florindo hailed from wealth and extreme abundance. He wasn't a businessman; he was a multicontinental gadabout. Tillie was born a businesswoman. As was his nature, Flo was content in showing a little profit, which Flotill was doing, then spending the rest of his time in the pursuit of pleasure. Florindo had a huge family fortune as a safety net, while Tillie knew the gravy train could end for her with one bad turn of events of that pear-shaped Italian fruit.

To any expansion into more products, Del Gaizo said, "No!" citing in his argument the recent spinach riot that Flotill had dodged. In his estimation, Flotill avoided that riot because Flotill concentrated on a single successful product, pomodoros. He refused to make additional investments into the company. Tillie was "think walking" ways to buy out the Del Gaizo interest in the company. If Flo didn't want to play, then he'd best get out of Tillie's way. The stress on the relationship between Del Gaizo and Tillie Weisberg was enormous.

Left to right: Louis Weisberg, Tillie Weisberg, and Florindo Del
Gaizo, 1937. With her husband (who didn't mind the arrangement)
on her left and her love on her right, Tillie impishly smiles.

FLORINDO DEL GAIZO (1873–1937)

As his father had before him, Flo died unexpectedly and suddenly on August
23, 1937, at 485 Ocean Avenue, Brooklyn. He was sixty-four years old. This
six-story brownstone was the place Tillie and Louis Weisberg had called home
since 1932, at least on legal documents.

Flo's obituary stated that the home belonged to him. Del Gaizo may have
purchased this property as Tillie's place to scram to when his wife was in town.
According to documents, Louis Weisberg lived at the property full time.[36]

---

36 Free housing may have been another reason Louis was so accommodating to his wife's affair. It is unknown if Weisberg was in residence when Del Gaizo passed away. However, it is the
author's opinion that Louis and Tillie Weisberg were never legally married.

Regardless of Florindo and Tillie's marital arrangement, Tillie felt every inch the bereaved wife. She prepared a lavish funeral service at Campbell's Funeral Church[lxxxviii] three days later.

If one had to be dead, Campbell's was the fashionable place to do it. Campbell's was good enough for heartthrob Rudolph Valentino's body and many other affluent corpses. To Tillie's credit, she gave the *real* Mrs. Del Gaizo billing in the *New York Times* obituaries and all the other major papers from coast to coast.[lxxxix] For many of the couple's acquaintances, the obituary naming Elvira Del Gaizo as *the wife* was a startling disclosure, since Flo and Tillie were assumed to have been married, which they were—just not to each other.

Elvira Del Gaizo did not attend. She was at the Del Gaizo villa on the winding, scenic Via Tasso Number 256, awaiting Florindo's remains. She dispatched her husband with the opulence of a crown prince.

Mrs. Elvira Del Gaizo, her seven children, and hundreds of mourners gathered at Naples Cathedral, completed around AD 1360. The magnificent Gothic-style basilica entombed kings and saints alike. It is the home of holy relics, martyrs, and miracles.[xc] Elvira Del Gaizo's send-off trumped Tillie's affair, hands down.

As she had learned from her past, Tillie suffered in silence and looked for the positive in this misfortune. She began scrambling for money to fund the 1938 season and to buy out the Del Gaizo family's interest. Tillie would not forget her love and gratitude for everything Flo had taught and given her. She vowed to credit him for her opportunities and to cherish his memory for the rest of her life.[37]

WHAT NEXT?

Tillie met with Luigi Del Gaizo after the grand funeral. Since photographs still exist of the assemblage of mourners outside the cathedral with the marquee calling upon all to "pay homage to the Great Florindo Del Gaizo" and

---

37 Tillie spoke of Del Gaizo so often that the tale became a rut-worn, embellished Cinderella story that she told, including her literal last words in public.

the interior of the cathedral with Florindo's ornate casket raised on pillars toward heaven, Tillie was probably quietly among the multitude of mourners, snapping the pictures herself. Europeans had long been indifferent to affairs of the boudoir. The Del Gaizo family had long known of, and liked, Tillie Weisberg. It was Luigi's guys, including Florindo Del Gaizo's son, who came to Stockton to help set Flotill in motion in 1934. Luigi enjoyed the fact that Tillie listened to him. Tillie was like a sponge, soaking in ideas to build affluence. Luigi was aware that Tillie had strictly, religiously followed in Luigi's late father's business footsteps and that she was in mourning for his wayward brother, too.

Again, luck from misfortune greeted Tillie. Luigi Del Gaizo had nine other factories in operation, five outside Italy, and all were losing a little money. He could use a bit of immediate cash. Luigi feared that war was coming and that he might lose the American business anyway. Luigi sold the business, including all rights to the Flotill name, to Tillie Weisberg for $72,000.[38] Luigi and Tillie remained friends and associates. Flotill and Tillie would supply product and support, should Luigi need it, and he promised to return the favor.

Tillie piecemealed the funds from several sources to make the Del Gaizo payoff work. Tillie was an expert at applying "if there's a will, there's a way."

Mr. A. Sala, vice president of the Stockton branch of Bank of America, stated, "Mrs. Weisberg paid [the Del Gaizo estate] $22,000 from her Flotill bank account she had with [Bank of America], $45,000 was advanced from Pacific Can and $5,000 was advanced by Mrs. Weisberg from her personal account."[xci] The $45,000 loan from Pacific Can was made using the last of Florindo Del Gaizo's clout.

Upon hearing of Florindo Del Gaizo's demise, at least one customer—P. Pastene & Co. Inc., a business neighbor and supplier on Hudson Street, New York—felt they were likely to receive a less-than-acceptable product now that a woman was completely in charge. Pastene & Co. demanded a discount on their remaining contract. Pastene airmailed a response to Tillie's phone call, October 1, 1937.

---

38 In 2016 dollars, $72,000 is equal to around $1.2 million.

Dear Mrs. Weisberg,

We were favorably impressed with the attitude you took in our telephone conversation of this morning...We appreciate the confidence you expressed when you said you'd accept our decision as to what we consider a fair market value for merchandise...we will let you know what would be a fair price for you to bill us on the contract, bearing in mind that we want first of all merchandise of good quality, the best you can pack. We have been in business long enough to know that quality is remembered long after price is forgotten.

—Pastene & Co. Inc.[xcii]

Tillie and her pomodoros exceeded expectations after Del Gaizo died. In fact, there was again too much product. Her customer base was impressed and growing by satisfied word of mouth. The taste and quality of the Italian pear-shaped tomato was superb.

Luigi Del Gaizo sailed from Naples to New York on the SS *Conte Di Savoia* on February 3, 1938, to visit Del Gaizo's Inc., still in New York. Luigi's listed occupation on the ship's manifest was "Wealthy." Luigi was likely going over paperwork and ideas with Miss Weisberg. Perhaps he wanted a last look at his brother's American life. Men who consider themselves "wealthy" as a job description rarely run simple errands.[xciii]

Chapter 5

TILL WITHOUT FLO, PYRAMID POWER, AND THINGS JUST KEEP GETTING WORSE

Swearing was just not done when the "lady of Flotill" was in the plant. Ever! Tillie had a melodious speaking voice. Butter wouldn't melt in her mouth most days. But Mrs. Weisberg was infamous for her "hell hath no fury like a Tomato Queen scorned by a supplier" vulgarity on the phone in her office. Tillie's profanity was born of necessity. It was for show: a verbal defensive tactic in the offensive testosterone filled world of industrial business. Tillie would begin all negotiations with class and style, which usually was effective. However, hers was a business that portions of a penny often made the difference between profit and loss. Each supplier from sugar to transport trucks had to be precisely coordinated and priced with precision. Nearly daily, Tillie faced at least one disreputable man who determined he could outsmart, finagle, flim-flam and cheat her. When etiquette failed; inflamed expletives often worked.

No one ever summoned the courage to inform Mrs. Weisberg that her profanity-laced utterances carried throughout most of San Joaquin County when she was riled.

As far as anyone knew, Tillie Weisberg was divorced. Some days she was Mrs. Weisberg; other days she was Miss Weisberg. When she was a miss, there was usually an attractive man in her sights.[39]

Everyone noticed, after Florindo Del Gaizo passed away, that Tillie and Lloyd Dunivan became very close friends. The gossip was rampant. The single and unattached Lloyd began escorting the boss lady to and from the plant and the fields: wherever it was she wanted to go. He was with her constantly. This was understandable, since Miss Weisberg was in mourning for her friend and business partner. Her worries must have been great burdens to her.

Soon, Lloyd was driving Miss Weisberg to and from her home for work. Drive-by snoops noticed that his car was a permanent fixture in Miss Weisberg's drive way. Ralph Garcia thought that perhaps Mr. Dunivan's car had broken down.

When Tillie appeared at the plant on a Saturday in jodhpurs and riding boots and Lloyd in jeans and a cowboy hat, followed by a stable delivery of a dual-horse trailer containing two riding horses that Tillie had named Traveler and Trixie, rumor became fact. Lloyd was covertly nicknamed "the Cowboy." Tillie and Lloyd regularly surveyed the plant and the fields that supplied the plant on horseback. As Ralph said,

> We men all respected them both. They were both single. Miss Weisberg was still relatively new here from New York. She didn't seem to have any friends at all, not one. She had five or six hundred people working directly for her or waiting around in an area outside the plant hoping for a job [a sort of tent city]. She was supporting us all during the Great Depression, and I was garnering more supervisory duties and skills as [their] big love affair was going on. Miss Weisberg deserved a little happiness. I guess Mr. Dunivan gave that to her.

This didn't stop the crew from making jokes about Tillie and the Cowboy out "horsing around" and "rolling in the hay."[xciv]

---

39 The author restates, for clarity, that it is likely Tillie and Louis Weisberg were not legally married.

Lloyd "the Cowboy" Dunivan and Tillie Weisberg
front and center of the Flotill crew, 1937.

THE HEISER BOYS

Tillie's "pick yourself up, dust yourself off, start all over again" philosophy continued to calculate new paths to conquest, but barely squeaking by, loan-wise, meant that she could make no mistakes over the next few years. Mother Nature was going to need to cooperate at 100 percent, and Tillie must employ not just good but excellent help. The weather was out of her control (other than crossing her fingers and praying), but she did hold a few aces in her hand as far as help was concerned.

The best employees were both hard to find and expensive. Tillie seemed almost supernatural about business opportunities: she could see possibility where the person of average vision would swear it didn't exist. She was never one to wait for opportunity to knock. In fact, with her will, she went right out, took opportunity by the hand, and dragged it through the door.

So it went with two of her nephews, Arthur and Albert Heiser. Arthur had recently graduated from Cornell University with a degree in law, and

Albert was ready to leave school and bring his effervescent charm into the workplace as a top-notch businessman with a specialty in sales. Arthur loved the idea of practicing law but stated that "young Jewish attorneys were a dime a dozen." Saul Heiser, the eldest nephew, became a medical doctor; he was the only nephew who never worked at Flotill.

The three boys were intelligent, upstanding citizens any mother or auntie would be proud of. They were sweet kids who always returned Tillie's affection. On one Mother's Day, when the entire family still lived in Brooklyn, twelve-year-old Arthur Heiser clamped on his roller skates and brought Chips a bouquet of flowers he'd purchased himself.[40]

Tillie loved her three nephews. She was grateful that Beatrice had given birth and raised great children, saving her the trouble.

Hiring her two youngest nephews had several benefits. Tillie expected more devotion from family than anyone else on earth. She knew how bright these boys were and that she could, often shamelessly, manipulate them in ways a standard employee would not tolerate. In return, they would always have a great-titled job as long as she and Flotill lived.

At home, the relationship was personal, and Tillie was Chips. At the office, woe unto the nephew—or anyone else—who referred to her as anything other than Mrs. Weisberg. Even as they aged and became husbands and fathers, she thought of them as kids. At home and at the office, as an endearment or in rage, Tillie referred to them as "the boys."

Several employees would say later, "We knew the company was run by a woman, but it wasn't something anybody felt directly. Arthur and Albert Heiser were the visible, vocal leaders of office meetings and directives. We never answered to Mrs. Weisberg. Oh, boy, we all knew Arthur and Albert did answer to her. The Heiser boys were the bosses, but Mrs. Weisberg was *the boss!*"[41]

---

40   Tillie was so touched that this flower delivery still made Arthur Heiser blush seventy-plus years later.

41   Stated by Harry Rosen, "Doc" Weast, Ralph Garcia, and Rosie Munoz.

PYRAMID POWER

*In order to remain a queen one ought to stand just above
her subjects so as to evoke awe and respect*—Tillie Lewis[42]

Tillie knew most men were not comfortable working for a woman. Rather
than fighting the facts, she set up the top of her business model as a pyramid.
She was the peak: the summit of the Flotill hill. The Heiser boys were directly
below her. The rest of the company was the middle.

Tillie did not think of any employee being below herself and the Heisers
as being at the bottom. At Flotill, there was no bottom. Everyone was a valuable part of her Flotill family, but she was definitely the queen—the Tomato
on Top!

Tillie was never known to reprimand any employee. If there was a problem, she had her secretary call Arthur or Albert Heiser into her private office
and then closed the door. Tillie stated often, "A female boss should never
criticize a man." Instead, she ordered her nephews to do that duty. Arthur
became Tillie's right-hand man, her second in command, who handled the
problems on the floor of the plant. Tillie would be free to play "good" gal
to Arthur's "tough" guy. Albert was just too good humored a soul for the
task. If a customer needed to be schmoozed, Albert was the right man to do
it. Tillie's great-niece Barbara Heiser later said that "Uncle Al made everybody feel like they were the only person in the room, he was so genuinely
engaging."

Arthur was the complex, serious soul who would often leave Tillie's office
appearing to bear the weight of the world on his slender shoulders. Workers
on the floor stated that they often watched Arthur, after a session with Mrs.
Weisberg, walking double time, head down, forehead creased, mouth soured
into what would become a nearly permanent frown.[xcv]

---

42 Tillie designed her office so that she was elevated slightly higher than the tallest seated man.
Visitors' chair legs were always shorter than her throne-like seating. It was a subtle, silent expres-
sion of her rank.

Nephew Albert's wife, Helene Heiser, later said, "Second in command, Arthur was smack-dab under her thumb." Helene continued:

Tillie stepped on toes. Nobody in the family loved her all the time. It was awful if she turned her eyes on you. I was her private secretary for two years. Chips could swear like a truck driver, then pick up the phone to speak to someone very professional, sweet, and ladylike, then hang up the phone and begin throwing things...right back to swearing about work.

It had to be so hard for her. Intellectually and power-wise, she was the only woman in a world of all these men.

Most men adored her. She'd have all these men doing things for her. They'd stay late working on a project in the days before overtime. They'd drive her places and clean up after her horses—anything she needed.

I know she used her femininity. I wonder if a woman could do what she did without using the power of her sex? I doubt it. That's just not the way the world worked.

HARRY ROSEN

Harry Rosen left the William Randolph Hearst Cannery in Oroville per the invitation of his former boss, Jim Dempsey.[xcvi] Harry said, "Dempsey had been fired from Hearst for hitting a worker. Dempsey ended up with a black eye and got "the boot" to boot." Dempsey asked Harry to come on down to Stockton to work for "the Jew lady."

Harry interviewed with Art Heiser, who hired him as a chemist. Harry later reflected, "Arthur Heiser was my boss, to whom I answered to for about sixteen years, and who tore up my written letters of resignation on two occasions when I thought the load was more than I could handle. Arthur helped me prove that I could handle it...Tillie Lewis was, with emphasis, *the boss*, my boss, Arthur's boss, everybody's boss!"[xcvii]

Everybody knew Tillie Weisberg was too smart to expect any man to regularly report to her, except her two nephews. Everyone reported up the ladder to the Heiser boys, and *they* reported to Miss Weisberg. A smart, industry-wise broad? Harry expected this dame to be one ugly shrew.

On Harry's first day on the job, he was introduced to a few nice enough fellows. After handshakes and welcomes, the guys went to their various positions, leaving Harry with two men, one of whom was clearly ignoring Harry's repeated inquiries about what he was expected to do. The other man then piped up, "Rosen, you're going to have to learn some sign language. Miss Weisberg hired this deaf guy. She hires anybody who is able to do the job. You're going to find yourself working next to women, Mexicans, coloreds, Jews, and all kinds of handicapped."

Harry was more than a little stunned at the news. He was still scratching his head in wonder when he saw a small contingent of suited men following a pretty young woman. "Who's the cute chick?"

"That cute chick, Mr. Rosen, is our boss."

Harry was slack-jawed as Mrs. Weisberg cheerfully shook his hand and introduced herself. She welcomed him to her Flotill family.

Mrs. Weisberg turned her attention back to her crew and clicked away in her high heels, leaving a trail of the sweetest perfume Harry had ever smelled. Harry smiled, "We could all smell that Parisian perfume before we could hear the tappity-tap of her fancy footwear. The boss always looked, and smelled, like she'd come straight out of Hollywood. Wowza!"[xcviii]

PAT STANCO

Tillie stopped into the Chicago Flotill office on her way to New York and the original Flotill on Hudson Street. A wholesale salesman named Mr. Stanco was placing his orders. Stanco had been a buyer since Florindo Del Gaizo was the sole agent of Del Gaizo Products. Tillie was grateful to Mr. Stanco for sticking by Flotill through the years.

Tillie asked how he and the family were doing. Stanco was distraught. His son, Pat, had rheumatic fever and heart problems. The boy was in need of a drier climate if he was expected to live. Mr. Stanco had barely completed his last sentence before Tillie embraced him in a little hug and whispered, "Then we'll just get him out to California and into Flotill."

Pat Stanco was a sickly seventeen-year-old kid when he stepped off the train in Stockton as the newly hired payroll clerk. On Mrs. Weisberg's orders, Bill Puliston, from the front office, picked Pat up at the station and delivered him to the Wolfe Hotel, his new home for sixty-five dollars per month. Tillie had originally intended that Pat would stay with her and her nephew Albert, but the son of her Boston wholesale broker, Jimmy Berger, just as needy for a job in California as Pat was, beat him to the spot.

Harry Rosen was staying at the Wolfe, too. He was rooming with Bob Rosin, whose mother acted as Mrs. Weisberg's personal clothes shopper whenever she was in New York. Stockton's upscale store owners didn't appreciate a Jewish lady trying things on in their establishments, since at least one gentile lady had been overheard stating that she "wouldn't buy things a Jew had worn." Mrs. Weisberg far preferred the selection Mrs. Rosin chose for her, anyway.

Bob Rosin said his mom would have piles of clothes for Mrs. Weisberg to try on, on the bed in a fancy hotel. Mrs. Weisberg would say yes or no to hundreds of dollars in dresses. Bob said he was another addition to Mrs. Weisberg's yes pile when his mom had asked Mrs. Weisberg if she had a job for him.

It seemed like Mrs. Weisberg was running a grown-up "Boys Town."[43] She knew what being in need and broke was all about.

The Wolfe Hotel guys became fast friends. Jimmy Berger and Pat Stanco were walking around downtown when Mrs. Weisberg spied the pair. As Pat later said,

> She couldn't miss us, since the sole of Jimmy's shoe was loose. It was flopping all over. He nearly tripped on it. Miss Weisberg stopped to inquire what in the world was wrong with the shoe. Jimmy apologized, embarrassed, and promised he'd buy new shoes the next pay

---

43 Founded in 1917, by Father Flannigan as a city of hope, training, and care for orphaned boys.

period. Miss Weisberg put her hand to her heart, "You mean I don't pay you boys enough to keep you in a pair of shoes?"

Mrs. Weisberg gave all of us a ten-dollar bonus the following day, "to buy shoes," and a permanent little raise in pay.

The four of us Wolfe Hotel guys talked over beers that night. One topic, after ruminating over the cute local girls, was "What was with Miss Weisberg in hiring this hodge-podge of characters from all ends of the country, Mexicans, Japs, coloreds, Oakies, Catholics, and Jews?" Harry Rosen said, "We all have a few things in common. There's not a lazy rounder in the bunch. Mrs. Weisberg expects we won't let her down in a pinch. I suspect we won't. Choosing the right people [and] treating them right. That's one smart lady."[xcix]

Stanco continued, "She wasn't always a saint. She was a shrewd, tough businesswoman. I overheard Mrs. Weisberg on the phone speaking sweet-as-cherry-pie charming to Longview Fiber Company, somewhere in the Northwest. Five minutes later, she's shrieking at some other man at Hershel Cannery on Eight-Mile Road. She was giving him the riot act...vulgar language and all. She had the ability to change direction in an instant."

She called Pat into her office, before he left for home, to bring her a pot of coffee and a pastry. She was buried in paperwork and pointed to a silver carafe and matching silver tray of Danish pastries. Pat brought the refreshments when he noticed that the sterling set was engraved with the letters WA, for the Waldorf Astoria, where she stayed all the time. "I think she pinched it," Pat confessed with a laugh.

He left the front office wondering how late she'd work that night. She was usually the first one in every morning. He'd heard her refer to this place as her baby. She took care of it and all the Flotill workers as if they were her family. In return, people broke their backs to please her. She rarely needed to ask them to. That's what you did for family.

A few weeks later, sorting-line worker Connie Munoz won the Stockton Cannery Queen contest. Connie was a beauty. Miss Weisberg helped her cinch the competition by dolling Connie up in an expensive gown, a shimmering tiara, and what were probably real diamonds. Connie had to give them back after she won, but Tillie told Albert he could take the new queen out for a spin in her huge, cream-colored convertible. Pat was dating Connie's sister, Rosie Munoz. The Munoz girls were Catholic, which meant that those sisters went together and were home early: no hanky-panky with the Munoz girls.

Al Heiser decided they'd go live it up at the 276 Club. Off they went on a warm summer evening in that gorgeous car with the top down. Beyond the College of the Pacific,[44] there was nothing but rice fields to the north; way out at Swain and Pacific Avenue was the 276 Club. Al said there was a nice bar, good food, and great drinks.

The foursome didn't get to find out. Patrick wasn't twenty-one yet. He was still slender and was growing healthier, but the club could see he was obviously a teenager and threw all four of them out. This was Stockton in 1939. There just wasn't anyplace fun to go. They were four young friends in the boss's car using the boss's gas. They settled for enjoying a long, slow ride home.

TILLIE WEISBERG, YOU'RE UNDER ARREST

Troubles of all types loomed for Tillie. The dark cloud that hung over this terrible Depression had ground everyone in the country down. Nerves were frayed. It was a politically and personally isolationistic, every-man-for-himself period in time. Yet Tillie Weisberg held firm to her ideology of maintaining loyal employees and ignoring ethnicity, culture, race, gender, and religion. This ideology was going to cost her.

Local white Christian men were used to being at the top of the hiring food chain, no matter their ability level or behavior. Verbal bullying and physical beatings of other employees were not acceptable in Stockton, but racist and bullying behavior occurred all over the country, especially when jobs were so precious and rare.

No bullying would be tolerated at Flotill—not with Tillie Weisberg in charge. A job with Flotill, or with any of the canning plants, especially full

---

44 Now University of the Pacific (UOP).

time, gave most people a better-than-comfortable lifestyle. Most folks cur-
tailed their tongues and opinions in order to stay employed at this diverse
company.

Tillie dismissed a few ruffians from Flotill. They'd been warned. Tillie
did not want to send anyone out into the cold if she didn't have to. These men
were let go for repeatedly using unconscionable racial slurs and fighting in and
off Flotill grounds with other employees.

From 1930 to 1941, with no end in sight of the Great Depression, losing a
good, solid job was devastating. These creeps whom Tillie dismissed were not
going to tolerate losing that job to some Mexican, Negro, Jew, or woman. The
men called the police with trumped-up charges after Miss Weisberg refused to
overturn her decision to let them go and no one else would hire them.

Tillie was arrested on November 28, 1938. The Stockton Police originally
accused her of fraudulent corporate bookkeeping; the accusations would later
become much more grave than that.

It was a very polite and low-key event as arrests go. The police did not
take her fingerprints or mug shot. She was asked for her height, to which she
responded, "Five feet four and a half inches in high heels." She spent no time
in a cell; she was quietly humiliated instead. The police noted that she had a
driver's license but didn't drive. It is unclear who drove her home.

The charges were technically dropped on March 2, 1939, due to lack
of jurisdiction. Nonetheless, the FBI requested Stockton Chief of Police H.
A. Vogelsang to conduct a preliminary report on the lady. Her home was
staked out, her mail monitored, and her employees investigated. The report
would not be finalized until July 19, 1941—more than two years later. Tillie
Weisberg was under serious investigation.

The arrest and the time spent in questioning at the police station certainly
had to be upsetting to Tillie, yet she never complained to a single soul or
missed a beat pushing Flotill ever forward.[45]

---

45 The author uncovered Tillie's arrests from police department records and Freedom of
Information Act reports.

ALL EYES ON TILLIE

As part of her advertising genius, she flaunted her classic femininity and wealth rather than downplay it.

Demure? Never! Secure and sure? Definitely.

She convinced consumers that the homemaker should be a creature of discerning tastes. Tillie was usually her own cover girl. She was the model for women who cared about providing and preparing the safest, best-tasting, lowest-priced, and healthiest dinners (and lifestyles in general) while wearing a pretty dress, heels, and pearls.

As the completely immersed, take-charge, no-nonsense head honcho of an ever-growing company, she knew she was the exception to every rule. Men brought home the bacon, but women made it a meal. Therefore, she pitched herself as a homemaker first and a businesswoman second. She redefined the "feminine touch," reminding housewives through her nation-wide ad campaigns that only another woman understood the enormous value of the home, which centered on the quintessential American table.

> As a woman, I recognize that other women demand quality above everything else…My company was founded and operated by a woman…For women because [only] a woman fully appreciated the universal feminine demand for the highest standard possible and insisted that quality-first, last and always be served…I lead all other brands as the accepted criterion for quality.
> —Tillie Weisberg, President of Flotill Foods[c]

Before Tillie's campaigns, most housewives didn't realize they required a "criterion." And fewer still knew what a criterion was, yet Tillie seemed to be looking out for homemakers. Tillie had full-color magazine ads, catalogues, and huge grocery store displays full of canned delights that seemed certain to be better than anything made by some company run by men.

Unlike the other famous women of food, such as Betty Crocker, Sara Lee, and Aunt Jemima,[46] Tillie was a real woman, not a fictional character. Tillie personally answered questions and fan mail and made numerous public appearances.

Tillie developed booklets that taught the homemaker how to set herself apart in the most cherished, yet underrated, of all positions, that of wife and mother. Tillie's professional photographs and simple instructions taught ladies how to properly set tables from casual luncheon buffets to formal affairs, all featuring Tillie's specific products in the recipe section of the booklets. Later, these free booklets became the first twenty-one-day diet plan in the world, known as Tasti-Diet. These, too, were mailed free, directly to the consumer's home, just for dropping Tillie Weisberg a request. An actual fan letter won a happy customer a spot-on Tillie's VIP mailing list, winning free coupons and bringing these very important customers health along with promotional updates.

GOSSIP AND ANTI-SEMITISM FROM BECHLOFF'S

The upper-crust ladies enjoyed pinning up, curling, and letting down their hair, guard, and gossip at Bechloff's Beauty Salon. A decent Christian woman was not about to share this intimacy with a Jewess. What next? Colored women? Certainly, not!

The regular customers objected to Bechloff's serving Tillie at all. They were assuaged with the shop's agreement to keep a separate set of combs, brushes, rollers, and pins exclusively for Tillie.[ci] They were not about to share personal grooming tools with a Jew.

These women were dependent upon familial wealth and/or the fortunes of their husbands. Tillie was an unattached, self-absorbed, whirlwind woman of business, building her own future without a man or family funding.

---

46   Betty Crocker was a General Mills brand name from 1921; Sara Lee was the name of company founder Charles Lubin's young daughter; Aunt Jemima was a fictional "mammy" figure modeled after an actual former slave.

These women came to relax as much as to primp. They wanted to talk about their children, their husbands, household duties, and whomever was not in the room. With Tillie Weisberg, they had absolutely nothing in common. Remembering Tillie, several Stockton people later commented,

Lady #1: "Yes, I knew that Tillie Lewis. I couldn't stand her. Why? Number one, she was a Jew; you know...pushy, loud, but sweet. She was very nice but with all that typical Jew behavior. As soon as she moved into 1581 San Joaquin Street, she brought the rest of the Jews with her...Listen to this! One day [Tillie] is standing on the sidewalk waiting for that chauffer to pick her up in a limousine, showing off for the neighbors. And she was wearing a full-length mink coat, high heels, and *blue* jeans. Can you imagine?

Lady #2: "I heard Tillie tried to get a one-million-dollar life-insurance policy placed on her life. She told the insurance agent, 'If Betty Grable can insure her legs, then I should be able to insure my life.' The insurance man made my uncle promise not to spread that around, but it was quite a joke here [in Stockton] for a while. But since they're all gone, I'm sure it doesn't matter anymore." [Whispers] "She dyed her hair...taboo in those days. She had that done at *Bechloff's* [emphasizes word]. She had her own hairdresser and special chair that nobody else could use.[47] That hairdresser was one of Tillie's only friends in town."

Lady #3: "When I was barely eighteen years old, I was a nighttime switchboard operator in Stockton, in 1940/1941. Often, Mrs. Weisberg would call all over the country, late at night, to speak to men late in the evening. My parents said, 'Tillie flaunted everything; she was brassy and a Jew.' I'm not sure about that, but we all knew she was rich. Part of my job was to check that the line was still in use.

---

47 Discrimination against race and faith was common nationwide. Tillie's hairdresser was courageous in devising a compromise to appease the salon's anti-Semitic customers while still serving Tillie's beauty needs by keeping items for Tillie marked and separate.

I confess I heard Mrs. Weisberg's husky voice talking pretty sweet to men in New York and Chicago a lot. It was a thrill to hear her calling. I guess I should have been fired, but it was such fun, and it was Tillie Weisberg, after all."

Lady #4: "I was a kid, too. I remember the doctor sold her the house but not the [entrance] lions of Italian marble. There was quite a scuffle over who owned those darned lions. Miss Weisberg was very aggressive and domineering. She was a pushy woman [whom] we always thought was Italian. Tillie spoke to the whole neighborhood in Italian; of course, she was Italian. Tillie invited a group of us girls in to join her for lunch. I'd heard people say there was a Catholic chapel with a baptismal font in the house. Ridiculous! That was the room we had lunch in. I remember it was stenciled beautifully with a little water sink in it, so there was no need to walk to the kitchen for a glass of water. A maid answered the door, and Tillie walked down the stairs dressed formally, for lunch! In my eyes, as a teenager, she was not a lady. She was a businesswoman! Definitely *not* a lady."

YES, IT CAN GET WORSE

The ghost of the 1932–1933 Merced start-up failure was still haunting Tillie, who fought to keep that bankruptcy quiet while in search of new funding. Tillie was ready to buy another plant and expand into multiple products.

Joseph Capolino Food Products Corporation, which represented Ripon Canning Company, felt that this was their opportunity to pick a final legal bone with Mrs. Weisberg[cii] after Tillie's Merced Flotill Company fiasco had adversely affected Capolino's bottom line. Capolino filed a lawsuit against Flotill Products Incorporated. Their contention was that Mrs. Tillie Weisberg's Flotill of Merced bankruptcy should not have cleared the way for Mrs. Weisberg to immediately prosper from Flotill of Stockton.

The food industry is a closely-knit brotherhood. Capolino was aware of the financial problems that Tillie had faced since the death of Florindo Del

Gaizo. A letter from Gillian Jones of the law offices of Levinsky & Jones stated at the time that the "lawyers appear to have little hope for the success of Tillie Weisberg or Flotill. At this point not litigating and saving further attorney costs is the recommendation." Jones added, "PS. You have probably already been advised of the difficulties Mrs. Weisberg now finds herself in [from Del Gaizo's death]."ciii

The Capolino case was dropped in March of 1939, but not before the same disgruntled workers began to complain to Jones about being laid off in 1937. These men tried unsuccessfully to sue Mrs. Weisberg merely for the sake of vengeance. They promised to speak out against Flotill to benefit Capolino. That was not going to hold any weight in the Capolino lawsuit, since it was clear that the reasons these men were let go were for everything from normal, seasonal layoffs to fistfights on the plant site. Gillian Jones had no interest in these men or their claims.

Dissatisfied that the Capolino lawsuit had dismissed them as irrelevant and that the Stockton Police Department wasn't interested in their gripes, the four men found an ear much higher up. These fellows decided to complain to the FBI.

Local employers were aware of the problems that, as E. L. Wilholt, president of the Stockton Savings and Loan Bank, put it, a "disgruntled employee bent on getting even and some State Official who is endeavoring to make a record for himself"[48] can cause a company or an individual in times of terrorism by the witch-hunt fear of anti-American activity. This was now happening to Tillie, and most Stockton businesses knew it.

In early March, both Wilholt and George C. Wollenberg of the Stockton Merchants Association congratulated Tillie on beating the Capolino rap. As Wollenberg wrote, "The Stockton Merchants Association [was] greatly pleased that a settlement was made in your recent legal controversy. We knew that the situation was very complicated and not as serious as some assumed."

Florindo Del Gaizo had now been dead two years. Tillie ran a full season more successfully than in the two years when Florindo was involved in the

---

48   E. L. Wilholt of Stockton Savings and Loan Bank congratulates Tillie for standing up to legal bullies, March 3, 1939.

company. The improvement in production was due to favorable weather conditions and the training, advice, and experience provided by the Del Gaizos. Tillie knew the victory was still partly due to Flo.

War was now looming in Europe; Mussolini was rattling sabers. Obtaining additional funding from the Del Gaizo family for 1939 was just not going to happen. Luigi Del Gaizo and his family were as anxious as the rest of Europe about escaping the wrath of Mussolini and Adolf Hitler. Would Mussolini hand Italy to the führer? Del Gaizo-Santarsiero had to look out for itself. Tillie was on her own with Flotill.

Tillie was back to the nightmare of finding the money to keep her baby afloat. Flotill was precious to her. She had no doubt she would be fantastically triumphant if she had the chance to expand, thus bringing all the fruits of the Central Valley into multiple plants and providing more local jobs and greater profits for all. But the banks in Stockton did not agree. Tillie was without a man backing her. Pacific Can was not blind to the positive jump in her production but could only offer a weakly worded letter to try to interest their East Coast connections. The following letter from Pacific Can Company President E. F. Euphrat to Thomas Bowers, vice president of the Bank of the Manhattan Company, on Wall Street, was written on March 7, 1939.

> My Dear Mr. Bowers:
> This will introduce Mrs. Tillie Weisberg of the Flotill Products...
>
> We have enjoyed this account since its inception and they have made a wonderful showing, so much so that Mrs. Weisberg has now found it possible to take over this entire corporation.
>
> We personally are not satisfied with [Flotill's] banking connections and I am of the opinion that it may interest you.
> Sincerely,
> E. F. Euphrat[civ]

Tillie went begging for funding—from banks to box companies, churches to the silver screen—she humbled herself to everyone she could think of. On

April 14, 1939, a Mr. Sala of Bank of America wrote the following letter to Eugene J. Wait, vice president of loans in San Francisco.

> Dear Gene:
> Mrs. Weisberg of Flotill Products, Inc. called and left with us [a] financial statement of the corporation we are enclosing.
>
> She would like to have us finance her entire operation for the coming season. She states she will require from [$400,000 to $500,000] on the same basis as last year. She also asked for a $25,000 open credit of which $8,000 is to be used for advances to growers and the balance to open the cannery. The open indebtedness would be paid immediately from the sales of the first pack.
>
> When Mrs. Weisberg purchased the Del Gaizo interests, which amounted to 85%, she paid them $72,000. Of this amount $22,000 came from the Flotill bank account with us, $45,000 was advanced by Pacific Can and $5,000 was advanced by her personally. The $45,000 from Pacific Can was a personal loan to Mrs. Weisberg, repayable $15,000 yearly and as collateral the Can Company has in its possession the entire stock of Flotill Products, Inc. However, [Mrs. Weisberg] explained this may be rearranged so that the Can Company will take a chattel mortgage on the machinery but this has not been definitely decided.
>
> The Officers Committee here, in reviewing the statement, felt there is no basis for open credit but would be interested in making advances on warehouse receipts to responsible buyers if the loans could be properly secured. If the price of tomato products remains the same as in 1938, 70% of the warehouse receipt basis would be ample but it might be wise to advance less than the full 100%, on the DTIs [debt-to-income ratio], especially where shipments are made to brokers...

Tillie had already financed Flotill to the hilt. Bank of America said no, and all the local banks refused her. Tillie remembered the banker telling her of the refusal and adding, "In addition to the financial issues, Mrs. Weisberg, what if you get a headache and can't come to work?"[cv]

Tillie contacted Hollywood from her Ziegfeld days. Her pleas were either ignored or were passed on and rejected in chain-reaction style, as was the case with Don Lieberman of Coronado Films Inc. of Hollywood. Lieberman sent a wire to Tillie's home at 1581 North San Joaquin Street, followed by a long chatty letter in which he completely ignored the fact that she had asked him for a loan. In a third connection, Lieberman advised Tillie to send her financial statements off to his father, Don Lieberman Sr., in New York. He closed with, "There is very little more to say now, except that Charlotte and I wish to thank you again for your hospitality during our visit to Stockton, and we both hope to see you soon again." His father also chose the ignore Tillie totally tactic; he never responded to Tillie at all.

Tillie wrote to one of her cardboard-box suppliers, Eugene Singer,[cvi] at his home; she poured out her need for his help, both financially and personally. She told him she was so desperate that she was ready to hock her Lord Harry Clifton diamond and all her possessions to save Flotill. Eugene answered with ideas from his office on Star Corrugated Box stationery dated April 17, 1939.

Eugene Singer was an executive with a company that provided boxes for Flotill. He and Tillie may have had a brief affair after Del Gaizo died, according to Albert and Helene Heiser. In any event, Singer and Tillie remained business friends for life.

> My Dear Tillie:
> Your letter of Saturday just reached me. I have written Willie [his brother-in-law] per copy attached and also sent a letter to Issie regarding the situation in general.
>
> Can assure you now that we will work out your corrugated case requirements so that you will have all the cases needed.
>
> About your ring Tillie, I would hold this thought as a last resort as the interest charges are so terrific on a loan of this kind. Let us wait a few days to see what we hear from Willie and Issie and then if

nothing breaks from there or in any other direction, we will go into a huddle and see what can be worked out. You know my position.

When you write again address me here instead of the house. Everyone fine. Love from all.

As Ever,

Eugene

Tillie noted at the bottom of the letter: "Answered 4/19/39." Sweet Eugene was going to bat for her. She wouldn't forget this. She wouldn't write him at home again, either. People were quick to misunderstand friendships.

On April 17, 1939, Eugene Singer wrote to his brother-in-law, William "Willy" Crouse, who resided in a suite at the Wyndham Hotel in New York.

Dear Willie:

You might be surprised to see a letter from me, but I feel that it is important to have you consider whether or not it would interest you to make an investment out here with the thought of benefiting yourself as well as helping Tillie Weisberg…Everything is lovely here and your sister [Eugene's wife] is in grand shape generally. Best from all.

Cordially,

Eugene Singer[cvii]

In June, Tillie convinced Pacific Can that she was good for another small loan to keep her as a customer for life. They typed out an informal note for $4110.29 at 6 percent interest, all due September 1, 1940.[cviii]

Tillie ran out of ideas and acquaintances to hit up for money. She turned to a higher power. She prayed for a miracle at all churches, temples, and synagogues in the area. Every little bit helped. Agabeg Occult Church Inc. in Stockton agreed to loan her $3,000 for ninety days at 6 percent interest. Tillie personally typed up a short loan note dated July 3, 1939. The church handed her $3,000. Tillie paid her Flotill employees, secured product, and created enough profit to pay off the loan in full on October 2, 1939. Saint Mary's

Catholic church would follow, loaning Tillie $1,000. Tillie paid the money back quickly; her gratitude would last forever.

AND SHE'S SAFE

Eugene Singer's recommendation and polite pressure tactics won Tillie an audience with a bank ready and willing to go out on a limb for Tillie Weisberg and her baby, Flotill. Tillie took the train to New York with her fingers crossed. The Banco de Napoli was a longtime lender to the Del Gaizos and was a friend of Eugene Singer and others. Tillie remembered,

> When I went into this little bank at Broadway and Spring Street, a tall, thin, distinguished man asked for my financial statement. I said, "Well to be absolutely honest sir—if I were you and I saw my financial statements, I would not loan me the money, either. But if you want to trust a great company and a woman of integrity, I'd go ahead and make the loan. And I swear, if you ever need anything from me, I'll help you 100 percent.

That tall, thin, distinguished man who signed the documents that day was Claude Young of the Banco de Napoli in New York. Tillie obtained the loan to produce the 1940 pack and begin the process of buying another plant outside Stockton to pack far more than just tomatoes.

She promised herself that this time would be the last time she'd need to go begging.

She was certain she'd learned the error of not doing enough research with Flotill of Merced in 1933. Tillie always remembered those who helped her when she was down and out. She never, ever forgot a kindness. If she had to be a borrower, she'd be an exemplary one. She paid her loans back on time—absolutely—and early if at all possible. The next time she needed funding, there would be no crawling. She vowed to obtain loans because she was a solid citizen of business—a marketable commodity.

She later stated in *Reader's Digest*, "I learned thrift early in life. Since then, I've never bought anything I couldn't pay for in 10 days. They say that's not smart…but carrying debts on my shoulders is too much trouble. It clutters your mind."[cix]

THE SPAGHETTI CELEBRATION

After her financing victory, Tillie returned to the Flotill suite at the Park Central Hotel. Eugene Singer had assured her that the loan with the Banco de Napoli was a sure thing and that she should be ready to celebrate. Cautiously, in case Singer was wrong, Tillie did not prepare for a gala. To be safe, in case she would be disappointed, Tillie invited her three nephews to a homemade spaghetti dinner that she prepared at the suite herself. She told them she'd spring for an evening on the town at a swanky nightclub if all three boys found suitable young ladies as escorts. All three young men not only complied but would soon marry each of their lovely dates: Saul and June, Arthur and Lucy, and Albert and Helene.

The girls had been forewarned that Tillie, the boys could call Chips, was the Tomato Queen of California. The girls were to address her as "Mrs. Weisberg." Their best manners were expected of them.

The young ladies were terrified, but Tillie approved of the three girls immediately. She gave them a genuine smile followed by a tour of her closet stuffed with recent purchases from Paris. The biggest surprise was dinner. Mrs. Weisberg prepared a humble pasta topped with simple tomato sauce served on fine china, along with crystal glassware and Irish linens. Mrs. Weisberg, enjoying her spaghetti, told the kids that dessert would be a little fancier than this.

A uniformed chauffeur then arrived in a limousine and drove them to one of the nightclubs near Central Park.

No matter the occasion, Tillie made every social gathering a classy and memorable event.[cx]

Helene Heiser later recalled, "It's funny [that] the three guys married all of us girls. Chips approved of us, I guess. Arthur graduated from Cornell

University with a degree in law. Saul was a medical doctor, and my Albert and I were sent off to work in the Flotill Chicago office to get experience in sales. Al went further, in his education, to learn agriculture at Cornell. Except for Dr. Saul and June, we all were going to follow in Chip's footsteps."

Throughout her life, Tillie showered her family with wonderful events more than she did with gifts, but family gatherings and vacations were known as more performance reviews than casual, laid-back affairs. There were rules for dealing with Chips. Tillie didn't have friends. She had acquaintances. True friends took time to be developed and nurtured—time she devoted to business. The people who were close to her accommodated her—family included.[cxi]

The subject of Auntie Chips and her own lack of offspring was taboo. In any event, according to everyone in her family, Tillie bore no biological offspring—discussion closed—but Chips's numerous facelifts (and other cosmetic battles with gravity) and her lovers were delightfully fair game.

Tillie's new luxurious Stockton office with her painting
by New York artist Mordi Gassner, 1940.

ASPARAGUS STRIKE

In April of 1939, at the height of asparagus season, the Filipino Agricultural Laborer Association (FALA), led by seven thousand Filipinos, the primary pickers of the tender asparagus crop, and the American Federation of Labor (AFL) struck the California canneries to push toward unionization in every cannery plant.

Flotill was affected by this strike, since the company's Filipino workers loyally supported their brothers who were not enjoying the benefits of working for the more progressive Flotill. Memories of some of the strikers are recorded in the *Stockton Record*.

Dean Devlin: "In Stockton, Filipino workers in particular became synonymous with asparagus cutting, considered one of the toughest crops to harvest."

Jimmy Ente: "The hardest work that I ever done was asparagus. You had to get the asparagus out of the field because during the hot days, that sun would soak up the liquid in the grass, the asparagus. We called [asparagus 'grass'] in those days. And if you got it to the wash house dry, they weighed it, see, you get paid by the weight. And they want to make sure you got that grass into the wash house but if it was late, the guys going to get mad because you didn't pick it up right away.

"When working in the grass, the wind was blowing up the peat dust, you couldn't see your hand in front of your face. I wore two pairs of pants, three shirts, a bandanna over my head, and scarf, and goggles. Yeah, goggles. And you had to tie your shoe strings around your shoes, because if the peat dirt would get up into your pants leg, you're going to itch like crazy when you sweat.

"After you finished work in the fields and get into the bunkhouse, you'd have to sweep down the bunkhouse. So you'd get all that dust outta there. That was miserable."

Dawn Mabalon: "There are very racist arguments that farmers make about Filipinos doing this work, because [for example] they're shorter and therefore they're closer to the ground.

"I'd like to think that you know, the ways that workers were organized in terms of home towns and in terms of provinces and the relationships that these men had with each other and the obligations that they had to each other, really contributed to the efficiency they had in their work [;] they had a reputation for being extremely skilled workers."[49]

Dean Devlin: "For picking 100 pounds of asparagus picked a day, Filipino workers received just 90 cents,[50] less than half the amount paid to their white counterparts. This hard-earned cash was often sent to waiting parents and family members back in the Philippines."[cxii]

At one point, the Flotill office manager, Harry Turnbull, asked Pat Stanco to get his hind end out in the yard before fisticuffs broke out between a female worker and Mrs. Weisberg. Mini Lope, on behalf of the cannery workers' union, was verbally taunting Mrs. Weisberg as she was entering the building. Mrs. Weisberg stopped and stood her ground. The tension felt like a catfight was about to break loose. Mini was riling women up and shouting at Mrs. Weisberg for more money. Mrs. Weisberg's usual smile was a grimaced mask. The two women stared, unblinking, for a frightening moment. Mini Lope growled, "More money." Tillie hissed, "No!" and abruptly stormed into the office.

Tillie had already set Flotill wages above those of other plants to avoid strikes. She was deeply disappointed in her workers for threatening to strike.

---

49 Evidence shows that the Filipino workers of Stockton were exceptionally good workers at whatever task they took on; asparagus picking is just one example of the difficult work they did well.

50 In 1939, nine years into the Great Depression, the average American worker in all vocations made eighty-nine cents per hour, or $1,850 a year. Source: "Television History—The First 75 Years." Available at http://www.tvhistory.tv/1939%20QF.htm.

Tillie did far more for her Flotill family than other companies at the time did, according to interviews with former workers.[cxiii]

The ladies on the line and the seasonal workers were paid by the box: the more fruit, the more money. Since Tillie sometimes worked side by side with the ladies on the peeling and sorting line, as a method to both calm her herself from the stress of running the whole show and a nifty way to sniff out any potential strike problems that might be shared by a chatty gal standing elbow to elbow with the Tomato Queen, Tillie knew that the senior workers would bully the newer girls into taking a place farther down the line, where they would get the smaller fruit (and sometimes no fruit at all), thereby earning much less money. Tillie initiated mandatory rotation in the line so that all workers would have an equal chance to earn money. The workers also knew that Mrs. Weisberg would silently stand on the catwalk above the lines to check on both quality and fair play.[cxiv]

Still, the Flotill strike struck. The workers left to picket, not to pack it. Tillie rolled up her sleeves for real to sort and pack fruit, as did the entire front office. Soon Stockton big-wigs were donning aprons and overalls, peeling fruit elbow to elbow for Flotill.[cxv]

No matter the gossip, digs, or social slights, Stockton had Tillie's back when it counted most. She needed help. Help arrived from the top end of local business, academia, and everybody in between.

With Tillie's blessing, one of her Japanese workers (who did not wish to be counted among the "Flotill Filipino deserters") wrote a letter to the AFL that included a personal note from Tillie to the AFL president, William Green; the writer protested "the inequity of the situation."[cxvi] Mr. Green did not respond, and the strike dragged on.

Tillie noticed an article in *Variety* titled "News of the Show World"[51] that lambasted Hollywood labor union leader and infamous Chicago mafia extortionist Willie Morris Bioff. For several years, the Hollywood unions had been under the thumb of Bioff, who counted among his calling cards Molotov cocktails tossed into businesses that objected to a little payola.

---

51 *Variety* kept Tillie current on news, parties, and gossip about her former Ziegfeld pals who were now in Hollywood.

Arthur Ungar, a journalist for *Variety*, took on this firebombing criminal through his courageously penned updates in the magazine, which finally put Bioff behind bars at Alcatraz.[117] He railed in one article,

> Willie [Bioff] proudly boasts he never worked in theatre. Why should he, when he knows how to scheme and negotiate? Willie is bad news, because Willie only negotiates one way and that is for Willie. [Now] convicted of pandering, [he] brags that [he] never served a sentence, because he had it fixed.
>
> Willie won his point, but had to call in Meyer Lewis of the AFL to do it. Lewis, who has a reputation for fair dealing, no doubt was the reason peace was brought about and a strike averted. The rank and file of the unions, including members of the IATSE [International Alliance of Theatrical Stage Employees], have a profound respect for Lewis. But for Bioff, nothing but contempt.[cxviii]

Bioff served ten years in Alcatraz for racketeering and extortion before the Chicago mob blew him—and his car—to pieces in November of 1955.

Tillie contacted the "fair dealing" and profoundly respected Meyer Lewis of the AFL directly. Lewis got the go-ahead from his boss, William Green, to unionize the Flotill plant run by Mrs. Weisberg in Stockton after finishing up the union mess in Hollywood. Meyer Lewis arranged a meeting with the lady president of Flotill for the following week. Meyer was often quoted that he "expected to see some dried-up old hag running the company, not the delightful young lady" he encountered. It wasn't love at first sight. It was more "Let's make a deal" at first sight.[cxix]

ADD A DASH OF MEYER

Since it was clear to Meyer Lewis that Flotill already exceeded the standard for working conditions and compensation and had one of the most broadminded and ethnically and gender-diverse managerial styles he'd seen to date, the only thing left to negotiate was where to take the alluring company president to dinner to discuss more pleasant matters.

Tillie Weisberg thought Meyer Lewis was a charming and formidable fellow, even if he was portly, balding, and a little too married. He seemed to be flirting, and he was Jewish—something Lloyd Dunivan was not.

Tillie was delighted that Mr. Lewis was so enamored of her company's operation. Meyer stressed that he'd never seen an employer as invested in his or her employees as Miss Weisberg was. He believed that her progressive programs were a first in the industry. By the evening's end, the two were negotiating Meyer's requirements if he were to accept a full-time position with Flotill in California. His wife and family were conveniently and comfortably living in Manhattan near Greenwich Village and were accustomed to his cross-country business adventures.[120]

They settled the strike details over cocktails and dessert. A few weeks later, Tillie hired Meyer Lewis as general manager of Flotill.

Meyer Lewis proved to be of service as a threat to union trouble. He was clever and charismatic. He carried himself with a manly confidence that seemed threatening to men and attractive to the ladies, including Miss Weisberg.

Rumors spread that Meyer Lewis had connections to the mob. Some said that he had bumped off more than a few characters who'd gotten in his way, but nothing could have been further from the truth. Meyer was a tough cookie with a tender middle. He was no pushover, but he was not a thug either. According to Arthur Heiser, Meyer most likely spread those mob-guy rumors himself.

Meyer's known criminal activities included peeking at an opponent's hand during a card game and sneaking fresh fruit off the Flotill line and popping peaches straight into his mouth. Photographic evidence of his absconding with apricots may be seen from a reprimand written on the back of a photo by a teasing worker on the apricot line. Meyer's hulking presence and strength as a union labor leader made him the right choice to become Tillie's new general manager.

TILLIE'S COMMON-SENSE HOUSING

Tillie spoke about common sense throughout her life and career. During the Depression years, it made no sense to her not to help accommodate the very people she needed to work for her. The uncommon boss she was saw how her employees often struggled to retain a place to lay their heads and transportation to get to work.

Tillie kept an eye out for structures where her Flotill family of workers could live comfortably. As was the case from Tillie's childhood memories of Brooklyn with immigrants, the Stockton workers tended to stick to their own linguistic, ethnic, and socioeconomic groups, which made it tougher to set up one specific area for Flotill housing.

Throughout the Great Depression, the poor set up tent cities, auto camps, and shantytowns near businesses and in unincorporated areas, reminding Tillie of a ground-level version of her own childhood of tenement misery. Just as in early 1900s Brooklyn, discrimination was prevalent in Stockton, even at the bottom tiers of society. The city had a "color line"; people of color were not permitted to live north of Weber Street.[cxxi]

Filipinos—nearly all men because of discriminatory regulations—built their own community in South Stockton. They set up businesses and organizations of all kinds to meet their own needs: restaurants, hotels, grocery stores, barber shops, and social clubs. The area was, and is, known as Little Manila.

The large contingent of Japanese immigrants stayed in Japanese-friendly hotels (where agricultural laborers could stay in the winter), the Buddhist Temple, a Christian church or two, a Tenrikyo church[52], and Nippon Hospital. Some of Tillie's Japanese employees quietly discovered their own free housing by occupying abandoned boats in the Port of Stockton. These boats were solid, weatherproof, close to work, and there was always the fresh fish supply for supper. With a little elbow grease and something from an authority to give them the legal right to be there, the boats could make very

---

52 A faith originating from the teachings of a nineteenth-century Japanese woman named Nakayama Miki, known to her followers as Oyasama.

decent housing for her Japanese employees, even if they had to pay someone a little rent.

Tillie authorized the office manager, Harry Turnbull, to contact the California Office of Immigration and Housing to see if, with her positive recommendation of character and financial assistance for the fix-up jobs, her Japanese employees might win approval to rehabilitate and inhabit any legally abandoned vessels. They were denied. Tillie then pushed beyond the local agent and wrote to California Governor Olson himself. Governor Olson's office flatly refused the idea.[cxxii] The governor seemed adamant about getting the Japanese out of California if he could. Tillie found a deep affinity for these gentle people who seemed to openly love her; Tillie finally just looked the other way and kept mum on the subject, since her boat-people seemed content with conditions as they were on their floating abodes.

A MORE PERFECT UNION

Meyer Lewis was instrumental in helping Tillie create the first full-union contract in the history of agricultural labor in the United States. They were photographed formally writing labor history by setting the Flotill standard into writing. As Tillie wrote, "I am happy to be the first industrialist in the agricultural field to place my signature to such a progressive and humane contract which will be an instrument of progress for both employer and employee…It has always been my ambition to work in harmony with labor and through an agreement of this kind which means better working conditions and working operations both parties cannot help but benefit materially."[53]

---

53 The union-labor contract was real: Tillie raised the standard. Flotill ad propaganda created by Tillie Weisberg. Printed in the *Stockton Record* and various periodicals.

... writing labor history ...

Signing the first full union contract in the history of agricultural labor
in the United States

"I am happy to be the first industrialist in the agricultural field to place my signature to such a progressive and humane contract which will be an instrument of progress for both employer and employee.

"It has always been my ambition to work in harmony with labor and through an agreement of this kind which means better working conditions and working operations both parties cannot help but benefit materially."

Sincerely,

Tillie Weisberg

President

FLOTILL PRODUCTS, INCORPORATED
STOCKTON, CALIFORNIA

The newly hired Meyer Lewis, left of "The Boss," Tillie Weisberg, signing the most progressive agricultural-labor contract in the country.

Chapter 6

TILLIE A SPY?

The FBI's top man at the time, J. Edgar Hoover, was deeply immersed in rousting suspected subversives. From anonymous Austrian grandfathers who delivered ice in the neighborhoods of Brooklyn to the millionaire J. Paul Getty, everyone and anyone might be plotting against the Stars and Stripes. The FBI whet the appetites of bigots, snitches, and rats with the offer of anonymity cloaked in the sweet cheese of supersecret G-man status. Many people invented tales of espionage to seek revenge or just to become "Informant A" or "Source D" on a classified FBI document, somehow enjoying the fun of being interviewed as if they were big shots.

It didn't help Tillie that on Christmas Eve of 1937, she filed for US trademark approval for a new brand-name label for her Italian customers called Conquista,[cxxiii] complete with a male silhouette of a uniformed and straight-armed saluting fascist.[54]

Under orders from the FBI, Tillie was informally arrested, again, on November 20, 1939; her original Stockton Police Department accusation of fraudulent corporate bookkeeping had been upgraded to "acting as an agent of a foreign government." Tillie Weisberg was being investigated as a spy.

---

54 Until Italy joined forces with Germany, Tillie was a food supplier for the nonpolitical Del Gaizo-Santarsiero Company and did pack under popular Italian labels, but she did so nearly exclusively for the US East Coast, not Italy.

The FBI report synopsis of the crime and the suspect was dispersed to the Stockton Police and to nine federal agents: two in New York, two in Chicago, two in Miami, and three in San Francisco.

FBI File# 100-1432

Synopsis: Subject corporation (Flotill) to have been originally been financed from Italy; that some of its owners now reside in Italy and most of its productions are labeled in Italian. Subject Tillie Weisberg president and treasurer, reported to be daughter of German father and Italian mother and strongly pro-Fascist. Subject XXXX employed in laboratory and strongly pro-Fascist bragged
most of production of the company (Flotill) went to Italy…

This investigation was based on the complaint below that was received by the San Francisco office of the FBI from "Source A," who furnished the following information.

Harry Turnbull, office manager (former narcotics agent and addict[55] from Alameda County, I am told) now with Flotill, plans to crowd mixed groups of Japanese into old boats at Stockton (in the port waters) and employ them in the canning of tomatoes. He and his employers, Mrs. Tillie Weisberg, are urging Governor Olson[56] to overrule the Immigration and Housing Agent in this matter. Mrs. Weisberg is a reported special agent of Mussolino [Mussolini].

Source B complained as follows:

Tillie Weisberg because of her Italian sympathies. Subject's partner is a Mr. Florenzo [Florindo Del Gaizo] and she has a picture of Mussolini

---

55   The author found no indication that Harry Turnbull was involved with narcotics as either agent or addict; she only found more unsupported accusations.

56   Governor Olson was concerned about Japanese immigrants before the attack on Pearl Harbor. Olson told the Tolan congressional committee that he favored the wholesale evacuation of people of Japanese ancestry from coastal California.

in her office which she compels people to salute. Since subject has a contract to furnish food to the United States Army, Complainant fears what might be put into the cans. Subject has many South American export contacts. Is flagrantly violating the Federal Wages and Hour Act and boasts about it. Also subject has big parties at her home, inviting younger women employed in her plant. Complainant thinks she may be debauching them. Complaint describes Mrs. Weisberg as follows:

Age: 40 years
Height: 5' 3"
Weight: 130 lbs.
Build: Medium
Hair: Bleached blonde[57]
Mannerisms: Very rough
Speech: Rough and vulgar...

Source C complained about:

XXXXX who is employed by Flotill who made very pro-Fascist remarks and noticed Source C's American Legion button stating, "We Italians will take care of the American Legion." Tillie Weisberg frequently calls this Italian into her office and asks him what is going on in the plant. Weisberg and the Italian speak in either English, Italian or German[58] and brags most of the cans are going back to Italy and labeled in Italian...

The FBI contacted the Stockton police chief to investigate further. Chief Vogelsang replied that the subject, Mrs. Weisberg, had already been arrested

---

57 Tillie was at no time a bleached blonde. Her red hair was an important part of the red-tomato queen campaign.
58 Tillie was fluent in English, Italian, French, and Yiddish.

on November 28, 1938, but that the case had been dismissed on March 2, 1939, due to lack of jurisdiction.

Vogelsang's report for the FBI of November 29, 1940, concluded that Tillie Weisberg (referred to as "Subject") had no likenesses of Mussolini in her properties; the report did state that Florindo Del Gaizo's portrait resembled Il Duce. It further stated:

Subject's father was supposed to be German and Mother Italian.

Subject was still married to Louis Weisberg who claimed to be a New York publicity agent but earned his income at "Moosalina Products Corp." grocery merchant in Brooklyn, New York.

Subject had a "handy man named Lloyd Donovan residing in her home" along with another fellow "Marcus described as: about 25 years old, very dark and swarthy."

Subject recently dismissed both a "Negro driver and Negress cook but had discharged them in favor of two German refugees." The man is named "George" the woman not known. This couple sent a great many telegrams with "Tillie" at home and with her absent from the city. [Vogelsang indicates he is to receive a copy of suspicious telegrams.] The German couple at "Tillie's" are not supposed to be able to speak English but deliverymen have talked to them and their speech is very good and very careful as to what is said.

Subject is reported to have made five trips to Europe and left for Florida immediately after the local canning season finished. She was supposed to meet a man named "Kippernose" [Sam Kipniss] …Tillie registered on 9/28/39 gave her party affiliation as that of a Republican.[59]

A follow-up report states that:

---

59 FBI-ordered police report on Tillie Weisberg by police chief H. A. Vogelsang, November 29, 1940. Section 563 of the penal code, repealed in 1947, addressed "bailments" and corporate account fraud. Information according to attorney Jeffrey Heiser, March 9, 2011.

Tillie's 1938 [personal] salary was $20,000.[60] The photograph that resembles Mussolini is of Florindo Del Gaizo [deceased] and Mrs. Weisberg has taken said photo home to San Joaquin Street, Stockton.

Subject's sister: Beatrice Hockheiser; husband: Louis Weisberg will be further investigated by New York office. Kippernose is Sammy Kipnis: Miami office will investigate his Long Island, NY and Jacksonville, Florida homes, properties and business, activities and reputation since Mrs. Weisberg meets with him.

Stockton, California will place a mail cover of mail addressed to Flotill Products, Inc. and upon Tillie Weisberg, 1582 N. San Joaquin Street, will follow-up and report results of such cover. Also bank accounts and those residing in home at 1581 N. San Joaquin Street home of Mrs. Tillie Weisberg.

WHAT WAS TILLIE UP TO?

The two German refugees at her North San Joaquin Street home mentioned in the report were George and Thea Froehlich, Tillie's chauffeur and housekeeper, respectively. They were Jews who had fled Hitler's atrocities in an Underground Railroad–type system of American Jews saving European Jews. Even though they were educated to do much more than they currently were doing, to be able to stay in the United States, they served as Tillie's domestic help while they worked to obtain permanent status. George Froehlich spent the rest of his working career at Flotill as an accountant, and Thea Froehlich became a favorite schoolteacher in Stockton.

In secret, Tillie financially assisted in the escape from Europe of several Jewish families, whom she then brought to work at Flotill. News of the generosity of a wealthy Jewish-American spread, and letters for help from terrified Jews written in both Yiddish and German started to reach Tillie. Tillie translated and replied to the Yiddish letters, and George Froehlich replied to the German ones. These were some of the questionable letters and telegrams the Stockton police were referring to. After World War II had ended, Tillie

---

60   This was equivalent to around $340,000 in 2016 dollars.

and George continued to answer requests for aid to the Jews who were now settled in Israel. The Froehlichs told the author Reva Clar that they had fled to America when Hitler's Nazis took power. In addition to everything else Mrs. Weisberg did, they recalled Tillie welcoming Jewish servicemen to her home at Passover.[cxxiv]

The negro couple mentioned in the police report who were dismissed from Tillie's home were hired at Flotill as a general mechanic and line worker. Several of Tillie's mysterious Florida trips were to see Lord Harry Clifton, in addition to Sam Kipniss. Lord Clifton was still a good friend. The canary-yellow-diamond affair had been shipboard on that singular voyage long ago. Tillie was too old for Lord Harry, and he was too fancy-free for her tastes. He enjoyed Tillie's company and her innate business sense. He used Tillie for advice, and Tillie had bragging rights to royalty. From 1938 through 1940, Lord Clifton was busy investing in property in sunny Florida. Florida real estate was a bargain, if one had the money and one was willing to gamble that prices would someday begin to rise again.

Lord Harry was frittering away his eight-hundred-year-old family inheritance at lightning speed. The Lytham Town Trust stated,

> Harry…dissipated his inheritance. All 2,500 acres, the Clifton Hall and its park. This last Clifton Squire had an unhappy childhood… He was able to get at capital of the estate. He kept permanent suites at the best hotels and was well known as an eccentric. He plundered the Clifton estates to support his extravagant life-style and wild schemes with complete and utter selfishness.[cxxv]

Tillie, and many other friends and acquaintances, enjoyed Great Gatsby–style good times with Lord Harry. But invest in swampland in the land of the alligator? Tillie Weisberg's advice was a resounding "No!"[61]

Tillie traveled many times to Italy. She was still making tomato products for the Del Gaizo firm. She was well aware of how much she owed this fine family. Another benefit was that the Italians knew how to dress

---

61   History of Lord Harry Clifton, available at http://www.lythamtowntrust.org/

in style. Tillie stopped worrying about buying clothes in California and instead had her shoes, bags, and dresses custom made while she relaxed in this beautiful, ancient place. And she would pop into Paris while she was in the neighborhood.[cxxvi]

Chapter 7

ONCE UPON A TIME, THERE LIVED A TOMATO

A local amateur camera bug who had the necessary time, talent, and equipment began to film places and things he found to be interesting all over San Joaquin County.[cxxvii] He especially enjoyed filming working machines and items being manufactured. He asked Miss Weisberg if he could film her Flotill operation in action. Tillie agreed, but she requested that he film her tale of success as a Cinderella story first—then he'd be welcome to shoot camera footage of the cannery.

Tillie's idea was to make a Disneyesque film short. The film was to begin with Miss Weisberg in her office being handed a full-color storybook of a happy little pomodoro tomato and its magical journey through the Flotill plant and into the homes of grateful homemakers.

The photographer, who simply wanted footage of the manufacturing portion of Flotill and not the ridiculous woman running the place, left most of the footage of Miss Weisberg on his cutting-room floor. Tillie was livid with the result. Tillie would orchestrate all further filming of her company.

KEEPING HER WORD

On September 27, 1940, Mussolini signed the Tripartite Act with Germany and Japan. Italian-owned banks and businesses began to leave the United

States, including the one that had loaned Tillie the money to save Flotill when no other bank would—Banco de Napoli.

That little Italian bank where Claude Young, the kind loan officer, worked was now going under. Claude hadn't forgotten that Mrs. Weisberg had made a promise to help him if he ever needed it. He needed that help now. He'd made a few inquiries and had learned that the redhead had done very well for herself. Her firm was on solid ground in a nice, decent, community where he thought he might raise his family. Claude called Mrs. Weisberg in California. He spoke to Tillie briefly and explained that he needed a job and that he sure hoped she'd be able to accommodate him. Tillie told him not to worry. She kept her promises.

Claude and his family were soon on a train bound for Stockton, all expenses paid by his new employer. She'd hired him on as chief financial officer of the firm.[62]

In January of 1941, *Western Canner and Packer* magazine still had no official place for a woman in its business-speak. It boasted the following in its "Men in the News" section. Tillie had just redecorated her offices and was anxious to brag about it.

> Mrs. Tillie Weisberg—the auburn haired young lady who jumped from Wall Street into the canning industry in 1934...returns from New York to the most unusual head office in the canning business...the new head office will have red and white leather walls, air conditioning, fluorescent lighting, dressing-room, lavatory, bar and fireplace. Currently the largest exclusive canner of tomatoes in the United States, Flotill will add asparagus and spinach this year.

Tomato red—from her hair to the walls and custom furniture wood—Tillie paid homage to the pomodoro and announced to all who entered that Tillie Weisberg was the Tomato Queen. A working fireplace, air conditioning, full bar, and deluxe dressing area were fixtures just as foreign to industrial buildings as was the lady herself.

---

62 He remained with Flotill for the rest of his working life, retiring in 1968.

Tillie's secretary wrote in a journal that, as of February of 1939, Mrs. Weisberg was divorced from Mr. Weisberg. This is certainly what the secretary was told, but it wasn't a fact. In order for the company to incorporate, the truth (or at least a version of it) needed to be recorded regarding marital status and more. April 9, 1941, Tillie Weisberg had to officially document that she was still

married to Louis Weisberg, who has no financial interest in the holdings of his wife, now or in the future. Tillie is 40-ish, German of Austrian decent. [She] was bankrupt for six months in 1932, claiming stock market losses…the company was originally a branch of the New York office of Flotill but now the reverse is true. Flotill of Stockton has branch offices in New York and Chicago for sales purposes. Florindo Del Gaizo, deceased Aug. 23, 1937 [was] owner [of] 85% of the company stock which reverted to the Del Gaizo Estate. In March of 1939 all of the Del Gaizo interest was sold [to Tillie].[cxxviii]

THE FBI FOLDS
J. Edgar Hoover himself directed the closing investigation on Flotill. He ordered the file of Mrs. Tillie Weisberg "to be closed—failing to reflect any information indicating that the subjects are acting as agents of a foreign principal." At this point, Tillie Weisberg was making a national name for herself by being precisely what she was—Tillie was as American as the apple pie she would surely pack if only Stockton grew apples.

TILLIE THE TORNADO
The salesmen for Packomatic happened to have met with Tillie on a day she was caught "peeling tomatoes along with the help, working in her office at high speed, long-distance calling to New York and New Orleans before dashing off to the boiler room to resolve a problem with the equipment"; meanwhile, the Packomatic team was trying to keep up with her. Flotill had just purchased

two Packomatic case-sealing machines. As per Packomatic magazine, 1941, Miss Weisberg commented that she'd made "eleven round trip aeroplane trips to her New York office alone the year before and had personally sold every case of product from the previous year's pack." Packomatic released a photograph of Miss Weisberg dressed in jodhpurs, riding boots, a riding jacket, and her signature pearl necklace at the rear section of the Stockton plant with her two riding horses, Traveler and Trixie.[63]

TWENTY QUESTIONS

At the end of the 1941 tomato season-pack, Tillie sent out a happiness-themed newsletter with a questionnaire attached to her employees. Most everyone filled it out and returned it, since Miss Weisberg stated, "We want to try to assist those on whom good fortune may not smile too often during the months until next season. It is our desire to try to assist not only you who have worked with us but also your families, by trying to add a little happiness in your homes." The questions asked for employees' contact numbers, marital status, and family details. It asked for details about their children, including their names, birthdays, schools, and grades; it asked if children were interested in musical instruments or singing, or joining the Boy Scouts or Girl Scouts, or if they were Campfire Girls. The form ended with, "If we build a new plant at Isleton would you prefer to work there or in Stockton?"

Tillie used detailed questionnaires for every new hire from this point forward. She was diligent about maintaining personal involvement with her employees to let her Flotill family know that she really did care about them.[cxxix]

If there was a possibility to hire a seasonal worker for anything else during the year, Tillie would call and offer her people the job. Her landscaping and small jobs around her properties were handled by trusted Flotill employees or their children.

This call list came in especially handy when the Japanese attacked the United States at its naval base in Pearl Harbor on Sunday, December 7, 1941. War meant a lot of canned food, now!

---

63 Tillie named all her pets with *T* names and embellished and embroidered everything she could with her initials.

Chapter 8

WAR, STRIPPERS, BRACEROS, AND DOING YOUR BIT

War, like all adversity, meant opportunity for somebody. Every problem has a solution, and that solution usually makes money. Soldiers were going to be hungry. Tillie geared up to start feeding troops immediately.

It was instantly wartime. Many of her young male workers would be joining up to do their duty. Some workers moved on toward Mexico for the season or for the holidays. Others simply enjoyed the time off. She, along with most businesses, was decidedly short-staffed for this national emergency. Having those recently acquired questionnaire responses proved invaluable to her.

Tillie called for all available single ladies who would work through the holidays. She needed them to strip off the original Flotill labels. Only girls who were willing and able to be 100 percent committed to working long hours and had zero responsibilities to family or a spouse would be considered for this duty. Tillie's first war-campaign plan needed immediate action.

Tillie sketched out a stick-figure idea she gave to a local printer. Her concept was a red, white, and blue all-American "Flotill loves the USA" label for her new "Flotill Feeds the Troops" campaign. The printer returned the rushed patriotic depiction of tanks rolling across the label. It was perfect. The "label strippers" quickly tore off the peacetime Flotill labels and pasted on new wartime Flotill labels. The girls were alone stripping these cans, but the boring task was made more fun when the church-going and highly proper yet spunky young ladies jokingly decided to refer to themselves as the "Flotill strippers."

They were making good money, but they felt locked away all day, with nothing on the radio but Christmas music. The girls were one "Jingle Bells" or "Silent Night" away from dashing out the door.

The patriotic Flotill label Tillie created to boost morale in a can stripped of its peacetime label and relabeled in all-American uniforms by the "Flotill strippers."

As a lark, they called a local DJ to tell them of their plight and to request some big-band swing, like Glenn Miller, Artie Shaw, or Tommy Dorsey.[64] When they explained that they were the Flotill Strippers from the Tillie Weisberg plant in Stockton, the DJ was more than happy to comply. He dedicated every nonholiday song to them.

First thing the next morning, the warehouse doors were thrown open by a smiling Mrs. Weisberg along with a reporter who happily snapped photos of these sweet young lady "strippers" placing labels of Flotill patriotism on hundreds of cans of food destined to feed our boys in harm's way.[cxxx]

On December 14, 1941, armed with foodstuffs, a red, white, and blue feeling Tillie sent the aforementioned AFL president, William Green, a lavish Flotill Christmas basket filled local treats, wine, and those patriotic canned goods. She was unabashedly schmoozing for a war contract. On January 2, 1942, Green sent "Nellie Weisberg" a thank-you letter for the Christmas basket of Flotill products but misspelled her name.

---

64 A heartthrob named Frank Sinatra was Dorsey's lead singer.

Tillie responded to Green with a copy of the memo to her employees in which she gave them a 5 percent bonus in addition to a 10 percent allotment for each employee who purchased war bonds *and* finished the season or was laid off by the company or was inducted into the military. Green would not forget her name again.

From 1940 to 1942, Tillie went from FBI suspect for un-American activities to US superpatriot. Green responded to Tillie personally:

Miss Tillie Weisberg, President, Flotill Products.

My Dear Miss Weisberg:
I cannot find language which would adequately express my feeling of appreciation of the fine service you rendered our Government when you advised your employees that you would pay a five per cent. bonus in War Savings Stamps to each and every employee who completes the processing season and who authorizes a ten per cent. pay-roll deduction for investment in War Savings Stamps and Bonds...

Your offer five per cent. bonus furnishes a strong incentive to complete the current season...[Your] plan means your employees will have saved for use in the difficult post-war period...I commend you most highly upon your action which was voluntarily taken...

I am particularly proud of this advanced step in employer and employee relationships.

With kind regards and best wishes, I am sincerely yours,
W. Green
President,
American Federation of Labor,
Washington, DC[cxxxi]

William Green sent Tillie's letter off to US secretary of the treasury Henry Morgenthau Jr. Green wrote to Morgenthau on July 9, 1942: "I wish all employers throughout the country would take similar action...I hope you find it possible to write Miss Weisberg, commending her upon the fine patriotic service she has rendered the nation at this particular time." Tillie, along with most other canning companies, had joined the battle by feeding the troops with a well-negotiated government contract; in addition, Flotill continued to pack for the nation.

AND THEN THEY WERE GONE

The immediate idea of getting even with the evil empire of Japan, which had slaughtered our boys at Pearl Harbor, along with that Nazi madman who was using Mussolini as his puppet, left the country feeling gung ho.

Then again, the memories were still fresh of the first war against Germany and its wicked alliances. Much of the world, including Tillie, hadn't forgotten the precious time and loved ones lost not thirty years before. This was a nightmare. What if her nephews had to fight? Her friends? Her workers?

Yes, making canned food was a smart business for wartime. Armies do fight on their stomachs, as Napoleon Bonaparte said. But Tillie was aching for those who would soon be marching off to fight this war.

She, along will all other employers who hired diverse staffs, suffered the sudden loss of their Japanese employees. Executive Order 9066 forced Japanese-Americans to evacuate the West Coast. It broke Tillie's heart, and she promised she'd hire them back as soon as she was able; but for now, they were gone. Most fit young men (from the ages of eighteen through thirty-eight) were in uniform and gone as well.

Her nephew Saul joined up to take his medical skills to help where he was needed. The world was at war once again.

THE MODESTO PLANT

Tillie was thinking of building the new plant in Isleton because the property was inexpensive. With the new war-contract income, she could have Modesto instead. The Modesto deal would cost a lot more money than Isleton, but the location in Modesto was sublime. With the war-contract money rolling in, her attorneys advised her to go ahead with the deal. She was excited and raring to sign on the dotted line.

Her nephew Arthur Heiser had asked to speak to her in private. Arthur argued that the Modesto seller was a crook who was asking far more than the place was worth. Alone with his aunt he said, "Chips, that property isn't worth what they are asking. These guys are trying to flimflam you!" He slapped his hand with a hard smack on the desk for emphasis.

Tillie pushed forward and sat on the edge of her seat, deep concentration etched into her face. She jutted out her chin defiantly, slapped her right hand sharply on the desk as hard as he had, screwed up her face, and said with authority, "Then let'em go ahead and flimflam me—I'm buying it!" As Arthur later said, "It was the best move the company made, and she just knew it instinctively. She was simply amazing. The Modesto plant was a winner from day one."[cxxxii]

LOVE AND MARRIAGE

Tillie needed to move toward marriage in her personal and professional life. Being known as a divorcée was wearing on the already thin skin of Central Valley society. The Cowboy had seemingly run out of rope and any potential for the future.

Dunivan had been butting heads with Meyer Lewis for Tillie's attention for some time now. The gossip was now outside the plant and was dribbling toward the ears of the beauty-parlor bunch and Tillie's housewife-wholesome customer base. This was not acceptable.

On the "Lloyd Dunivan for a mate" plus side, he was unmarried and had no children, and Tillie loved him. On the negative side, he wasn't Jewish. Tillie was not devout to her Jewish faith but she was, as she said, "Jewish-minded." She was not keen to marry any man who was not of her faith. The other problem was bigger: Lloyd wanted children and a traditional life.

Then, on July 11, 1942, Lloyd married the twenty-eight-year-old Jaquelin Kappenberg in Stockton, thus officially ending the affair with Miss Tillie on his own terms.[cxxxiii] It is unknown if Lloyd delivered the news at the office, but it is likely that he did, since Tillie seemed blindsided.

The end of the romance with Lloyd sent the unflappable Tillie running to the main floor employee's ladies' room for a serious cry. The women who worked the floor asked no questions while they swiftly cleared out of the bathroom. They silently shuffled past their bereft boss and got right back to work without a word. The line ladies gave one another shakes of their heads, sidelong glances, and shoulder shrugs in feminine secret code to convey that they understood heartbreak when they saw it. They could hear Miss Weisberg sobbing over the running washbasin faucets that she hoped would drown out the sound of her sorrow.[cxxxiv]

Tillie lost no time in demoting Lloyd and replacing him with Meyer Lewis. The *Flotill Notes* newsletter from August of that year mentions that Meyer L. Lewis was the new assistant to Miss Weisberg as well as general manager of Flotill, while Lloyd was downgraded to supervisor. Soon, Lloyd and his new wife would leave both Flotill and Stockton.

The fact that Meyer was married with two sons was a familiar problem. Tillie had been canoodling with the married Sam Kipniss for years. It seemed that all the powerful Jewish men of business were married.

It wasn't that Tillie was a serial home-wrecker. She did want to find her own man—she just couldn't afford to make a manhunt her full-time job. In her defense, she had been looking for the right guy. Tillie was truly a world traveler. She was a flirt. She wanted one man in her life, with the only drama in her world focused on Flotill. Still, she could not find an eligible bachelor who would fit into her world.

Now there was a war on. Tillie's love life was going to have to wait. At the moment, Tillie was busy building Flotill into an empire. She'd let the men vie for her affection. No rush: he who made himself eligible first would likely win her hand.

Tillie designed several advertising campaigns including one that featured herself at a blackboard teaching homemakers to buy Flotill's less expensive tomato paste and add water to create tomato sauce or tomato juice. One can of Flotill tomato paste plus two cups of water made sauce; four cups of water made juice. And both saved the family, in those difficult times, money. Tillie Weisberg and Flotill were there to help.

Tillie cranked up for the war effort, set up a draft office on site, and assisted essential workers, like Harry Rosen, in obtaining deferments.

Harry resisted the deferment. He promised he'd take a temporary deferment and wouldn't leave Tillie in the lurch. Harry agreed to set up the new Modesto plant for Tillie. He intended to fight for freedom, to do his bit, enlisting along with his brothers in arms, as soon as possible.

To entice local women and other workers, Tillie remodeled the Stockton plant with $200,000 in improvements. This included buying buses to shuttle workers from their homes to the plant and back for people who had no form of transportation. Women who couldn't work because they had small children were bussed, kids and all, to the plant.

If the crew was diverse before, it was even more so now. During wartime, Tillie invited anybody who was clean and sober to work. Tillie had already established that race, religion, and genders were simply going to get along; any physical handicap that could be worked around and accommodated for was. The deaf could work near the louder machines; the elderly could take naps. Jennie Panelli, one of the adorable can-label strippers who worked just after the attack on Pearl Harbor, recalled a beautiful little woman named Elizabeth who still brought a smile to her face.

> Oh, Tillie just hired everybody who was nice and decent then. Little Elizabeth, we called her "Itsy Bitsy," stood on a stack of Flotill fruit boxes so she could reach the conveyor belt. Bitsy was no bigger than a minute and such a lovely girl. She was a midget but looked like a precious doll and was just as productive as the rest of us. Sure, we stared at first; then we forgot about her size. Goodness, the whole place had blacks, whites, Mexicans, Asians, and the like. We were all just Flotill workers happy to work for Tillie.

The WWII years kept employees working on-site both day and night. The plant was a home away from home for many people. The Flotill family was solidified by having on-site day care for the workers' children, including toys, games, and a full-time children's caretaker. A nap area was set up for the elderly or disabled staff, along with those who were willing to work double shifts and needed a well-deserved rest. The cafeteria offered affordable hot meals or cold sandwiches, lively conversation, and never-ending card games.

The card tables—this was the one place and time everyone would groan if the boss lady turned up. Tillie would either accidentally distract the players with a polite gossipy visit or hang over a shoulder and unintentionally give away a player's hand. Tillie did not have a poker face and often spoiled the game by making a positive or negative comment, much to the players' dismay. Tillie never sat at a table as a player. She didn't gamble on anything aside from Flotill.[cxxxv]

Her new general manager, Meyer Lewis, did not have this rule; he loved to play cards. Meyer was known to hustle to be first in line on get-rich quick schemes, including high-risk ventures and gambling—especially card games. For Meyer, gin rummy became an addiction.

TILLIE'S GREEN PHAETON: LANA TURNER HAD THE RED ONE

In a grand gesture, Tillie placed her coveted new kelly-green 1940/41 Chrysler Phaeton in front of her Stockton office on blocks with a "Save Rubber" sign in the window. She never drove it again.

The car was one of only five that were built, since the war needs took precedence over building luxury automobiles. The red one belonged to the movie star Lana Turner. Tillie knew the Chrysler family personally. When Walter Chrysler passed away of a stroke in August of 1940, Tillie attended the memorial service. After numerous somber eulogistic statements by mourners that "life is to be lived fully and lived well," Tillie decided to purchase the sumptuous vehicle at the wake, sight unseen. She decided on the green color because it complimented the color of her red hair.

Tillie's green Chrysler Phaeton convertible. Only five were built,
due to the war. The actress Lana Turner got the red one.

Tillie sent Meyer Lewis to Detroit to personally retrieve the Phaeton as
it rolled off the assembly line. Meyer told his sons that "the car drew a crowd
wherever [I] went. [I] was afraid to sleep at night for fear someone would steal
or damage it."cxxxvi The car arrived in perfect condition, although Meyer was a
little worse for wear from worry. Tillie posed in front of her San Joaquin Street
home in the kelly-green beauty, much to her heart's delight and her neighbors'
dismay. As far as they were concerned, this was just another example of that
"Jew broad" showing off.

KEEP 'EM EATING
On August 6, 1942, Tillie officially opened the Modesto plant, even though
many people had been fully employed at the facility for months. Tillie wanted

the plant in perfect running order before inviting in photographers and dignitaries with her picture-perfect public image and all the pomp and circumstance she could muster. She ran her new "Keep'Em Eating" campaign for national and troop morale, combined with Flotill's old motto of "Quality in Quantity."

Tillie sent out a letter on embossed "Flotill Products, Incorporated, of Stockton, California" and "99 Hudson Street, New York" letterhead to officially welcome all her new employees to the Modesto plant.

"FELLOW EMPLOYEES: This day marks the real 1942 opening of the Modesto Flotill Cannery for what we are sure will be a most successful season for all of us.

We all have a great job to do...production of food is just as important as the production of ships, airplanes, guns, tanks and bullets during this national emergency.

The Flotill Company is obligated to our government, our armed forces and our fellow citizens to provide canned foods of QUALITY IN QUANTITY.

We have arranged a full season for you and hope you will be with us and enjoy a happy term of employment through peaches, pears and tomatoes from now through November.

Welcome to our FLOTILL FAMILY and let's all...

"Keep'EM EATING."
Sincerely yours,
Tillie Weisberg

Tillie posed in an article/photo opportunity called "With Her Hand on the Switch of Achievement" while about to switch on the Modesto plant's main conveyor belt, backed by city councilman Carl Stanley, chief of police E. E. Arrington, chamber of commerce secretary Bob Kimmel, fire chief George Wallace, and judge J. Lee Robertson. She developed patriotic, newsreel-like advertisements in which locals were implored to come and do their duty and work for Flotill; they were shown at movie theaters that ran directly after the actual Hearst Company newsreels.

The *Modesto Bee* announced in a headline, "Extensive Improvements Were Made and 1,000 Persons Will Be on the Payroll." The story reported, "Miss Tillie Weisberg states she has spent $350,000 to acquire, rebuild and expand the old Pratt-Low plant on 9th Street, Modesto. Modesto will can apricots, peaches, pears, fruit cocktail and other seasonal products… New manager, Arthur Heiser said preference for jobs will be given to Modesto residents."

Tillie's August 1942 *Flotill Notes* newsletter promoted war-bonds sales, rubber drives combined with ride shares, and blood drives, all in the Tillie way: "Every pint of blood donated saves the life of one of our boys who has risked his own." The rubber drive stated:

> Here's how you can fulfill two patriotic duties in one easy gesture. We have set up routes to the canneries, made a master map, and indicated on the map where each worker lives in Stockton and the surrounding counties.
>
> The purpose for this study [is] to arrange to have workers with and without cars join together to save rubber, gasoline and automobile service…
>
> …It is the desire of the Rubber Administration…to give cooperating employees retread tires or tires as needed for cooperating.
>
> Be a good Neighbor—Save gas!
>
> Help the War Effort—Save Rubber!

Vol. I   Stockton, Calif., August, 1942   No. 1

Hitting the Bond Bull's Eye . . .

"I cannot find language which would adequately express my feeling of appreciation of the fine service you rendered our country when you advised your employes that you would pay a 5 per cent bonus in War Savings Stamps to each and every employe who completes the processing season and who authorizes a 10 per cent pay roll deduction for investment in War Savings Stamps and Bonds."

MISS WEISBERG

That is an excerpt from a letter received by Miss Weisberg, the president of Flotill Products, from William Green, president of the American Federation of Labor.

Naturally we're all very proud of this recognition received from the AFL president. The cooperative effort of the Flotill employes and management in this effort to aid the Government has become an item of national prominence. Flotill Products, in full cooperation with its employes, was the first organization of its kind in the country to set up the voluntary 10 per cent pay roll deduction plan and, so far as we know, the only firm to effect the 5 per cent bonus.

Here's the way the Bond Bonus works:

The 5 per cent bonus is given by the company in addition to the 10 per cent allotment made by each employe for the purchase of War Bonds. This will add 50 per cent additional to the money you set aside.

The bonus will be paid to every employe who finishes the season; or who works until laid off.

It will also be paid to those who remain at work until inducted into Government service.

The combined and cooperative effort between the management, the workers and their union brought both to the firm and

Suggestion Box

What are YOUR ideas? Have you any suggestions to make that will be of benefit to Flotill Products? What can be done to enable Flotill to be of more service to the Government war effort? What can we do to build a better Flotill family?

Your ideas may be of great value. We would like to hear them. A Suggestion Box will be set up at both the Stockton and Modesto canneries. Prizes will be given each month for the best ideas and some of them will be published in "FLOTILL NOTES."

Put on your thinking caps. Write out your suggestions and drop them in the suggestion box. Don't forget . . . many a shining light has been hidden behind a bushel.

to the union the Treasury Department's coveted "Bull's Eye" Flag.

James G. Smythe, State Administrator for War Savings Bonds, in his letter to Flotill informing us of this honor, said in part:

"You are helping to set a pace here in Northern California which — if equalled by all business firms—would put our billion-dollar-a-month quota 'on ice' for the duration."

Secretary Morgenthau has personally written commending this action.

We can inform you with pride that, working together in this issue of patriotism, you and your company, as a unit, has set a precedent in war effort for labor and management throughout the Nation to follow. The thousands of dollars that you will lend your Government this year, coupled with the $75,000 that your company will add to that amount, will help to give Hitler, Hirohito and Mussolini a very bad time.

Produce! Produce! Produce!
And Cook the Axis Goose

A Housing Project

This is war! And, of course, all of us are coping with problems that are new and without precedent. Prices go up. Rents go up. There is a concentration of workers in various areas of war effort that presents housing problems due to congestion. Those problems must be met, and Flotill has concerned itself to be of benefit to its employes wherever possible.

We want to help you, who are helping us do a good job in feeding the nation and the armed forces, to be as comfortable and as secure in your private lives as is possible under the stress of this great wartime effort.

Flotill has a project under consideration that, if successfully worked out with the housing authorities at Washington, will bring about the construction of eighty housing units adjoining our Stockton plant.

The project when and if completed will house about 400 of our employes with all proper home facilities within walking distance of the plant. We have already acquired 20 acres of land next to the cannery where the houses will be built.

The plan at present is tentative. We are working on the program and expect to have good news real soon.

Our aim is to provide, if possible, comfortable homes at the lowest possible cost to our Flotill employes.

Flotill in Uniform

Flotill people are going to war along with the other young men of the Nation. Here you have the names of just a few former employes who are in the services. If you know of former employes who are wearing the uniforms of Uncle Sam, send them in to the editor.

Capt. Lawrence Poundstone, U. S. A., at Santa Ana, California.

Corp. Frank W. Kurtz, U. S. A., at Washington, D. C.

Sergt. Jimmy Berger, U. S. A., in New Zealand.

Frank Elias Garcia, Merchant Marine, San Pedro, California.

Tom Raymor, Air Base Squadron, Fort Riley, Kansas.

The *Flotill Notes* newsletter, written and created by Tillie Weisberg, who wrote several newsletters during the war years to lift the morale of the busy crew.

LIBERTY SHIP BLUES

No matter her tireless recruitment campaign, Tillie was losing workers to Bay Area shipyards for better wages; the misogynists who loathed working for a woman now had an option to bail. As Clifford Stevens of Manteca, California, later remembered,

> My dad was L. H. Lawrence Stevens. He worked for Tillie's Modesto plant in 1942. We were so poor he had only a bicycle to ride to work. He was a master mechanic [and a] forklift and truck driver. He was a man of all trades. He told Miss Weisberg he was going to Richmond to make more money. She begged him to stay and promised him another five cents an hour if he would stay another year. He stayed until 1944 and "always thought she was a bitch who was difficult to work for." When the Richmond shipyards promised government housing, we all up and moved to Richmond.[cxxxvii]

To compete with the Liberty Ship builders' higher pay (which included housing) in the Bay Area, Tillie announced her intention to combat the higher rents that had been forced upon her employees by greedy landlords.[65] She hoped to build eighty housing units on twenty acres that Flotill owned behind its plant. This was a battle that Miss Weisberg lost: she had no backing to create affordable housing from the city or federal government. With housing prices rising, keeping employees and making production deadlines was a nightmare task for Tillie and her nephews, Arthur and Albert.

Arthur later stated, "Available employees were few. We had the Flotill busses and the day care to bring in local housewives who wanted jobs, but there were just not enough local people left to work. We began to use those busses to drive daily to Pleasanton to pick up sailors who had not yet shipped out as day workers and paid them in cash. Everybody was in a jam to find enough workers through the war years."

Tillie eavesdropped on gossip in the lunchrooms and on the lines. She asked workers what they hoped for and what they needed in order to keep

---

65 Some landlords raised rental rates near places of business all over the country.

them at the plants. Miss Weisberg was known for her generosity and loyalty. That year, at Christmas, she gave every employee 20 percent of their annual pay as a bonus.[cxxxviii] Tillie resorted to incentives in multiple forms. Tillie's holiday dance party at Matteoni's in Stockton and the Odd Fellow's Hall in Modesto gave goodie boxes as gifts to workers that included nylon stockings, which were rationed during the war.

While some of the gals admired the "Rosie the Riveter" look of working girls in overalls, that was just too sloppy for Tillie. But if wearing slacks was going to make her Flotill gals feel better about their employment, then so be it—a relatively small concession might yield big rewards in job satisfaction.

Tillie began to wear stylish slacks to work on Saturday; other women could follow her pant-wearing lead but only on Saturdays.

Tillie made some of her workers' small loans for weddings, bar mitzvahs, and *quinceañeras*, as long as they promised to remain at Flotill for the whole season.

She began giving out pink "Tillie-stamps" as loyalty incentives, similar to the "S & H Green" stamps that were popular at the time.[66] The Tillie-stamps replicated S & H stamps except for the tomatoey color and the caricature of Tillie on the stamps. An employee could earn Tillie-stamps for attending work daily, working overtime, coming in on time, bringing in a new employee, or submitting an idea to the suggestion box—in other words, pretty much any reason could earn an employee Tillie-stamps.

Tillie set up a little store in the cafeteria where employees could use their Tillie-stamps to purchase extra Flotill canned goods and items that were rationed during the war, such as nylon stockings and bags of sugar and chocolate. Harry Rosen later recalled, "She had to fight to get workers for her business to survive and give them what they wanted to stay at Flotill, including nylon stockings." Sometimes she went much further to help a valued employee. As one article put it at the time, "The wife of an employee ran off to Mexico with their two kids. Tillie paid his way to Mexico and back to bring the wife back, and help resolve their issues. The couple are happily still together."[cxxxix]

---

66 These were a popular grocery-store loyalty incentive at the time. People could collect stamps in S & H booklets to earn points toward a catalogue of items, from coffeepots to jewelry.

Then there was the group who stayed for the love of Tillie—those employees who simply adored her and wouldn't think of deserting her. After all, they figured, this war wouldn't last forever, and the employees who stood with her would surely be rewarded. Tillie had proved that time and again. Tillie built her own positive and legendary reputation for her innovative ideas through deeds and the media, including the episode in which her steam-train idea saved the canning season, her frequent solitary "think walks," and her stress-release tomato-peeling episodes alongside her workers in which she wore obviously expensive dresses and glittering diamond rings. New workers would comment "Miss Weisberg, you are going to dirty that ring." She would laughingly respond by holding a tomato aloft, the juice dripping down her silk sleeve onto her glittering hand. "Honey," she would say, "this tomato is what bought me these things." She'd continue to chat with the "girls" until she was calmed. Of course, they loved her.

ONE MILLION CASES OF TOMATOES

On November 15, 1942, posing for the newspapers with a few members of her "from the beginning crew"—Lloyd Dunivan, Joe Mariani, Leo Landuci, and E. Mariani—Tillie smashed a California champagne for the cameras to christen the one millionth case of tomato paste.

She cracked open the bubbly against the Flotill crates wearing a Peter Pan–collared satin blouse, pearls, a large orchid corsage, and stylish wool ladies' slacks. After the first pack, in 1935, Tillie had been horrified by Del Gaizo's Italian crew showering her similarly in a surprise celebration, ruining her silk blouse and taking momentary control of her photo opportunity. This time she had planned for the event to the last detail, including an identical change of clothes as backup. In addition to the invited newspapers, Tillie hired her own photographer to capture the moment. With the war now in full swing, Tillie knew she wasn't likely to garner any press coverage if something major occurred. Tillie left nothing to chance where self-promotion was concerned.

One million cases of tomatoes were later celebrated by a champagne christening from Tillie. Prebubbly photo, left to right: Arthur Heiser, Tillie Weisberg, Albert Heiser.

The December 1942 edition of *Flotill Notes* featured a cartoon Flotill tomato can, in uniform, soldiering across the cover page. Tillie editorialized,

As I speak with you of a sincere, heartfelt appreciation, I do not mean in the first person alone…It is a much broader and more universal sense that I wish to express myself at this holiday time.

We have all shown—every one of us who has worked together during the past season—a vast appreciation of the fact that we are free citizens of a free land…as free citizens it has been our privilege to serve our Government and that we have served it well. We have turned out hundreds of thousands of cases of nourishing food…to be used [by] our men at war…and to helpless men, women, and children who would [otherwise] suffer the agonizing misery of malnutrition and starvation.

Yes, my fellow workers, we have done a good job. And that knowledge alone should, at this Christmastide, bring a solace to our hearts and a warmth of cheer to this holiday that we observe this year during the heat of a barbarous war and a world turned asunder with devastation…

I appreciate what you have done and wish every one of you, individually, the best of Christmas cheer. I think of the loyal Flotill veterans and inexperienced townspeople of Stockton and Modesto and the faculties and student bodies of the College of the Pacific[67] and the other schools who responded to our call for help…I think of every individual who played a part in helping Flotill to avail itself of the privilege of producing tons of food for the world and I feel very proud and very humble and very inspired all at the same time.

At this Christmas season, with the world at war, my wish for you all is that the spirit of peace and good will…will rise above the din of conflict and roaring tornado of destruction and will enter your homes, hearts and lives. May this war end soon…May peace come back to this earth…A fine Christmas to every one of you and may God, who watches over us, bless you all…A Merry Christmas and Victorious New Year.

THE BRACEROS

The Flotill newsletter promised farmers that "a special service in the Field Department has been inaugurated under the direction of Miss Weisberg and General manager, Meyer Lewis, to assist farmers in securing farm help, trucks, etc., and to assist farmers at absolutely no charge for this service."

---

67 Numerous College of the Pacific faculty, students, and spouses of faculty went in to work for Tillie's Flotill to help feed the country and our military.

This was the bracero program, which had been created by executive order in 1942 in response to many growers' argument that World War II would bring labor shortages to low-paying agricultural jobs, especially since their Japanese workers had been incarcerated. They were right: labor was epidemically short.

Ralph Garcia was assigned to take the train to Texas, where he was to collect Mexican laborers to work for the farmers who supplied Flotill and other canners. Legally, farmers and agribusiness owners were required to provide free housing and good, inexpensive food for these "guest workers." Tillie made a point of insisting upon more than just decent facilities for these men. The bracero program had a reputation for poor treatment of the workers. Ralph, a Mexican himself, assured Tillie he would personally see to it that this would not be the case for the laborers under the Flotill roofs.[cxl]

Ralph said it broke his heart to see most of his Mexican brothers clad in sarapes made of rags and wearing strips of old tires tied with rags to their feet as makeshift sandals. Ralph's first stop was for shoes and shirt fittings for his new crew. A few farmers and growers thanked Tillie in writing:

Your bringing in Mexican Nationals was of great benefit to us. If it had not been for this labor our crops would have suffered immeasurably. The men did good work and Flotill Products is to be congratulated on this contribution to the war effort.
—K. G. Stark

We feel indebted to Flotill Products for the cooperation which was afforded outside growers in allowing us to use the [Mexican] Nationals. We fully understand the expense and trouble that was necessary to arrange for bringing the Nationals in, as well as the daily routine of housing, feeding, [and] caring for them.
—E. A. Couture[cxli]

On December 24, 1942, at the age of twenty-nine, Harry Rosen wrote an office memo in which he formally advised Tillie that he was going to serve his country:

> ...to do my bit to preserve that form of government which allows people like you—people with energy, ambition, and ability to rise to the top of their chosen field regardless of race or creed.

> With kindest personal regards.
> Harry Rosen.

Harry donned his army uniform and shipped out.

TILLIE, THE ILLEGAL WAR PROFITEER?

The government was keeping a vigilant eye on all those who profited during wartime. Under President Roosevelt's Office of Price Administration (1942–1947), Tillie's two Stockton plants and her two New York distribution branches for food products were sued for $1,277,033. Tillie was accused of overcharging by three times the amount allowed by government regulations. Tillie was deeply hurt by the allegation that she was cheating her country in such dire times. The Flotill books were immediately opened for exhaustive examination. The government leaked the complaint to the newspapers to deepen her distress.

The OPA did not prevail, however, since prices—from the beginning of Flotill's service to the issuance of service rations—were negotiated between Miss Weisberg and the proper government authorities; in addition, agricultural products were not under the jurisdiction of the OPA.[cxlii] It was the impeccable financial records kept by her dear front-office men Claude Young, George Froehlich, and Patrick Stanco that easily cleared Tillie's good name.

Tillie made money because she worked every moment of her waking hours to consider more ways to legally earn a profit. The more opportunities she made to earn money, the greater the number of local people who would stay gainfully employed. Businesses like Flotill were creating a solid middle class of homeowners from former day laborers and migrant workers. Flotill was an economic and lifestyle game changer for a better life for many in the Central Valley.

For Tillie, she could afford to buy the compound she had her eye on in Palm Springs—that she nicknamed P.S.

PALM SPRINGS

The estate house at 657 North Via Miraleste in Palm Springs was 7,517 square feet, it had nine bedrooms, and it had seven and a quarter baths on 1.79 manicured acres. This would be her hideout and playground.

Here, she entertained Lucille Ball and Desi Arnaz, the Marx Brothers, Fannie Brice, Sophie Tucker, and numerous other stars, along with her family members.

Here, she hid out from the troubles of Flotill, had quiet time in the massive swimming pool, and played tennis and ping-pong.

Tillie was terrific at ping-pong; she coerced family members and guests alike to play against her. All her nieces-in-law were required to play whenever Tillie commanded. She played to win (as with everything else she did) and took no prisoners as she gleefully slaughtered her competition.

Tillie used the Palm Springs estate as a place for rest, recreation, and recuperation in privacy from facelifts and other beauty treatments. Her sister, Bea, cared for Chips after facelifts and dermabrasion. Tillie treated Bea to facials, chemical peels, and spa days. Tillie ended up with gorgeous white, porcelain skin, according to Barbara Heiser; Helene Heiser agreed: "The facelifts and treatments made all the difference in her looks. Her skin was all peaches and cream."

Utilization of Asparagus Waste for Penicillin Mold Culture Indicated

Commercial-Scale Experiments at Flotill Explore Use of Liquor and Pulp Residue From Asparagus Butts

EXPERIMENTS of several years' duration on a laboratory basis on utilization of asparagus wastes are having their first commercial-scale trials at the plant of Flotill Products, Inc., Stockton, Calif. At this plant, for the first time, manufacture of concentrated liquors from canning lines has been made to determine suitability of this material as a medium for the culture of useful bacteria molds, such as penicillin.

Penicillin is a recent development of medical science, and its value as a drug for the treatment of a wide variety of diseases has been adequately proven. As a result, the present tests at Flotill have the dual purpose of serving humanity through development of a satisfactory medium for culture of the penicillin molds, as well as providing the food processing industry with a means of making useful disposal of material which would ordinarily be wasted.

WRRL Initiates Work

The current commercial trials at Flotill are being made through cooperative effort with Western Regional Research Laboratory at Albany, Calif. WRRL first began its work on utilization of cannery wastes in 1941. The aim of the first experiments was to determine if asparagus wastes could be used as a biological culture medium. Experiments on a laboratory basis had been conducted in Albany, and once these had determined the possibilities of asparagus wastes as a culture medium, efforts were made to contact local California canneries and to interest them in the project on a commercial scale.

Word was passed out to canners through Major W. S. Everts of Canners League of California, who mentioned the WRRL work on asparagus juices. So considering the extreme value of penicillin to medical science, and need for large-scale manufacture of the drug, Miss Tillie Weisberg, president of Flotill, offered to place the facilities of her plant at Stockton at the disposal of the WRRL researchers.

Contact of Flotill with WRRL was made through Don Martinelli, general superintendent, who got in touch with Dr. H. D. Lightbody of WRRL, and arrangements were completed to get the project under way. Under the agreement, Flotill planned to provide the laboratory with 1,400 lbs. of concentrated liquor for WRRL experiments, and to pack for the balance of the year whatever material was possible for commercial-drug laboratories who were interested in using the liquor for penicillin culture and extraction.

How asparagus liquor from waste butts fits into the penicillin picture is best explained by Dr. Irvin Feustel, senior chemist in the biochemical division of WRRL, who has been conducting the experiments. Dr. Feustel and John H. Thompson, assistant chemical engineer of the laboratory, have been working with Flotill in getting commercial extraction of the liquor into operation.

According to Dr. Feustel, corn steep liquor is now commonly used for penicillin mold culture. Experiments at WRRL determined that asparagus juices might be used for these purposes. First, because of the vital growth factors in the product, and second, because of nutritive factors which are essential in rapid growth of micro-organisms. Experiments since 1941 convinced the laboratory researchers of the possibilities of the product for biochemical uses.

Production Method

Extraction of the liquor is fairly simple

A USEFUL DRUG from a cannery waste! This looms as an excellent possibility following experiments conducted at Flotill Products, Stockton, Calif., in cooperation with Western Regional Research Laboratory at Albany.

At top, Miss Tillie Weisberg, Flotill's president, examines a test tube of concentrated asparagus liquor, while Dr. Irvin Feustel (left), senior chemist, biochemical division of WRRL, and Don Martinelli, Flotill superintendent, look on. On the table in front of them is a pile of asparagus butts, normally wasted, from which the liquor is extracted; the dried pulp residue from the butts; a decanter of raw juice; and a tube of this same juice after filtering and before concentration. The concentrated liquor is shipped to laboratories as a medium for culture of penicillin molds, and interest has been shown in the dried pulp residue by paperboard manufacturers.

At bottom, acres of asparagus waste. To prevent this waste is part of the purpose of the present experiments.

Tillie built a state-of-the-art laboratory whose primary purpose was to raise the standard for food safety beyond that of any other canned-food company, in addition to creating penicillin from asparagus mold.

HARRY IS LABELED

Harry Rosen was now serving in the trenches in Germany. He opened a box of rations and found a can of Flotill spinach. He mailed a letter and the label to Tillie. She responded to him on August 19, 1944:

> My Dear Private Rosen,
> You can't imagine what a source of pride it is to have you send us our label, and to know that we have helped our boys, at least by trying to supply them with food...
>
> A movie was made of the plant recently and shown in Stockton theaters in an attempt to recruit cannery workers...I'm sure you would have been proud to see it, as I was. All my best wishes and God bless you,
> Yours most sincerely,
> Tillie Weisberg

Tillie included a glossy magazine pamphlet of the successful asparagus-penicillin project in her letter to Harry.

Tillie purchased the peat-rich Medford Island in the Eastern Delta, west of Stockton, to grow asparagus for $250,000.[68] At a meeting of the Canner's League, a scientist spoke about the potential to utilize the waste product of asparagus to make penicillin. Tillie immediately volunteered her plant for the project by purchasing the equipment to create a new laboratory for research and development under the direction of the US Department of Agriculture.

Miss Weisberg said at the time, "If we can do something for humanity by placing our canning facilities at the disposal of Research experts whose findings may result in increased production of penicillin, our compensation will be in the knowledge that we are helping fight against illness and injuries.[cxliii]

Further compensation lay in potential government business and further profitable usages for what formerly had been agricultural junk. Asparagus butts (i.e., the tough, nonedible stems) not only successfully cultured the

---

68   This is equivalent to $3,303,000 in 2015 dollars, according to inflationcalculator.com.

antibiotic, but asparagus enzymes could cold-proof beer.[cxliv] Innovation, foresight, and maintaining a state-of-the-art laboratory at Flotill was the new standard.

LOANING THE LADIES

Tillie continued to struggle to keep workers on the lines through every means necessary. Her campaigns for employees now extended into academia. While most of the middle- to upper-class women of Stockton were not inviting Tillie Weisberg to tea, their husbands were well aware of the economic devastation Stockton would suffer should the Flotill plant fail. The professors of the colleges volunteered their wives for Flotill duty. The ladies worked long, legitimate shifts and were, for a few months, "missing in action" as far as their husbands and families were concerned. At the end of the season, College of the Pacific professor M. R. Eiselen revised the lyrics to "My Bonnie Lies over the Ocean" and sang along with an assemblage of other beleaguered professorial husbands this playful lament:

My Bonnie is working for Tillie
My Bonnie fills cans with puree
My Bonnie thinks housework is silly
Oh bring back my Bonnie to me.

The mending is piled to the ceiling
The dishes are stacked in the sink
My Bonnie is somewhere out peeling
A million tomatoes, I think.

Her apron is stained with their juicing
Her hands are encrimsoned with gore
Since tomatoes have started producing
She doesn't live here anymore.

I think if the judge is concurring
I'll get me a final decree
Imagine my Bonnie preferring
A pear-shaped tomato to me.[cxlv]

ONE-MAN BAND

Tillie had been enjoying the company of Meyer Lewis fairly exclusively throughout the war, but she was not ready to commit to him—he was married, for goodness's sake. During the rare times she did make free time for herself Tillie dated whomever she chose to date and certainly didn't need to report her activities or travel plans to Meyer.

To pressure Tillie into a more committed relationship than she wanted with the wedded Meyer, he threatened to move his wife and two boys to California. That was fine with her. Tillie, through Flotill, paid Mrs. Meyer Lewis's and her sons' relocation fees to a fine home, complete with servant's quarters, to the beautiful Berkeley Hills in California.

Meyer got the point that Tillie wasn't ready to settle down with him. Still, Meyer was rarely home at the new Berkeley residence to enjoy the house he filled with musical instruments and knickknacks.

The new home of Meyer and Elinor Lewis was decorated with miniature carved wooden figurines of musicians, a Steinway grand piano, and a complete set of drums, in addition to attractive furnishings chosen by Elinor.

Meyer's youngest son, William "Bill" Lewis, recalled that nothing topped the moment when he watched his father deposit a one-man-band set into his office/study. Bill doesn't recall his father ever playing that single-unit train-whistle contraption operated by a drum, cymbal, and bellows, but the high-spirited Meyer Lewis certainly must have had a go or two at it.

AUNTIE CHIPS

The nephews and their wives began to have babies. The holidays—in fact, every event—would be bigger and better at Auntie Chips's place.

Saul and June had a baby girl whom they named Judy on October 13, 1944. It was no surprise that Tillie orchestrated formal newborn photographs to be taken at her own house; what did surprise the new parents was that they were relegated to standing in back while Chips sat in front with the new little sweetheart cuddled to her chest.

June was not happy to be bested by Chips in this breach of protocol, but Saul soothed his wife, as was his way. At least he was a medical doctor and didn't live near, or work for, his demanding aunt, like poor Arthur and Albert did.

Chips simply couldn't wait, even for Thanksgiving, to spoil the new baby girl. Chips had to beat everyone to the gifting punch.

On an embossed Saks Fifth Avenue gift card, Tillie penned to the baby on November 22, 1944: "Judy darling: A little early but this is your 'first' Christmas present from your loving Aunt Chips. And you *are* very beautiful."

Chips officially insisted upon being the center of the family's private lives, even if it took her bank account and checkbook to do it. There was never an off button or a stop switch for the redheaded, meddling captain of industry and now auntie-in-chief of Saul, Arthur, and Albert's private lives.[cxlvi]

Helene Heiser later recalled, "The first few years that Al and I were married, Chips made it clear that Saturday nights belonged to her. We were to make no plans at all for ourselves. We were either entertaining Chips, by herself, or we were guests of a Flotill event with Chips. She had us mingling, often, with Lucille Ball, Fannie Brice, oh…just everybody in politics, big finance and Hollywood."[cxlvii]

ENTER CLAIR "DOC" WEAST

In February of 1945, the war was not quite over, and Clair "Doc" Weast was working at Pacific Can Company for twice the money he'd ever made, with none of the fun. Doc's keen intellect, commanding presence, and sense of humor made him a delight to most people and intimidating to others. Doc was not happy with what he felt were "shenanigans" by his bosses. One of his superiors, a Mr. Caron, particularly irked Doc, who said, "Mr. Caron had tremendous respect for me, but he would be just downright mean to people working their heads off to do a good job for him."[cxlviii]

Mr. Caron liked to pull Doc off projects in order to parade him to sales-and-production-problem appointments. PhDs were rare in the food industry; a few people were fortunate to have high-school diplomas before 1950, so the fact that Doc Weast had a PhD was quite unusual and impressive. Knowing this, Mr. Caron used Doc as an intellectual weapon to embarrass clients into submission. Doc could "college-speak" customers into admitting that they might not know what they were talking about, after all, regarding a problem with cans from Pacific Can. This involved plants all around California. This is how Dr. Clair "Doc" Weast met Mrs. Tillie Weisberg in 1945.

Doc was proud of his PhD. His pride was one of humble delight in a task hard won, and he expected no less than he gave. Appointments, even casual, were to be made promptly on time, and commitments had to be met and promises kept. Although he could seem arrogant, in reality he was just finely organized.

He kept meticulous notes that he wrote in longhand and kept in labeled binders—notes about research formulas, all his ideas, song lyrics, and his boyhood memories of growing up "dirt poor with a dirt floor" in Big Oak Flat, California, of which he said later, "Big Oak Flat...was like grinding poverty in Appalachia, without the charm."[69]

Mr. Caron and Doc had just inspected a few minor issues with cans in Visalia. Caron was proud of the way they'd handled that complaint. Caron used Doc as an intellectual battering ram again and the customer took a beating on that one, which just tickled Mr. Caron and made Doc feel like a horse's hind end.

Driving on toward Stockton, Caron cleared his throat and said, "You ever meet the Jew broad? The gal who owns the Stockton and Modesto accounts? She's something—owns the place and runs it, too. She's griping that she's got major leakers. You just tell her that you examined the cans, and it's her cooking problem and not the cans. We'll bring her down a peg or two."

---

69 Big Oak Flat was no more than a few tents and dirt-floor shacks. Doc was raised in wretched poverty; yet, he recalled Big Oak Flat with deep affection years later.

Doc pictured an elderly hulk of a mannish broad running the show at Flotill. He was literally struck dumb by the beauty behind the carved mahogany desk who was perched like a queen and dressed like royalty in a green silk dress the color of spring grass. As he later stated,

My first opinion of Miss Weisberg was [that] she was a holy terror with a smile. Everything in her office was perfect, like in a movie, especially Miss Weisberg. Before this, I'd seen a lot of pretty girls. Miss Weisberg was a whole other animal. She had perfect hair, teeth, skin. I'd never noticed perfect makeup before, but there it was. Those eyes…big, liquid, a brown I felt I was falling right into…I said nothing at all. I couldn't. Miss Weisberg somehow dried up all my vocal fluids. I let Mr. Caron begin his pitch, while I just sat frozen.

Never raising her voice, with a *Mona Lisa* smile, Miss Weisberg explained that the cans in question had inferior seams or seals. The cans were leaking, causing the food she was packing to swell and burst. Miss Weisberg wanted the cans recalled and compensation for some spoilage and downtime. Caron chuckled, gave me a wink, and asked her to "Go get a man. That man could explain to her that she obviously just didn't cook the food at a high-enough temperature to kill the bacteria."

Oh, boy! Through that lip-sticked perfect mouth flew words I'd only heard drunken sailors use. Miss Weisberg cut the vile Mr. Caron down to size with a tongue sharper than any switch-blade knife. By the time she was finished, Caron was nearly in tears.

I couldn't stand the man, but I felt sort of sorry for him. Miss Weisberg had torn Caron apart [by] using both profanity and good science. The lady knew exactly what she was talking about regarding manufacturing seams, cooking processes, and everything else she'd just shoved down Caron's…throat. I was impressed on every level.

Caron meekly signed off on the cans and compensation [that] Miss Weisberg already had prepared before our meeting. That done,

Miss Weisberg nestled back in that throne of a chair and thanked us with a generous grin, as if butter wouldn't melt in her mouth.

Caron let me handle the Tillie Weisberg Flotill accounts from then on.[cxlix]

DOC'S TOP SECRET

On behalf of the army, Doc and his team at Pacific Can were now experimenting with various bombers and their crews, specifically the B-29, to possibly create a plane's own weapons in flight while en route to specific targets without blowing the whole thing out of the sky.

Their inquiry was this: what occurs when freezing, altitude-related temperatures are combined with the vibration of an airplane over a specified time period while carrying large, sealed canisters that contain various liquids and solids in such a way that these transported items would not combust until impact?

Doc flew with his latest and safest "secret product" from the experiment to the army quartermaster lab in Chicago. The "weapon" that Doc and his team had developed was a combination of sugars and heavy dairy products—it was a very tasty form of ice cream. The price of each delicious scoop would bankrupt the country before it killed anyone from obesity.[70]

The actual weapon that they developed and delivered that day was a form of chlorophyll (the green color in plants) that was used to create an infrared, undetectable form of camouflage paint to disguise our troops. Advanced camouflage was what the army was actually hoping for.

Doc Weast joked, "The army got to have their weapon and eat ice-cream, too."

The army wouldn't spring for a plane ticket home for Doc. On the train back to California, he befriended a man carrying several large sacks of groceries. He was a diabetic on a seriously restricted diet. The man carried his own

---

70 Doc and his team created products that they boldly tested on themselves as the "Guinea Pig Club." Doc earned his second nickname of "Pig" from his role as the first taster in this ice-cream test.

food wherever he went. He shared with Doc his displeasure at the medical community, along with his five loaves of french bread and a whole roasted turkey. They split the low-sugar feast and the stories of their lives, rumbling along from Chicago to San Francisco. Doc told the man that he was a scientist in the food-canning business.

The man roared at Doc, "Why can't you people produce canned foods that a diabetic can enjoy?" The fellow bellowed so hard that Doc forgot to ask the gentleman's name.

Doc didn't need any more berating to get his wheels spinning. He began to formulate a plan to create just such a product. He couldn't wait to get home and discuss this tasty diabetic-diet idea with his wife, Elsie.

Elsie held a master's degree in nutrition and chemistry. He and Elsie would put their heads together and cook up a healthy, sugar-free diet. They had no intention of sharing this secret diet with those stinkers at Pacific Can. For the time being, the Weasts kept this just an intellectual idea to volley about.[cl]

MOVING UP

On May 8, 1945, the war was over in Europe with Japan not far behind. The soldiers would return to work soon, and business was booming. Tillie really wanted to find a husband now that the world was finally simmering down.

Her attorneys counseled her that she just might not find true love and true wealth in the same pair of trousers. She was probably going to need to settle for a man of financial means or a man she loved, regardless of his bank account. If she chose love, it would be a good idea to settle her real estate and business holdings now to avoid a gigolo swindling her out of her fortune through community-property laws before she said "I do." It was clear that Tillie did not appear to be as lucky in love as she was with tomatoes.

Tillie was, without a doubt, rich beyond even her wildest dreams now. With all the products Tillie added to the plant through the war years, Flotill was now the largest tomato cannery in the country and the only one in the world owned and operated by a woman.[cli] That distinction was just for the tomatoes. Flotill, as she had predicted before Florindo Del Gaizo died, had grown far beyond the pear-shaped pomodoro since adding the Modesto plant and all the locally grown produce, she was now a megacanner of peaches, apricots, pears, figs, spinach, asparagus, and more. She was officially "Tillie of the Valley" in addition to being the "Tomato Queen."

She bought a resale mansion, for sale by owner, again negotiating directly with the owner in Italian. The mansion, built in 1928 for the J. E. Henry family, was located at 740 Willow Street at the corner of Baker. The four-bedroom, five-bathroom home contained 7,420 square feet of living space. It might take a few years, but she was going to turn the massive family home into a space to entertain everyone from politicians, to Hollywood stars, to her Flotill family and her own biological family.

Tillie sold the home at North San Joaquin Street. That house was a beauty, but it was not big enough for the entertaining she planned to do in the future. After the close of escrow, she took pretty much everything from North San Joaquin, including things that were, in fact, nailed down.

Tillie's removal of the two Italian marble lion statues adorning the entrance to North San Joaquin that had been placed there by the original owners, Dr. and Mrs. Craviotto, caused a neighborhood stir. Their North San Joaquin Street neighbors liked those lions right where they'd been since the home was built. They were a bit of a landmark.

Tillie repositioned the marble lions in her backyard gardens at 740 Willow. Later, she fictionalized a tale of how she had absconded with the magnificent felines straight out from under Mussolini's Fascist nose.

The greatest faux pas, according to the neighbors, was that Tillie pilfered all the magnificent wooden paneling and bookshelves at the North San Joaquin home in what Tillie used as a parlor, which was rich with thick velvet burgundy draperies and the aforementioned affixed woodwork. The San Joaquin Street buyers were understandably distressed at Tillie's breech of protocol and contract.

The mahogany walls were a significant selling point for the San Joaquin Street house Tillie was selling—so important that they served as the stunning backdrop for one of Tillie's largest portraits. The muralist, Hollywood set designer and portrait artist to the stars Mordi Gassner,[71] was commissioned in 1940 to visit Stockton and paint Tillie gracing that paneled parlor in a gown of gold, wearing Lord Harry Clifton's ring. Gassner liked the shelving so much that he brushed his signature into his rendition of the shelves rather than in the usual lower-right corner of the painting. Tillie decided the paneling and bookshelves were important to her, so she had them pulled off the walls of San Joaquin Street, without the buyers' knowledge or approval and stored at Flotill in a warehouse until Tillie found the time to place them inside the new house at Willow Street. Unfortunately, one of many Flotill warehouse fires destroyed the exquisite woodwork before they were installed.

To decorate 740 Willow, Tillie melded ideas from her past as a young woman who had been fortunate enough to stay as a houseguest at regal estates and hotels.

The mirrored front office off the entrance was an idea from the Countess d'Franco's[72] highly reflective Hollywood palace that Fannie Brice had rented in 1937 and that Tillie enjoyed (with her nephew Albert) as guests of Fanny's on several occasions.[clii]

Tillie's landscape design was a nod to Lord Harry Clifton's estate in miniature. Tillie hired landscaper and designer Paul Tritenbach, who presented Tillie with the final drawings on October 16, 1951.[cliii] The gardens were a myriad of paths that wound around and diminished to create visual distance and space. Some paths were grand, while others were intimate. Trellised arbors, fine statuary, gazebos, and an expansive rose garden filled the space with scent and color, while the Olympic-size pool was the central feature. An entire area was devoted just to roses, which grew with bright vigor and fragrance; Tillie's favorite flowers were roses, perhaps a sweet reminder of her mother, Rose.

Business entertainment was the main reason Tillie selected this large property. To accommodate more people, she added to the concrete patio

---

71 Mordeca "Mordi" Gassner (1899–1995) was a Jewish-American, Manhattan-born painter and muralist trained in New York and Italy. He also painted post-office murals for the Works Projects Administration (WPA) in the 1930s. He was considered a Surrealist.

72 Countess d'Franco, married to Count d'Franco, was an American heiress who enjoyed parties, luxury, and the company of handsome men.

and installed the latest high-tech outdoor sound speakers for both mood and dance music.

The formerly covered patio was transformed into a cocktail bar that would be serviced by professional staff, with the eternally happy-to-oblige Meyer Lewis ready to create a straight drink or mixed libation for guests.

Tillie collected and displayed Oriental carpets and antiques from her many excursions to China, France, and Italy, peppered with Tiffany lamps and vases. It was a courageously eclectic mix that spoke of wealth and good taste—similar again to that of Countess d'Franco.

Neighbors around Willow Street, who prefer to remain anonymous, believed that Tillie Lewis was "an heiress from an upper-class family situation out of Manhattan." Tillie spoke with a nearly British affectation. Her Italian was flawless and her French quite good. Her voice was feminine but deep and modulated with a clear crispness that hinted at boarding-school training. Tillie didn't engage in small talk, gossip, or pointless jabber, which increased her mystique. Tillie never spoke of her humble past with the neighbors. Instead, she dazzled them with her affluent present through her lavish lifestyle and events and the decor both surrounding and inside her home.[73]

How would the neighbors around Willow know she was Jewish? She decorated for every Christian holiday with panache. Along with her great-nieces and great-nephews, she invited the neighborhood children to numerous joyful Easter egg hunts in addition to Halloween and Christmas parties complete with splendid Christmas trees, lights, gifts, and Santas. No one ever mentioned, or perhaps even noticed, the menorahs that were polished, gleaming, and lit for Hanukkah among the holiday garland and mistletoe.

Being Jewish was seldom a good thing in Stockton. Tillie kept mum on her religion outside of her home and synagogue.

From her upbringing in the tenements, Tillie's first language was Yiddish. Now, she spoke her mother tongue rarely and only in private. When members of her family slipped into Yiddish in her presence, Tillie usually feigned ignorance.[cliv] As far as she was concerned, her impoverished past was finally kaput.

---

73 Former neighbor Rich Prather told the author that his parents had no doubt that Mrs. Lewis was a very wealthy heiress.

She had no desire to be reminded of it. She was a woman beyond "the now" who lived in the future—the "what's next?"

HARRY ROSEN "DOING HIS BIT"

Harry Rosen was on Omaha Beach at Normandy on "D-Day plus fifteen," where he was busy creating chemical weapons for Patton's army.[74] Harry wrote from Straubing, Germany,

> Dear All,
> Censorship over, now it can be told...Nov. 3, 1945, [we] kicked the ship-builders off. We had to help finish building our liberty ship. Rough crossing...I got very sick. We zig-zagged across the Atlantic with rumors of Subs flying fast and thick.
>
> We were at Wargrave, England playing ball and getting suntans until we were boarded into British ships, July 4th, wearing about 7 layers of clothing. Assault boats took us to Omaha Beach then to an apple orchard outside Mosles, France where we set up shop...doing "beaucoup" work.[75] Up all night hearing "ack-ack" from our pup tents from "the front very near us."

Harry detailed the Allied breakthrough at Metz, where the infantry took the town while his troop dealt with "sniping going on...artillery firing over our heads at the forts still holding out... [he could] 'see shells hitting Fort Driant from the school house his troop was holed up in.'" He continued,

> A German recon plane would come over every night at 10:00 p.m. We called him "Bed Check Charlie." New Year's Day, 1945, We had a big air attack and an armored outfit near us was strafed. We did a Hell of a lot of work while here.

---

74   June 6, 1945, was D-day; "D-day plus fifteen" was June 21, 1945.
75   The Chemical Warfare Service (CWS) mixed, created, and delivered gas, chemical, and physical weaponry, inventing/improving on the fly to assist General Patton's front line, in Harry's case.

Then came the Battle of the Bulge. We moved to Koerich, Belgium, Jan. 4th. We worked hard pushing back the Jerry advances and final cracking of the Siegfried line. We were on a marathon advance. At Aldsdorf, Germany we completed our work instrumental in the crossing of the Mosel. By March 17th–22nd we did our preliminary work to cross the Rhine.

The company crossed the Rhine April 1. We slept in the apartment of a German doll-factory owner who was caught making flying-bomb parts.

April 10th, we were the first Jewish troops to enter Ohrdruf concentration camp of which I have already written.

Neustadt on Eich was our next stop. The Third Army was ordered south just as we were supposed to join up with the Russians. We ended up at a cement plant at Berglengenfeld, April 29th. We had a real nice set-up here. The supply room was in the plants laboratory and I had fun snooping around. By May 2nd we ended here in Straubing.

According to Doc Weast, except for in the letter, Harry Rosen never spoke of what he saw in the concentration camps: it was a horror he wouldn't speak of. Harry ended his war service by following the Third Army into Dachau concentration camp and liberating eighty survivors.

The following quote is from another soldier who did speak of what he saw (and what Harry Rosen would have witnessed, as well) from the hell that was Ohrdruf, the first death camp the Allies entered. A. C. Boyd of the Eighty-Ninth Infantry Division of Patton's Third Army recounted the following:

On April 7, 1945, the 89th Infantry Division received orders to move into the German town of Ohrdruf, which surrendered as the Americans arrived. A mile or so past this quaint village lay Stalag Nord Ohrdruf.

When regiments of the 89th Division got to the camp, the gates were open and the guards apparently, all had gone, but the doors to the wooden barracks were closed. Lying on the ground in front were bodies of prisoners who recently had been shot.

When I went into the camp I just happened to open the door to a small room. Inside, the Germans had stacked bodies very high. They had dumped some lime over them, hoping it would dissolve the bodies.

I still have vivid memories of what I saw, but I try not to dwell on it. We had been warned about what we might find, but actually seeing it was horrible. There were so many dead, and some so starved all they could do was gape open their mouths, feebly move their arms and murmur.

There were ditches dug out in the compound and we could see torsos, lots of arms, severed legs, etc., sticking out. Many had been beaten to death, and bodies were still in the "beating shed." Many had been led to the "showers," where they were pushed in, the doors locked and then gassed.[clv]

EUROPEAN-AFTERMATH

Japanese-Americans all over the country were released from internment camps to their former residences on January 2, 1945. Many had lost their homes and businesses as well as their jobs. As she promised, Tillie welcomed her former Japanese workers back to Flotill. She was one of the first employers to do so. This kept promise was not forgotten by the local Japanese community.[clvi]

In Italy, the damage was heavy from the Allied bombings. Naples alone lost twenty to thirty-five thousand citizens by the time twenty Allied B-24s and two hundred B-17s destroyed essential buildings, including the Del Gaizo canneries and at least one church, built in 1310, the Basilica di Santa Chiara.[clvii] The Del Gaizo cannery in Teduccio was completely destroyed.

After the fall of Mussolini in July of 1943, and the end of the war in Europe in May of 1945, Luigi Del Gaizo was one of the first people to begin reconstruction through humanity's most basic needs. People needed to eat. He planted good food and canned it, just as he had done all his life. Luigi's distrust of Fascism and quiet support of his company over the Fascist govern-ment gained him the confidence of the people and support from the new democratic regime (which Luigi didn't trust, either).

In May of 1949, it was Luigi's devotion to his company and to Italian business in general that earned him the position of vice president of the Union to Rebuild Industry. He was back in banking and rising as a respected advisor and administrator when he died, on April 14, 1953, at the age of seventy.[clviii]

Tillie wept when she heard the news.

Chapter 9

THE VARSITY TEAM, WHAT'S NEXT, AND TYING THE KNOT

One of many talents successful people share is the ability to choose great staff. Tillie was the feminine pinnacle in this vital skill. Her two nephews who worked for her, Albert and Arthur Heiser, were absolutely invaluable to her success. That her sister, Beatrice, gave Tillie these two men as her right and left arms of stability freed her to use her uncanny abilities to foresee market trends and needs and to fearlessly jump on opportunity, even when traversing unknown paths. The Heiser boys were always there for her. They were her tether.

DOC WEAST

Meanwhile, Doc had had enough of the bad-tempered Mr. Caron. He let the can plants he visited, including Flotill, know that he and his PhD were available for hire. Tillie was told that Doc was looking for a new position. She had Arthur Heiser call him.

Within two weeks, Doc was working for Tillie Weisberg at Flotill. He settled into Harry Rosen's spot while Harry was still serving the country, followed by a little stateside recovery time.

Since he was married to his own accomplished wife, Elsie, who, as noted earlier, held a master's degree in food science, Doc was prepared to take instruction from Rosie Munoz, the sharp young-lady lab technician assigned to get him up to speed with the Flotill processes and procedures. Rosie prepared Doc for the idea that Miss Weisberg would expect him to do whatever needed doing at Flotill. His PhD was all well and good, but if the floor needed cleaning, he'd better be willing to clean it—and pronto.

ROSE M. MUNOZ

Rosie and her sisters Connie, Angie, and Cora Munoz all began working on the sorting belt at Flotill together in 1937. Rosie was eighteen years old at the time. None of the girls spoke English. Rosie was bright and inquisitive, and she noticed that the girls who spoke English were selected for the most interesting and best-paying jobs.

It was common knowledge that the boss, Miss Weisberg, wanted the girls on the floor to rise up through the ranks in the business. Rosie encouraged her sisters to learn English with her, as in a game. Rosie was not afraid to use her broken "Spanglish" at work. As a result, Mrs. Bolger, the laboratory supervisor, chose Rosie for advanced opportunities.

First, Rosie learned the laboratory weight-measuring devices. As was Rosie's way, she became expert at what every indicator tick on every sophisticated device was perfect and what was cause for alarm, regarding each product line. If a minute number of bacteria was growing to cause a quality issue, Tillie's laboratory was expected to rectify the matter immediately. Rosie was Mrs. Bolger's shadow, assisting daily in all aspects of the laboratory. Rosie was a sponge when it came to the intricate details of science, and her English was soon fluent. Speaking Spanish created a bridge to bringing more Mexican crew members into the higher-level positions. Rosie was a joyful, bright gift to the success of Flotill.

At times when Mrs. Bolger was sick or on vacation, Rosie Munoz was in charge of the lab. As Miss Weisberg suggested, Rosie was learning a real trade and earning good money as a Flotill laboratory supervisor. It was her responsibility to train Doc Weast, her new lab superior.[clix]

HARRY ROSEN

Harry found the war a manly, honorable, patriotic adventure, but he took some time to recover emotionally from the horrors he'd seen in the concentration camps.[76] Now he was worried that he may have waited too long to secure a position back at Flotill. He'd heard that some PhD had taken his position. Maybe Flotill didn't need him anymore.

He timidly entered the Stockton facility to a roar of welcome, and slaps on the back, by the crew. Tillie heard the commotion. Harry said, "Miss Weisberg and that perfume! I could smell her before I could see her."

A beaming Miss Weisberg greeted Harry while clickity-clicking in a full high-heeled dash across the plant floor to fling herself into his arms. "When are you coming back to help me, Harry?" she said before he could utter a word.[clx]

Doc Weast was now the head laboratory man at the Modesto plant. This was the facility that Harry Rosen had gotten off the ground for Tillie before he marched off to war to beat the bad guys.

When he settled in from his valiant war effort as a chemical-weapons specialist, Harry was assigned to turn that deadly skill into a healthful one, working as Doc's laboratory supervisor. The men became best friends and confidants for life.

Harry Rosen was welcomed back as Flotill's war hero; it didn't hurt that he was also a Jewish war hero. Tillie had a huge soiree planned at her home in Stockton for the ambassador from Israel, Abba Eban.[77] Fanny Brice, Eddie Cantor, and Sophie Tucker all showed up at 740 Willow Street to meet and greet with the ambassador.

---

76 Truth be told, like all decent people, he never stopped having the nightmares of those camps.

77 Abba Eban (1915–2002) was the Israeli foreign affairs minister, education minister, deputy prime minister, and ambassador to both the United States and to the United Nations. He was also vice president of the UN General Assembly and president of the Weizmann Institute of Science.

Tillie rarely allowed photos to be taken in the sanctuary of her private home. She demanded to be the center of attention, which was impossible with a cast of characters like this particular assemblage. Tillie's dismissal of private photographs of the rich and famous made her guests feel at ease. Because the Hollywood set considered Tillie "a good egg," Tillie received invitations to many Hollywood events—tit for tat.

On December 14, 1946, Harry Rosen received a handsome holiday bonus and an original signature on colorful "House of Flotill" stationery for his efforts; Tillie wrote, "It is my pleasure to extend the warmest of Season's Greetings to you. I have enclosed a check to show in a small way, Flotill's appreciation of the important part you have played in our family..."[clxi]

MEYER LEWIS

Meyer Lewis was of enormous value in many areas. He was a sharp guy. He truly shined in the social-events department as the Flotill event planner and entertainer. Meyer Lewis was seriously fun. He was a perfect complement to Tillie's serious intensity.

Tillie danced and drank a little. She did nothing to excess, except for work. She was the Flotill matriarch. Usually smiling, she was still restrained. People were careful about what they said in the presence of the Tomato Queen.

Meyer Lewis put most everyone at ease. He was pot-bellied, double-chinned, and charming. In defiance of his girth and gravity, he was as light on his feet as Fred Astaire on the dance floor. Ladies waited patiently for their turn to dance with Meyer Lewis, who was always complimented not only on his footwork but as a delightful, witty, intelligent gentleman. Even though several Flotill ladies admitted that they found Mr. Lewis quite attractive and even sensual, there was never any hint of misogynistic or sexual improprieties from the staff about him.[clxii]

Meyer Lewis was born Meyer Lefkowitz. He was the seventh of eight children, born in New York, to Louis and Bessie Lefkowitz, Russian Jews who had emigrated from Poland. Meyer may, or may not, have been a "Yankee Doodle Dandy," born on the Fourth of July, but like many first-generation

Americans, he claimed July Fourth as his official date of birth. Such a great number of immigrant parents were so very proud to live in the United States that a child born around their new nation's birthday was deemed to have been born on July Fourth.

Meyer always had a natural rhythm and love of a cool beat. He played the drums and loved to dance. Throughout high school he had led the school's band as the drum major, wearing a dark military-cadet-style uniform with bright-gold buttons, braided trim, and a patent-leather, feather-plumed hat.

When the stock market crashed in October of 1929, young, uninvested individuals such as Meyer didn't pay much attention—after all, the market had been up and down the last few years and always seemed to come up smelling like a rose. Another dip in the Dow sounded like the perfect time for the brothers Lefkowitz to dine, dance, and be devil-may-care on a "Cuban fiesta" cruise to Havana. Cuba had been feeling the crash coming since 1928. When Wall Street fell, Cuban prices dropped to frightening lows. The tension of revolution scented the Cuban air. On November 29, 1929, Phillip (twenty-three), Meyer (twenty-five), Herman (twenty-nine), and Joseph (thirty-three) high-tailed it home.[clxiii]

At the University of Minnesota, Meyer played drums unofficially. Officially, he was the band manager. Meyer Lefkowitz was instrumental in organizing the University Concert Band's one-thousand-mile tour of the South in February of 1930. There are no references to Meyer in the 1930 University of Minnesota *Gopher Annual*, other than as band and tour manager. Meyer does not appear in the listings of graduating seniors from the 1929 through 1931 annuals. There is no evidence that Meyer ever graduated or what his major was.[clxiv] Still, Meyer learned early the perks of business planning and orchestration while leaving the marching to everyone else. Meyer was happily off making personal trips on the university's dime to major cities to solidify the concert halls and accommodations for the university's band.

Heaven only knows how many unofficial cities Meyer enjoyed that were not on the final approved route. Nonetheless, Meyer schmoozed and greased the path so well that his band was greeted from Springfield, Illinois, to New Orleans, with banquets and parties both in the afternoon and evening and dancing at every single stop. Meyer's jovial nature opened doors for him and anyone lucky enough to be in his general vicinity.

The band's stay in New Orleans went a bit longer than planned when manager Meyer Lefkowitz went AWOL for a few days. According to the *Gopher Annual*, after Meyer "briefly absconded with the funds,"[clxv] he returned from his successful gambling spree with all accounts intact and paid the band's bills with enough to leave everyone who'd been aggrieved with a handsome tip, a handshake, and a promise to visit again, soon. Charm was Meyer's strong suit.

Back to 1947, Meyer was aware that Tillie's star was still rising. She was meeting more interesting (but always married) men. Tillie was actively searching for an unmarried one—a widower perhaps—to come her way. Then that darned Sam Kipniss began to show up again.

Without obtaining any promises from Tillie, Meyer Lewis began formal divorce proceedings against his wife, Elinor, and downgraded his family into a somewhat lesser neighborhood. According to Meyer's son Bill, the new house was still very nice, but his mother never forgave Meyer for leaving her.

Tillie bought another plant in Stockton she called Penthouse,[78] which canned the higher-end products that Tillie was bringing into the fold. She was expanding into more perfect fruits and negotiating with Hormel to can their meat products.

A Mr. Francoeur wrote a letter to Tillie about one of the first Penthouse products to hit the grocery stores. This was the beginning of Tillie's food-related fan mail, which soon became a happy avalanche in the years to come.

Francoeur & Company, Inc.
25 Beaver St. New York, NY

To: Flotill Products Inc.
Mrs. Francoeur bought some of your canned apricots in Westport, Connecticut. They are by far the finest we have ever eaten. It so happens that my father-in-law has a place…Seven Springs Ranch…and

---

78 Tillie loved to obtain the most expensive hotel suites on their top floors, called penthouses: hence the name for her best products.

he knows you.[79] Our purpose in writing is simply to compliment you on a very fine product.

Very truly yours,

P. M. Francoeur[clxvi]

ISRAEL

On May 14, 1948, the State of Israel officially came into being. Tillie's father was to enjoy this blessing only briefly. Jacob Ehrlich died in September, only four months later. He was buried in the soil of his Israel.[clxvii] It is not known if Tillie attended the service. She did call upon the rabbi, her family, and Harry Rosen to attend a somber memorial at the house on Willow to bless the life and passing of Jacob Ehrlich. Bilha lived another ten years in the Holy Land and was buried next to Jacob.

On her future world travels, Tillie stopped to pay respect to her father and gave generously to Jewish relief causes in Israel.

THE FBI, AGAIN

Tillie purchased a new warehouse in Modesto just as the hot Central Valley weather was creating the perfect glut of products. Prices fell drastically, and cost cutting was on the horizon. Flotill had to let several employees go; Arthur Heiser even unexpectedly asked Harry Rosen to leave, since he was no longer needed. Harry had to clear his things out that day. Doc was miserable; he really felt that Harry had been given the shaft.[clxviii]

While other canners were struggling to obtain financing, thanks to Tillie's government contacts, Flotill managed to obtain a large-enough loan from the Reconstruction Finance Corporation (RFC) to grow.[80] At the Penthouse

---

79 Francoeur refers to his father-in-law's impressive custom estate, Seven Springs Ranch, with its expansive land holdings in lush Cupertino, California, to which Tillie had often been invited as a guest.

80 The RFC was a program for government lending to essential American businesses that operated from 1932 to 1957. The RFC also sold obsolete army aircraft and ships for personal use or for scrapping.

plant, Flotill began to pack corned-beef hash for Hormel as well as a Flotill canned spaghetti to compete with Chef Boyardee.

At least one person at one of these "other" canneries determined that Tillie Weisberg—only a dumb divorcée, after all—must be using illegal, immoral, or perhaps even communist methods to continue her success. This confidential informant, referred to as "T-1" in FBI case file #49-116118-18, contacted the FBI.

The FBI assumed, since Miss Weisberg had been under their scrutiny from 1938 to 1941 (case closed by J. Edgar Hoover himself for lack of evidence), it couldn't hurt to open a pending file on this dame. No harm in keeping their eyes and ears open, since "when there's smoke, there's fire."

The government had just lent Mrs. Weisberg a sizeable chunk of money and sold her a couple of used army supply ships. The ships were making a lot of trips along the coast, into international waters, and to Cuba. Perhaps something was rotten with Miss Weisberg after all.

Then Tillie had a fabulous new "what's next?" big idea that could make a fortune: she would use the bulk of the RFC loan to buy Lone Star International Foods in Edinburg, Texas, specifically to can Mexican pineapple. Ever since the end of the war, Hawaiian pineapple prices had gone through the roof; Mexican and Cuban pineapple was much more affordable.

The RFC loan made growth in other areas possible. Arthur Heiser called Doc Weast in and requested his services to officially run the Stockton plant. Doc was by now used to the fact that Tillie didn't give a hoot if you had a PhD or a high-school diploma: you were expected to do whatever jobs were necessary. Nobody told Tillie no. Not ever.

Doc had one request: "If I'm going to be doing magic running a plant slightly outside my educational grade of food chemist, I want Harry Rosen back working here as my second in command." Doc's wish was granted—he and Harry were together again, working through what Doc called "the glory days for Flotill."

DEATH BY SPINACH

Tillie wanted more product, and she wanted it cleaner, higher quality, and faster than ever before. It didn't matter to Miss Weisberg that the machines and processes to accomplish these feats had not yet been invented. She expected everybody to come up with ideas and solve issues. Miss Weisberg would stop by to ask about "progress, not problems."

Doc, Harry Rosen, and Rosie Munoz created a spinach-specific conveyor belt that drummed in water, thoroughly washing out the sand and grit. The first test went awry when a big glob of spinach got stuck tight inside the contraption. Rosie Munoz suggested that they rake it out. Tiny as Rosie was, Harry was even smaller. He was chosen to walk the slimy wet belt, test rake in hand, reach in, and pull. It worked for the spinach but dragged poor Harry into the mechanical works. They thought Harry just might be a goner. Happily, he was fine; he was just covered in Popeye's favorite food. They referred to the incident as Harry's "death by spinach" affair.

Conveyors were the apparent answer to the speed they needed. Doc and Harry tried a similar technique on the fragile asparagus stalks. The problem with asparagus was cutting off the tough, woody ends. Harry and Doc scratched their heads as nice clean stalks came through quick as lightning, but the butt ends were still intact. Previously, all asparagus was babied by hand from the fields to the plant, where they were then cut (also by hand) in small lots with sharp knives. Asparagus was becoming too expensive to can. But there was no way the guys were going to confess to Miss Weisberg that they were stymied.

What to do? Coffee break and "noodle it?" Tillie took her famous think walks; they'd take a think break. In jest, Doc suggested using a guillotine, to which Harry exclaimed, "band saw!" They had a mechanic come up and help jury-rig a band saw to the edge of the conveyor belt while avoiding electrocuting the inventors/guinea-pig crew. The thing was a success.

By the end of that summer, Doc and Harry had invented an automatic tomato peeler using water and Harry Rosen's specialty: chemicals. The result was that the ladies on the line were no longer burning their hands-on steam-heated tomatoes or cutting their hands while removing the skins. All fruit and vegetable lines were plagued with accidents that caused pain and suffering for the ladies on the floor and required regular burn care. That problem for the gals was nearly a thing of the past.

Miss Weisberg congratulated the innovators, calling them "miracle workers." Of course, there was a handsome bonus from the grateful Tillie.

Doc later wrote, "Tillie expected creative thinking on your feet. Everybody worked harder for Miss Weisberg because she was both intimidating and inspiring. All the people of her plants worked long and hard, not just for money...*no!* Nobody wanted to let Tillie Weisberg down. For the men and women alike, it was a thrill to win a smile from the beautiful boss because she made us all feel so darned special."clxix

MEYER TUCKERED OUT

Meyer determined to make good on a ground-floor investment, hoping to prove that Tillie was not the only wise owl in the tree. He met the automaker Preston Tucker in Chicago in 1947 and invested all his savings in what Tucker called "the car you've been waiting for." Meyer, along with 49,999 other investors, was certain this futuristic marvel of automotive engineering with the "Cyclops" third headlight was a sure thing.

Tucker produced a total of fifty-one cars. Tucker was closed down by the Securities Exchange Commission (SEC) and the justice department in January of 1949.[81] Meyer, and the others, lost their shirts.

Meyer's monetary blunder did not go unnoticed by Tillie. When he mentioned that he had even gotten behind on his child-support payments due to the failed Tucker deal, he met Tillie's icy stare. Through clenched teeth, she told him that he'd need to wait for payday, or he could stop into bookkeeping and apply for a loan through Flotill, with interest. Tillie never personally bailed Meyer out of any financial situation. He, like all employees, would need to visit the Flotill front-office accountants.

---

81 An open letter from Preston Tucker from June 15, 1948, is available at http://www.hfmgv.org/exhibits/showrooms/1948/letter.html.

Flotill paid well enough to support Meyer's ex-wife and two sons in what most folks would consider luxury and still have enough cash to spring for a fancy gift once in a while to soothe Tillie. After losing the dough in the Tucker deal, if he couldn't be investment savvy, he wanted to do something gallant.

Meyer feared he was losing her to another suitor. That gent from the past, Sam Kipniss, just might sweep Tillie off her feet before Meyer did. On a Flotill business trip to Chicago, Meyer asked the advice of the head secretary, Nettie Galluzzo, about what gift a gal like Tillie Weisberg might really like—something she didn't already have that would be different and special.

Nettie mentioned she'd seen an amazing set of tomato-red alligator-skin luggage in the window of one of Chicago's most stylish stores, Arnold's on Michigan Avenue. In fact, when Nettie spied the suitcases, they immediately made her think of Miss Weisberg. Meyer clapped his hands. Tomato-red alligator luggage? Perfect! He asked Nettie to purchase the luggage and have it wrapped for immediate shipping. Nettie included a lovely gift card with the package, composed and signed by Meyer Lewis, before she sent the gift off to Stockton.[clxx]

WHAT'S NEXT FOR 1947?

Tillie was on a thinking-out-loud walk through the plant, inviting workers to contribute a "what's next?" idea. She was hoping for a great idea to mull over on a much-needed few days of vacation in Palm Springs, where Tillie and Bea were going to enjoy a few rejuvenation spa days.

Doc cautiously mentioned his idea for a low-calorie diabetic product line. Tillie stopped and looked Doc directly in the eye and said, "Talk to me when I get back from Palm Springs."

Tillie took her break, and Doc went home to talk to Elsie. Doc knew that Miss Weisberg needed a new "what's next?" idea right now.

Tillie's nephew Dr. Saul Heiser created a family vacation photo album at Chips's Palm Springs compound. Saul caught Tillie relaxing in shorts and lounging with his mother, Bea, at the "outer garden area" as well as playing serious ping-pong (in a dress and heels) against her nephews' wives in the "inner garden area." Tillie was still a serious ping-pong competitor; she'd become quite good at the game and pounded the ladies at the sport. Tillie was a gleeful winner and a poor loser. The entire family knew it was never a good idea to "outshine or win" at anything when it concerned Chips.

Featured in the album is Tillie showing off the plant to Saul and his wife, June. Saul was the medical doctor of whom Tillie was as proud as any biological mother could be.

Saul's photos included a shot of the conveyor-belt line of ladies sorting tomatoes, with Chips smiling as the fruit rolls past. Saul wrote, "1,000 girls & 1 brain." Not complimentary to the other ladies, but this was a private album just for Tillie. Saul was letting Chips know how proud he was of her, too.

Another is a pose of Saul, with brothers Arthur and Albert Heiser, flanking Chips. Saul commented, "Chips & her kids." These three men had wonderful parents in Beatrice and Sam Hockheiser. Chips was the cherry tomato on top.

THE DIABETIC DIET

Doc and Elsie Weast had been tinkering with the diabetic product in their Manteca home kitchen at 232 N. Lincoln Street. Doc and Elsie, both food scientists, had gone ahead and invented that sugar-free sweetener that Doc thought of on the train with the diabetic man. Doc and Elsie Weast intended to market the product to diabetics. The sweetener was made from the naturally occurring carbohydrate in fruit (called pectin) and saccharine, a synthetic sugar.[82] They simply could not afford to invest in the idea on their own. With Elsie's resigned approval, Doc pitched the idea to Mrs. Weisberg. He later said that "Mrs. Weisberg frankly both terrified and enthralled me" and confessed that he made a few practice runs for his speech in the men's room mirror before asking Miss Weisberg's secretary for a formal meeting with "the Boss." His knees were knocking while the idea—kept secret for far too long for Doc's

---

[82] Saccharine is two to seven hundred times sweeter than table sugar; it has zero calories, zero nutritive value, and it does not raise blood sugar.

liking—poured through his lips. Tillie's direct eye contact and broadening smile assured him that he had piqued her interest.

Tillie asked if Doc and Elsie had any samples to taste. He did not yet, but he promised he'd have samples for her to taste by morning. With a phone call home, Elsie mixed several different sugarless fruit-preserve samples using Doc's formula in order to impress Mrs. Weisberg.

Tillie leaned back in her chair, still holding the mason jar, closed her eyes, and stated to Doc, "Why market this to just diabetics? With the war over and rationing a thing of the past, everybody is growing fat. Let's put the country on a diet!"

Hallelujah! Doc had hit a home run.

Tillie immediately applied for the patent in Doc's name. The test pack of apricots was produced at the Modesto plant. It was going to take years and a lot of money to push this new "baby" through.

Tillie just knew it: delicious diet products were going to be bigger than postwar waistlines.

ELSIE WEAST

Tillie expected that Elsie Weast would sign on as chief "cook" for the new Tasti-Diet brand at Flotill, but Elsie declined. Elsie was absolutely not going to leave her two little girls, three-year-old Edith Claire and two-year-old Kathryn Ann. Elsie was a traditional housewife by Tillie's standards, but as an uncommonly intelligent woman from Modesto, California, who'd attained a master's degree at Berkeley on her own in 1938, she was anything but traditional by most standards of the day.

Sweet, kind, and exceptionally intellectual Elsie Weast was the only person Doc had ever heard of who refused Tillie Weisberg anything. The only person whom Doc had ever heard of who'd told Tillie no. But after a bit of cajoling by her husband, Elsie was willing to negotiate several terms.

* Flotill was to create a full laboratory test kitchen at the Weast home at 232 North Lincoln Street in Manteca at no cost to the Weasts.

* Elsie was to be paid a salary commensurate with her position as a research scientist, and Elsie would work around the napping schedule of the children.
* Doc would tote the product samples back and forth to the plant.
* Elsie would never be under any obligation to attend any meetings at Flotill.
* Miss Weisberg was to acknowledge that the Weast children would be Elsie's priority before anything else.
* The patent for Tasti-Diet would be in Doc's name (not Flotill's), and he would receive royalties for the lifetime of any products derived from Tasti-Diet in any and all forms that were created in the future.

Tillie agreed with the stipulation that, outside of agreed-upon royalties to the Weasts, Tasti-Diet belonged to Flotill and Tillie Weisberg. Doc and Elsie sold the marketing rights and the rights to the story of the creation of the first dedicated diet products to Tillie Weisberg, who could spin the story any way Tillie pleased.

While Tillie's attorneys worked on Doc's patent approval, Tillie sent engineers out to the Weast home to install a mini-lab upstairs in the attic space. A tiny combination electric stove/refrigerator/freezer unit was placed alongside a little sink, cabinets, and work counter.

First, using a derivative of pectin that would form a gel, Doc and Elsie made a line of low-calorie jams and jellies. The only sugar content was of the fruits' natural juices. Next, Elsie created salad dressings and mayonnaise containing no more than 10 percent oil, which was quite a bit lower than the enormous fat and oil content of other spreads. Pleased with herself, Tillie renamed the mayonnaise "May-Lo-Naise." The company included canned fruits and vegetables in the dietary line. Another company developed an imitation egg that Elsie dried for use in a pancake mix. These were absolutely delicious low-calorie, low-fat, low-salt, and low-sugar products, and they were all from the little Weast laboratory.

OTHERWISE ENGAGED

From 1939 on, Tillie made certain that she would conduct any remotely in-appropriate behavior far away: in Europe or at her Palm Springs compound. The truth was that Tillie was getting too old to put much energy into such nonsense. As Helene Heiser later recalled,

> Tillie was not a woman's woman. She liked men. I don't mean just in the sexual way at all: she just didn't associate with women. She had no interest in regular woman things. Really! What woman in those days thought like Tillie did about business, finance, success? No one! She never seemed upset about it [not having women friends.]
>
> I'll say it again: Tillie liked men; men liked her. At her social and financial level, most men interesting to Chips were married. That's just the way things were.
>
> In New York, P. S. [Palm Springs], and Europe, infidelity was common. Here in Stockton, oh boy! No way. [Shakes her head in disapproval at the long-ago memory.]
>
> Just before she married Meyer Lewis, she was still seeing that Sam Kipnis. Chips liked the intrigue. Tillie had been seeing Sam on and off since even before Del Gaizo died. Sam was the one she loved, but Sam Kipnis was not ever going to leave his wife.
>
> We didn't like Sam Kipnis much. He was pushy; [he] spoke and acted sexually [inappropriate], with this *huge* belly [makes a gesture in-dicating great girth]. We all knew Sam was [still] financially and emo-tionally involved with his wife. Sam was never going to marry Tillie.
>
> We liked Meyer Lewis. My oldest daughter loved Meyer. Meyer was fun and [now] available.
>
> Chips never met men in Stockton for an affair, but this time she got caught…Meyer Lewis had gone to her place on Willow, just a few blocks away from our house. We all knew that Meyer proposed, and Chips was putting him off until she had time to talk to Sam face to face. Tillie had given Sam the "marry me" ultimatum, and Sam was here now…both men at the same time. This, Chips did not plan.

I guess to avoid a scene in front of the neighbors, Chips jumped in her car and raced over here to our place. Sam Kipnis was right behind her in her car. Al and I were horrified. Goodness, we were just a young married couple ourselves. We didn't know what to do.

Chips ran in, locked the door behind her, and pleaded with us to hide her. Here [was] the grown woman—the Tomato Queen—crying, shaking, and begging to sleep on our sofa until this all blew over.

Sam was banging on the door and saying he was sorry, saying he was leaving, saying he had to go home. Chips didn't say a thing. She just stood there, tears in her eyes. Sam left.

A few minutes later, an angry Meyer Lewis was banging on our door. Tillie just turned away and dropped onto the couch, her chin almost in her lap, childlike. Al finally told Meyer to leave [and] that Chips wasn't here. I mean, her car was out front! Meyer got the message and left. Tillie stayed two nights. She didn't go into work.

The next thing we knew, she was on the phone planning the wedding with Meyer.[83]

Everyone was relieved [that] Mr. and Mrs. Sam Kipnis were not on the guest list.

For Meyer Lewis, he thought there was no down side to marrying Tillie. He'd be marrying serious money and would be living the life he dreamed of as the king of the Flotill castle. Tillie, even as she aged, was a sexy, vital, classy woman. He hoped that Tillie would forgive him his accumulating debts as a wedding gift. She did not.

For Tillie, it was simply time to settle down. Meyer and Tillie would marry, but first Tillie had to tie the financial knots. The vow to be richer was fine with Tillie; poorer was not going to be part of the deal.

Meyer Lewis would legally remain strictly an employee, separate from Tillie's properties, businesses, and bank accounts. As an employee, Meyer would receive a salary from Flotill throughout the marriage. All travel and

---

83   Since there is no evidence of Tillie's marriage licence or divorce decree from Louis Weisberg, the author maintains that Tillie was likely not legally married to Louis Weisberg.

luxury expenses would be on the company dime but, the marriage bed would be the only thing Tillie shared equally with Meyer—as long as he did not object to having no ownership in the mattress, box springs, or bedding.[clxxi]

Meyer quipped to his growing sons his advice on the fairer sex: "Everything in life isn't romance."[clxxii] Tillie and Meyer knew this was a sensible business marriage, not a passionate love match.

Groom Meyer Lewis and bride Tillie Ehrlich obtained their Los Angeles County marriage certificate on November 3, 1948. Tillie, who was originally born in 1896, would have been fifty-two years old at the time, but she'd altered that year (wanting to be more youthful for Florindo Del Gaizo) a long time ago.

Her *new* birth year was 1901. This would still have left her three to four years older than Meyer Lewis, who was born in 1904. Tillie wasn't about to let a little thing like the truth about her age ruin her wedding day. Tillie claimed on their marriage certificate that she was forty-three years old: a year younger than her spouse-to-be. Simple—Tillie had now been born in 1905.

Prewedding Tillie: The bride-to-be chauffeurs their bridal-party hostess Jeannette Brownlee around town, while Meyer Lewis, the groom, looks on approvingly.

Jeannette Brownlee hosted the prewedding shower at Palm Springs for the bridal party, and Jeannette and her husband, Clinton, purchased the wedding album for Tillie and Meyer. Jeannette was the closest thing to a friend Tillie had, yet her inscription in the album simply reads,

To you,
Dear Mrs. Weisberg.
With all of our love.
Jeannette and Clinton Brownlee.

Jeannette was photographed in the backseat of Miss Weisberg's newest convertible; she was being chauffeured, with the top down, by a smiling Tillie. Palm Springs must have been just as shocked, as Stockton was, to see the Tomato Queen driving a black woman around the local streets and avenues. The Brownlees were the only black guests at the wedding.[clxxiii]

Later, little Barbara and Nancy Heiser posed with Auntie Chips, all three in their pretty, new bridal-shower dresses. While the adorable girls smiled brightly in their ruffles and bows, Tillie appeared slightly dazed. Auntie Chips had just recovered from a visit to her Beverly Hills dermatologist for a bride-to-be dermabrasion facial. Now evidently feeling younger, she dared ask the girls, "How old do you think Auntie Chips looks?" Nancy Heiser proudly chirped, "About a hundred!"[clxxiv]

On November 7, 1948, Tillie Ehrlich-Weisberg became Tillie Lewis in Los Angeles. The newlyweds enjoyed congratulatory cards and telegrams from around the world.

Meyer and Tillie were married four days later, on November 7, 1948, in the sculptured gardens of LA. The bride wore an ankle-length silk lamé long-sleeved shirtwaist blouse with matching pleated skirt, gloves, and shoes with a hint of a red bow. Her petite hat matched her French lace veil. Her brother-in-law, Sam Hochheiser, gave her away.

The guest list welcomed friends and business associates from all across the country, as well as from Havana and Tokyo and other far-flung places. Family, Flotill staff, and a few celebrities were in attendance. Conspicuously absent was Miss Fanny Brice of 312 North Faring Road, Holmby Hills, California, and dancer Harry Pilcer. Both were invited, but neither responded to the invitation. This hurt Tillie deeply. Fanny didn't even send a gift or a telegram of congratulations.[clxxv]

George and Thea Froehlich, whom Tillie had saved from Nazi persecution during the war, were so deeply touched by their inclusion on the guest list that they kept their original invitation intact in a box of their most cherished belongings for the rest of their lives.[84]

The newlyweds' honeymoon included attending food conferences all over the country that, naturally, featured sumptuous samplings of edible bliss.

Meyer Lewis decided to leave automobile investments behind and to stick with the food industry in order to strike it rich on his own. He thought about Tillie's philosophy for success of "looking for a need to fill," but what need required filling? And how would he know it when it saw it?

It was at one such California specialty-product sampling that Meyer tasted his next venture: the Medjool date. The salesmen offered date candies, cakes, breads, and juices, each more delicious than the last. Meyer was entranced with the idea that date palms had existed before human beings; the darn things could grow in the desert with no care at all. Dates were a staple in Mesopotamia, he learned, and the palm leaves offered "360 uses," from baskets, mattress stuffing, and rope—there were hundreds of other ways to skin a date palm.[clxxvi] As far as Meyer was concerned, investing in dates was a sure thing.

---

84 The author owns George and Thea Froehlich's wedding invitation, a gift from their son for this biography.

Tillie couldn't argue that dates weren't delicious, but they were a specialty—a luxury or a holiday gift, at best. Tillie was not about to invest. If Meyer wanted to take out a loan from Flotill, he was welcome to see Claude Young at the main office and make arrangements in his name only—Tillie wanted nothing to do with the date business. An undisclosed interviewee later stated that:

> Meyer borrowed more money from Flotill and bought a nice Medjool date orchard in Indio, California. Meyer had no family money, so he always needed to borrow from Tillie for every little thing. The dates were delicious, but when things went a bit south, Tillie wouldn't help Meyer out. He was sinking deeper into her debt. While he was spending his time writing Tillie's speeches and being her stage manager, Tillie never supported his ideas or opportunities.[clxxvii]

As Tillie predicted, the date farm turned out to be a specialty item and not a necessity in an economy still recovering from World War II and soon to enter a war in Korea. The investment went bust.

Chapter 10

PINEAPPLE PIRATES, KOREA, AND THE MEASURE OF MEYER

It seemed like a great plan.

Banks L. Miller brought the idea, the know-how, the connections, and the notion of buying two used US Army surplus ships to Tillie; these ships could solve the fruit-cocktail problem she was currently experiencing by using Mexican pineapples. The ships would be used to transport pineapple and equipment. According to the Food and Drug Administration (FDA), a product may not be labeled "fruit cocktail" without the proper ratio of fruits, including pineapple "tidbits." Miller's prospectus pointed out that Dole of Hawaii had enjoyed a monopoly on pineapple products long enough, to which Tillie agreed.

According to Banks Miller, Tillie could enjoy not only the exceptional quality Mexican fruit but the byproducts of it (such as pineapple juice) without compensating the naive Mexican growers. He was selling his Texas canning facility (including its equipment), ready to continue to pack Mexican pineapple, just as he had done the previous year. He brought Tillie canned pineapple samples to taste and test, along with impressive records of his previous production. According to Miller, Tillie would be making more money than she could imagine, and at a discount price, since he was more of an idea man; Tillie was the brilliant businesswoman.

The Flotill lawyers, including Arthur Heiser, voiced their bad feelings about this Banks Miller fellow. Ignoring some of her advisors served her well in the past, this time, all agreed Tillie was buying trouble. She went ahead anyway. After obtaining the one hundred thousand dollar RFC loan (which she secured using Flotill and her Stockton mansion as collateral), on March 1, 1948, Tillie took over the plant in Texas[clxxviii] and sent the more than reluctant Harry Rosen to get the place running, Flotill style, applying the company motto "Quality in Quantity."

Harry had already lived through hell in the war; the conditions he found at Lone Star International Foods were a close second. The hair-raising flight to the site was a portent of things to come. Harry recalled later,

> It's certainly funny, at this juncture, to think of the near-death flight in that two-seater air antique that flew me into Mexico, sitting here now relaxing in my nice safe living room. But fifty-plus years ago, that crazy pilot—if he was a pilot—had never flown above fifty feet in his life. The lunatic pilot said, "I only know the way by following the dirt roads." There we were, hugging the ground, my eyes as big as saucers, scared to death. I figured maybe I wouldn't die if we crashed, since we were only a story or two high.

After a teetering landing, Harry hoped the worst was behind him. It wasn't. Harry wrote and telegrammed Doc Weast for help and advice. Nothing that Miller had promised Tillie was true. The plant, the equipment, the supposed contacts—even the fruit—was all a mess. After weeks of trying to clean and make repairs, the FDA inspector left for Washington, DC, in disgust. The only saving grace for Flotill was that the FDA inspector had no doubt that Harry Rosen was legitimately more distressed at the conditions of this plant than he was.

Nonetheless, the FDA report was a failure of enormous magnitude. Harry wrote directly to Miller and sent copies of the correspondence to Miss Weisberg and several others. In a May 24, 1948, memo[clxxix] to Miller, Harry Rosen wrote, "I know there are many changes you intend to make...I have tried to observe as much as possible in test runs May 19–21 and feel I should bring to your attention some things you may or may not be acquainted with." Harry detailed to Miller that the temperatures reached by the equipment he had sold Miss Weisberg were going to give the public botulism: "It is imperative, as you know, that each can reach a minimum temperature of 190 degrees to [ensure] sterilization. I am concerned that unless every possible step is taken to guarantee the proper processing of every can, we may be jeopardizing our pack by possible subsequent spoilage…" He made it clear that he intended to apprise Miss Weisberg of all the problems he'd encountered that might sully her good name in the industry—not to mention making the public sick, or worse. He continued, "Such memos to you of my observations and examinations will be written from time to time. This will keep you informed of the conditions as they exist and enable you to consider possible changes in operations and equipment for both the San Carlos [Texas] plant and the *Miss Tillie*." [85] The *Miss Tillie* and *Miss Tillie II* were the army ships being used for this new venture.

Harry had to be fuming, since he did not end with a polite closing or a signature. His name was at the top of the memo—that was good enough for this stinker.

June 17, 1948: Memo to Banks L. Miller from Harry Rosen

The Production Marketing Administration[86] is withdrawing its Inspector from this plant as of this date because of sanitary conditions existing in the plant. They will supply us with inspection service again provided we comply with the following recommendations.

* Approval of water system and purification with State or County Health officer approval…
* All fruit must be adequately washed…on all sides of the fruit.

---

85   The *Miss Tillie* was used as a floating cannery. The *Miss Tillie II* was used for ocean transport.
86   PMA followed the WWII wartime Food Administration. PMA dissolved at the end of 1948 into the FDA.

* The mezzanine floors must be curbed to prevent water and dirt from dripping to lower floors.
* All floors must be kept periodically clean.
* All doors and windows must be screened.
* Wash basins [must be] provided for employees.
* Refuse piles and stagnant water outside plant must be cleaned up and provisions made to prevent reoccurrence of conditions as they now exist.

I don't believe that any comment is needed as to the effect that such action by [the] Production Marketing Administration will have on our reputation. We have been given a "break" of a second chance when we have complied. This is contrary to their usual procedure. The conditions above [mean that the facility is] condemned. Not only are they contrary to good canning practice but the federal Food and Drug Administration inspection frowned upon his visit. I believe every effort should be made to prove that we too do not approve of the present sanitary conditions of the plant.

Harry and the rest of the Flotill crew knuckled down and scrubbed the plant clean, earning approval by the inspectors. Tillie Weisberg and her team truly insisted upon excellence and would accept nothing less. This project was way over budget, and they hadn't canned a single pineapple.

The pineapples themselves were unacceptable. They were full of mold or too juicy, and the flavor was lousy. The "naive" Mexican growers and government had their hands out for every bribe imaginable they could get from the people whom they considered foolish and greedy Americans.

Texan and Mexican plant workers from the previous year confessed that they'd had inferior pineapple the year before. They disclosed that Miller knew this, which thus spurred his plan to unload the problem pineapple plant. Miller started shipping in huge cans of Cuban pineapple, which he poured into his company's smaller cans to defraud potential buyers.

Back in Stockton, Tillie took another "think walk" to solve the problem. She ordered her workers to place the equipment to can the pineapples on the ship now christened the *Miss Tillie*. She told them to make it a sparkling-clean, floating cannery and to moor it off shore in international waters. She further instructed that the pineapples and workers should be rowed out to the *Miss Tillie* for packing.

The processing line had Mexican ladies in their aprons cutting and sorting fruit. The rowboats became a floating conveyor belt for people and supplies to the ship and from the ship to shore. The company avoided the filth of the Texas and Mexican plants, which was unacceptable by both legal and Tillie standards. In addition, international waters should halt the never-ending "little bites" that the not-naive-in-any-capacity Mexican authorities were taking from the hands that fed them. The Mexican officials watched in amazement as Lone Star, under the direction of the American boss lady, took to the sea and began production. Harry Rosen was actively supervising in an official capacity. Unofficially, he was certain that this hare-brained scheme was destined to land somebody in a Mexican prison. He was also convinced that his head would be first on the chopping block in that dark hole of despair that he imagined himself taking his final siesta in; he would be that "somebody" rotting away in a Mexican prison.

The *Miss Tillie* pineapple-canning ship; Harry Rosen and Meyer Lewis chat in front of the ship, just before Mexico arrested the Flotill team for piracy.

Harry telegrammed an official SOS. In flew Arthur Heiser and Meyer Lewis to the rescue to assist if any legal issues came up. Just as Harry had foreseen; gigantic legal issues came up.

Harry telephoned Mrs. Lewis to inform her that Arthur Heiser had been arrested by the Mexican government for piracy in Alvarado, Veracruz. An armed crew of Mexican police had boarded the *Miss Tillie*, demanded all personnel to the shore, and placed Art and Meyer under house arrest at a local hotel. What, one might ask, were the Mexicans doing during this standoff? A few armed soldiers were washing and hanging out their laundry on the ship lines. Later they smoked cigarettes with their feet up while enjoying the sunshine, rifles across their laps.

According to Harry, Tillie contacted her attorneys. She was not about to fly herself into the slammer, even if it was a five-star hotel with room service. The attorney assured Tillie that this was "nothing money couldn't fix; more palms just needed to be greased. The attorneys just need to know *which* palms need to be greased." In the meantime, she ordered Meyer, Arthur, and Harry to stay put: do not make a break for it, which was Meyer's original suggestion. Legally, an escape—no matter how great an escape it was—would officially make them pirates and international fugitives.

Meyer Lewis was popular for his keen negotiation skills and his playful spirit. This would be no exception. Harry Rosen remembered him as the ringleader in the drunkest few days he'd ever had on foot. The three hit every drinking establishment within walking distance of their hotel. Harry surmised that they may have caused a liquor shortage of historic proportion in the town.

When summoned back for their bailing out, he and Arthur Heiser dragged the 240-pound Meyer Lewis up the cobbled-stairs, scuffing the toes of Lewis's shoes on the rocks, much to Meyer's pickled glee.

The official word was that Meyer Lewis was to drive immediately to see the Mexican official in charge of the port, bringing hush money and a contract that Arthur Heiser scribbled up, per agreement, between said official and Tillie Weisberg. If the contract and cash were not in hand by 5:00 p.m., then the *Miss Tillie*, and all her equipment, would become the property of Mexico.

Harry Rosen later reflected, "Hungover Meyer drove like a bat out of hell; I acted as his eyes, since he was too bleary to see and I was too hungover to be of much other use. Arthur Heiser handwrote the contract over the speeding, bouncing terrain. I know there is a God, since I was praying up a storm and we made it on time [and] in one piece."

Even so, the whole pineapple-packing idea had gone adrift as far as Tillie and company were concerned. Tillie called a meeting in Edinburg, Texas that included Banks L. Miller—it was time Mr. Miller took some responsibility for this mess. Tillie knew she could file for bankruptcy on the whole kit and caboodle, but she was a woman of honor. She knew she owed her attorney, the printing company, the can manufacturer, and the US government. But she did not feel she owed Mr. Banks L. Miller a damn thing.

On August 28, 1948, Miller pled to the assembled group that none of this mess was his doing, and he expected a return on his investment. Tillie listened silently. She stood and quietly said, "It's bankruptcy." She straightened her skirt as she stood stone-faced and left for the Sherry-Netherlands Hotel suite in New York to take care of a few things.

Miller took care of a few things, too. He had equipment removed from the *Miss Tillie* as well as from the Lone Star plant. Under Miller's directive, the second ship just "went missing"; the *Miss Tillie* was run aground and left for vandals.

Then things got uglier. The FBI came in, undercover, to again investigate Mrs. Weisberg; they monitored Tillie's long-distance phone calls to and from Stockton, New York, and Texas, in addition to monitoring her air travel. The FBI created a sizable file a few inches thick and made the decision to take her to a grand jury, if J. Edgar Hoover approved, because she'd broken bankruptcy laws by paying her promised obligations to some of her creditors while she was still in bankruptcy. The agency alleged that Tillie had paid her attorney and her CPA, she'd paid Lehmann Lithograph for printing her labels, she was in the process of making arrangements to pay off her US government RFC loan, and she'd paid the Continental Can Company (Tillie was in big trouble for returning perfect, unused cans to Continental Can).

Paying off selected creditors is in violation of US bankruptcy law; not paying valued creditors was against Tillie's personal moral rule of law.

Tillie was legally wrestling with the FBI, which brought her (and her top executives) in repeatedly to make formal statements. She knew that FBI agents were watching her every move and keeping notes in triplicate. She pushed on. She was trying to do the right thing, but she was *not* going to pay Banks L. Miller. While the RFC had seen plenty of companies go bankrupt on them before, they had never seen a company in bankruptcy *trying* to pay them. Tillie was illegally still paying off her RFC loan, which had been folded into her bankruptcy under an umbrella clause. Further, she was applying for an RFC loan extension while under an FBI investigation in which she was accused of the crime of paying her bills. Distressed and clearly puzzled, RFC chief Paul Cotter contacted J. Edgar Hoover in this letter.

Reconstruction Finance Corporation, Washington, DC
January 24, 1949

To: Honorable J. Edgar Hoover
Director, Federal Bureau of Investigation
Washington, DC

Dear Mr. Hoover,
Re: Lone Star International Foods Company; Tillie Weisberg-Edinburg, Texas
This Corporation [i.e., the RFC] made a loan of $100,000 to the above-named corporation and Tillie Weisberg appeared as a guarantor. The corporation has gone into bankruptcy and we have been asked to give the guarantor an extension of time upon the pledge of additional collateral.

Incident to these negotiations, it has come to our attention that your Bureau may have the subject Weisberg under investigation in connection with some criminal matter. Prior to granting any extension

of time, it would be greatly appreciated if you could furnish us with the nature and status of any situation in which Miss Weisberg may be involved and which is presently under investigation by your bureau.
Very truly yours,
Paul J. Cotter
Chief, Investigation Section of RFC[clxxx]

J. Edgar Hoover must have approved of the requested extension, since Tillie got the loan and paid it off in half the time. The FBI case was closed on April 25, 1950, by assistant US attorney William Eckhardt, who acknowledged the interest of continued prosecution of this case by others; Eckhardt did not feel that a successful prosecution could be obtained.

Tillie's Flotill became the California food company to choose when the United States needed her. Her reputation for keeping her word to other businesses became legend. A deal was a deal with Tillie and Flotill Products.

Tillie sent Ralph Garcia and a small crew to find the *Miss Tillie* and clear her of anything salvageable, but there wasn't much left of her—she was a wrecked ship left to the tides. Meyer Lewis finally found the *Miss Tillie II* at an undisclosed location. Meyer moored the *Miss Tillie II* in Cuba. She was sold to help clear debts.

THE MEASURE OF A MAN

Meyer was as bright with his people skills as Tillie was with her business skills. Meyer undoubtedly bought more than a few rounds of the best booze and *apertivos* available for the Mexican police and guards, thus warding off disaster during the pineapple-pirate debacle, which easily could have included prison. Meyer was an expert at machismo etiquette who could create masculine comradery in spades. [clxxxi]

Tillie did find Meyer's inner negotiator-tough-guy persona very appealing. While they were in public, if things ever became sketchy, Tillie knew she could relax and let her man deal with any unpleasant situations. On one occasion, Tillie, Meyer, and his youngest son, Bill Lewis, went to see *High Noon*, the new Western with Gary Cooper, at the Fox Theater in Stockton. The three had just settled in when a preview of the Gene Kelly and Debbie Reynolds musical comedy *Singin' in the Rain* came on, which Tillie noticed was currently on the marquee down the street at the Empire Theater. She would rather see that, but the trio had to hurry. Leaving in a rush, Meyer collided with a young man on the street. The fellow made a disparaging remark, so Meyer yelled back at the man and brandished his fists, ready to knock the guy for a loop. Tillie was mortified and quietly said to him, "Let it go." Bill was stunned, uncertain if his father was bluffing, but his dad was assuredly standing his ground. Tillie tugged at her husband's arm, and they made it to the Empire in time to cool down over soft drinks and a hot tub of buttered popcorn.[clxxxii]

Once, Bill had been instructed by his mother to ask his father about his late child-support payments. His father was going to have to wait until his next payday to settle things, since Tillie did not make personal loans. This incident affected Bill's next visit via airplane: he was going to have to board using the less-expensive stand-by option to save money. Meyer assured his son that he'd handle everything and not to worry. When Bill boarded, he found himself to be the only passenger on the plane. Using different names, his father had called and booked as many seats as he could so that he'd be certain his son would obtain a seat at the bargain fare; the plane was empty save for his son.[clxxxiii] Tillie wasn't the only smart one: Meyer Lewis knew how to get things done, too.

The Lewises often threw extravagant affairs at home, but sometimes they took a dinner for a crowd on the town. The check was always enormous. After their wedding, Tillie always feigned that the tab was on her husband, much to the approval of the citizenry of Stockton. At least on the home front, Meyer Lewis appeared to have tamed the tigress. Meyer was generous to waitstaff, but he was not one to be taken advantage of. In private, Tillie would quickly calculate expenses to the penny; in public, this was Meyer's job. Tillie knew it wouldn't do to usurp her husband in front of an audience.

At one grand affair where they were hosting many guests, Meyer noted that the final bill had been presented to them with an egregious additional charge for liquor. This happened to be a rare evening in which none of the guests had ordered alcohol. The waiter explained that large groups were automatically charged a minimum for drinks. Meyer sized up the number of patrons who were enjoying the entire restaurant and requested a nonstop wine pouring to every table until the bogus fee had been taken advantage of in full. Meyer used the moment to announce a toast: "Another gift to the community from Mrs. Tillie Lewis."[clxxxiv]

Meyer was a natural marketing man. He easily set up social and business events with neighbors, newspapers, film stars, and heads of state. They all bought food, didn't they? They ought to be buying Flotill products, as far as Meyer Lewis was concerned. Meyer also handled Tillie's travel details and made certain that folks knew that they were in the presence of the world-famous Tillie of the Valley, the Tomato Queen, wherever they were in the world.

He loved to entertain clients in his meet'em and greet 'em style. He was a gregarious man who was smart and smooth in many ways. Fun, friendly Meyer could turn on a dime into a forceful, take-no-nonsense negotiator. He was the kind of guy who was willing to take a punch or deliver one as the situation warranted.

Meyer didn't care for the hoteliers of France or the rich food Tillie craved in Paris. He told Bill once that he preferred England: "If you hold out a handful of change to an English taxi driver, he will only take what he is owed. If you hold out a handful of money in France, you're lucky to get your hand back." Meyer was particularly rankled at the unending Parisian handouts for staff at the Ritz Hotel, which Tillie loved. Nevertheless, if his fair Tillie wanted Paris, Italy, Spain, or New Jersey, Meyer Lewis got her there in grand style worthy of a queen.

KOREAN C RATIONS CROWN THE TOMATO QUEEN OF THE WORLD

On June 25, 1950, early in the morning, a sleeping South Korea was attacked by the Communist forces of North Korea. On the following day, the United States began to send men to assist.[87] While President Truman and General Douglas MacArthur planned to keep the Communists contained, Tillie placed calls to her government connections with a plan to obtain as many government contracts to "Keep 'Em Eatin'" in Korea as she could.

Tillie had been the focus of governmental investigations for so long that local and federal officials knew her well. They were diligent in trying to find something negative about Tillie. The final governmental conclusion was that

---

87 The Korean conflict lasted from June 25, 1950, through July 27, 1953.

Tillie Lewis was the gal who paid her debts to her country and who created "Quality in Quantity" food products.

Tillie secured Flotill as the primary producer of C ration packing for the duration of the Korean conflict.[88] The majority of canned fruit and tomato products at the time came from her own plants, while sixty-six different suppliers from twenty-three states shipped tons of products to Stockton for thousands of local workers to assemble at the Flotill plants during wartime.

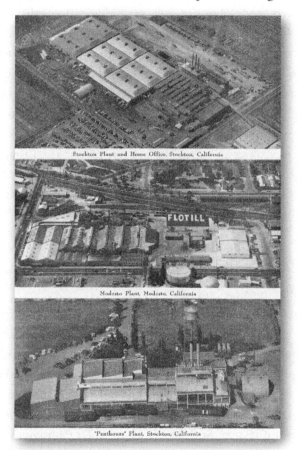

Stockton Plant and Home Office, Stockton, California

Modesto Plant, Modesto, California

"Penthouse" Plant, Stockton, California

Tillie's three can plants worked around the clock to
"Keep'Em Eatin'" in Korea and North America.

---

88 C rations, short for "combat ration kits," were a fully contained box of food and toiletry supplies for use in the field of combat.

Flotill was in full operation year-round now, packing sixty to seventy thousand C rations per day, in addition to canning for their regular customer needs. As a *Stockton Record* article[clxxxv] reported at the time ("B" refers to a bread unit),

> Each ration pack contains enough food to feed a soldier for a full day. Main meals are 8 small cans of food and a bar of soap. B-1 contains four crackers, cocoa powder, soluble coffee, dried milk and a tin of jam. B-2: four crackers, one cookie, two chocolate candy disks, coffee, dried milk and sugar. The accessory package includes a package of 20 cigarettes, two packages of coffee, milk and sugar, two books of moisture resistant matches, water purification tablets, a can opener, and three small packages of chewing gum, toilet paper and a polyethylene bag to protect contents from dampness in the field.
>
> A variety of seven menus have been prepared so that no soldier must have dreary repetitious meals every day. There are chicken and vegetables, beans with frankfurters, meat and spaghetti, ham and lima beans and canned hamburger along with canned fruit direct from our California orchards.

The *Stockton Record* article includes a photo of Flotill's lovely worker Ola Mae Williams displaying a ration pack.

Tillie often invited soldiers to her mansion, where she treated them as VIPs during wartime. GIs, both active and veterans—and conspicuously those from the Central Valley—began a letter-writing campaign to their governmental representatives to complement her on the chow. Soldiers' letters of compliments arrived in the Flotill mailbox with statements like, "Chicken and noodles almost like home" and "I was surprised...good roast beef."[clxxxvi]

New Hampshire senator Styles Bridges, then campaigning for his third term, brought a young amputee named Corporal Henry Needham for a taste testing of the ration products and to meet with Mrs. Lewis. The senator and Corporal Needham sampled the apricots straight from the can.[clxxxvii] Army officials ranked Flotill as one of the most efficient assembly lines in the United States.[clxxxviii]

SHE KNOWS HER TOMATOES

Time magazine interviewed Tillie in her suite at the Saint Regis Hotel in Manhattan. Tillie ordered two tomatoes delivered by room service. The waiter, impeccably dressed in a Saint Regis black tuxedo with gold-braid trim, handed the bill to Mrs. Lewis after setting down the sterling-silver tray. Mrs. Lewis exclaimed, "One dollar for two tomatoes!" She shook her head as she signed the check, then pointed a manicured finger at the server: "You tell Vincent Astor that these tomatoes cost him no more than five cents each. That's a one thousand percent profit." The waiter replied, "I guess you know your tomatoes." The man guessed right—Tillie Lewis did know her tomatoes.

As the article stated, "Tillie discussed the products that 'whiz by on conveyor belts she invented' and then she goes home every evening to prepare spaghetti with Flotill Pomodoros for her hubby, Meyer."[clxxxix]

If Tillie Lewis were Pinocchio, her pert little nose would be measured in yards, but the public enjoyed the idea that this titan of industry in peep-toe pumps could invent complex machinery; handle payroll; supervise two mansions, three gigantic factories, the twelve-hundred-acre farm on Medford Island in the Eastern Delta, and four-thousand-plus employees; and then go home and cook for her husband, just like any other housewife.[cxc]

Tillie began a country-wide newspaper article and advertisement "drip" that would last the rest of her life. Tillie's name was in some paper—at least one—in the United States every day. Drip, drip, drip—Tillie Lewis was advertised or glamorized every single day.

Tillie calculated every detail. The placements of her products were directed to be at the end caps of the grocery aisles. Her advertising displays were the biggest and most eye-catching to be found, with a pop-out Tillie Lewis happy to serve you. Also available were tear-off tickets to send directly to Tillie to get a coupon for free products.

Most of her ads requested the buyer to send a personal note to Mrs. Lewis about how much they enjoyed the product. Many began to write fan mail to her in response. Her secretary read every single letter, sending a company thank-you for the average letters and giving the more memorable ones to Tillie so that she could personally respond to the authors. These people remained on a campaign of updates and coupons for new products; Tillie let them know that they were her extra-special customers. Extra-special customers were usually extra-loyal customers.

One week in November of 1951, a headline in Zanesville, Ohio, read "Woman Heads Huge Canning Industry"; in Anderson, Indiana, in 1961, "Pomodoro Taste Made Woman Canner"; in Canandaigua, New York, in 1967, "Experts' Advice Rejected; Real Tomato Succeeds."[cxci]

Every week, somewhere in multiple Smalltownsvilles, USA, Tillie rehashed the very same rags-to-riches story on newspaper grocery pages, featuring store ads that coaxed readers to buy Flotill from the amazing Tillie, the Tomato Queen.

The Hotel Statler in Saint Louis presented a joint meeting of the women's and men's Advertising Clubs at one point in 1953 and printed full-page tickets to see Tillie Lewis and to "hear her story and explanation, her secrets behind her present advertising campaign: 'A WOMAN'S ADVENTURES IN A MAN'S WORLD.'" The ticket continued, "Men and Women Invited: BRING A FRIEND."[cxcii] The big news? For the first time, American men were coming to hear a woman give advice on business success.

Chapter 11

TASTI-DIET ROARS NATIONWIDE, THE MARX
BROTHERS, AND JIMMY DURANTE

FDA approval was taking forever but, Tasti-Diet was exactly what Tillie was praying for—delicious, different, and desired. Plus, Americans *had* actually gotten fat since the end of the war. The FDA's bureaucratic, red-tape heel dragging cumulated in adding about twenty pounds to the average American's figure. Misfortune was, once again, Tillie's fortune. Anticipating the positive outcome, Tillie had made a point of watching the portion sizes with her food and hadn't gained a pound. She now had the perfect product for self-promotion and girlish glory. The fictional Betty Crocker had been selling products for General Mills since 1921. Tillie decided she would be the perfect human face and figure of American fitness and femininity; she'd sell her Tasti-Diet to the world as a product that she'd created all by herself.

Because a Doctor put Tillie Lewis on a Diet—

YOU NOW GET LOW-CALORIE FOO
AS DELICIOUS AS HIGH-CALORIE FOOD

ally a New, Year-Round Way to
Normal, Healthful, Delicious Meals!

can lose weight, and *stay* slender, while enjoying regu-
als, including desserts, right along with the family!
because a Doctor put a remarkable woman on a diet!
woman was Tillie Lewis. Once unknown, now named
ca's First Woman in Foods. Written about in maga-
hundreds of newspapers. All because she did not like
less, limited diet—*and decided to do something about it!*
result is a *new kind* of low-calorie foods, created by
Lewis! Actually 36 Tasti-Diet Foods—including sweet
ts, salad dressings, jellies, chocolatey topping! *All de-*
. Tasti-Diet Fruits, for example, come to you in rich,
tasting syrup, made *without* added sugar! So differ-
from "watery" diet fruits! Yet they contain, on an
e, *less than half* the calories of regular canned fruits!
, adults who need to *control* weight, as well as those
ng, can eat complete, delicious meals the year round...
e the rest of the family!
n today to normalize weight *enjoyably*, the wonderful
6 Varieties" Tasti-Diet way!

TILLIE LEWIS
TASTI ♥ DIET
36 VARIETIES

'S TASTY—IT'S TASTI-DIET—DON'T ACCEPT SUBSTITUTES

TILLIE LEWIS, AMERICA'S FIRST WOMAN IN FOODS, explains the exclusive and pate
ces that makes Tasti-Diet Fruits sweet, delicious, firm —entirely unlike any
fruits. The famous "36 Varieties" also includes jellies, salad dressings, swee
SPECIAL FREE OFFER: For your Tillie Lewis Diet Plan Booklet—full of helpful m
ideas—write Tillie Lewis, Dept. L-1, Stockton, California.

Tillie's Tasti-Diet ad telling the world that because a doctor had put her on a diet, she'd personally created a diet so delicious that the only thing she gave up was pounds.

Beyond being frustrating, the diabetic diet patent-approval process proved to be stickier than the sugarless product line. From 1948 to1950, the only approvals the products obtained were for "Health Foods Stores Only." This was not good enough for Tillie. She wanted the first true major-grocery-store full line of diet products available nationwide. Her regular attorneys thought that health-food stores might be good enough for the diet line. Tillie told them, "I don't hire attorneys to tell me NO; I hire attorneys to tell me HOW!"

This sweet discovery of hers wasn't going to be produced in small quantities and hidden in obscurity in some little health-food store. She called in a new attorney, Arthur D. Herrick, to obtain approval by the Council on Foods and Nutrition of the American Medical Association (AMA). On January 2, 1951, the patent was approved.

Feverishly busy in her Manteca attic mini-lab, Elsie Weast was developing gelatins and puddings. Vanilla, butterscotch, and chocolate pudding were such delectable hits that they went straight into the grocery stores almost automatically; people from Canada to Florida were begging for more.

Tillie did enjoy the Tasti-Diet products herself and boasted about the chocolate pudding that was divinely delicious, especially in a pie shell. Flotill included a Tasti-Diet chocolate pudding pie recipe in many of its advertisements—never mind the calories in the pie crust.

Tillie requested Elsie to consider creating a written diet that would use as many of Flotill's products as possible. Elsie did far better than that—she calculated every calorie in each product and ingredient, then delivered the first twenty-one-day, twelve-hundred-calorie, AMA-approved diet in the world to Tillie Lewis.

Tillie's brand-new, state-of-the-art experimental food laboratory for
Tasti-Diet was also used to concoct whatever the next "What's next?"
might be. Elsie Weast was still chief designer, creating new Tasti-Diet
products at her Manteca home's minilab in the family's attic.

The Weast home could no longer contain the enormity of Tasti-Diet.
Flotill built a new laboratory and a plant in Stockton just for Tasti-Diet. Tillie
Lewis was selling the new product line and diet to doctors and hospitals across
the country. Her Tasti-Diet crew wore special Tasti-Diet uniforms. Tasti-Diet
was big! Then came Elsie Weast's Tasti-Diet colas. Tillie's campaigns included
free copies of the twenty-one-day diet and free bottles of soda.

As previously stated, Doc and Elsie Weast had sold Tillie the diet lock,
stock, and barrel, so fudging on the "sweet taste of success" story was Tillie's legal right.[89] Tillie exaggerated a sweet-tooth and "obesity" problem that she never
actually had; the doctor's warnings about her need to lose weight in full-page
ads and brochures in newspapers across the country were fabricated as well. The
Tillie tale was just a terrific marketing tool that she'd added to her repertoire of

---

89   The Weast's earned their agreed-upon royalties for the products that were sold, and Doc still
owned the patents.

fiction and made into fact by repetition. Doc Weast said later, "Mrs. Lewis told that story of her doctor, her weight gains, and her creating Tasti-Diet out of thin air so often, there's no doubt that she believed it herself."[xciii] He laughed and added, "Tillie spent more time and money perfecting her picture on the label than it took to create the products. There were at least three different caricature versions of herself. I recall the first one was just far too 'va-va-voom' for her public image. Meyer Lewis reminded her that she was selling diet products as a homemaker, not as a red-headed Marilyn Monroe."

Meyer was right.

Tillie knew she had to sell the entire package: it was imperative to have a wholesome, healthy image of Tasti-Diet equaling an attractive, svelte, and happy homemaker, along with solid science for the, usually male, doubting Thomases around the country. Tillie insisted that her marketing of Tasti-Diet be placed next to scientific articles about early death from diabetes and heart disease whenever possible.

Tasti-Diet booklet. Tillie sent the headline-shocking divorcée-to-be Lillian Korazen everything she needed to battle her husband (and her weight) while maintaining her dignity during her infamous "She's Too Fat for Me" divorce case.

The 1955 "She's Too Fat for Me" divorce case in Chicago was music to Tillie's ears when she heard about it. When Judge Cornelius Harrington ordered a Mrs. Lillian Korazen to lose forty pounds or else he'd proceed to grant her husband, Michael Korazen Sr., a divorce, "because Mrs. Korazen was just too fat," Tillie Lewis contacted the woman. Mrs. Korazen quickly lost the required forty pounds; gained new confidence, a great hairstyle, and smaller clothes; and was now having second thoughts about taking her husband back at all. Said Mrs. Korazen at the time, "This woman, Tillie Lewis, told me just what I could eat and what I couldn't. I haven't had one of my old headaches since I started on the diet. I hate to sound like one of those before-and-after advertisements, but I'm forty-three and I feel like I'm twenty-three…Now that I've got the hang of it, I'm not going to stop dieting until I'm down to 120 pounds. I wonder what my husband would say about that."[cxciv]

Tillie ran ads in *Stars and Stripes* newspaper's Europe, Mediterranean, and North Africa editions that appeared, not as an advertisement, but like an informative bit of news:

> Millions of women put on an extra pound with every extra bonbon they eat…but Tillie Lewis did more than moan about it. She created a new line of low-calorie foods because her sweet tooth got the better of her waist-line…Mrs. Lewis started working on this idea 10 years ago…now she's down from 147 bulgy pounds to 121…Tillie developed Tasti-Diet for medical reasons and just for the sake of appearances… [now you can] find low-calorie fruits, jellies, custards and puddings."[cxcv]

On the Tasti-Diet publicity tours, Meyer Lewis, always the entertainer, often the prankster, had identical suits made for him just for touring. They were constructed in big, bigger, and biggest sizes. Every other day he'd wear the larger size so he could demonstrate how he was losing weight right before the public's eye, bragging he was eating nothing but Tasti-Diet and watching the pounds drop off.[cxcvi]

On September 18, 1951, the *Stockton Record* ran the headline, "BOYS ONLY: No Girls Allowed in New Stockton Trade Club Launch." The story stated that multimillionaire captain of industry Tillie Lewis had not been invited to a party honoring Stockton's canneries, which the paper lauded as among "Stockton's greatest institutions for prosperity." Albert Heiser and Claude Young were allowed to represent Flotill. The audience enjoyed vaudeville performers who entertained the all-male sellout crowd of six hundred professional men.[cxcvii]

WOMAN OF THE YEAR, TILLIE LEWIS DAY, TASTI-DIET TOUR

Voted by the Associated Press as one of 1952's "Women of the Year," Tillie told one audience, "First look around for a need. Research how to fulfill that need with diligence: Know as much as you can about it. Know what you want and where you are going. Meet failure by getting up and brushing yourself off to try again after evaluating what went wrong. Give more than you get. Admit your mistakes. Appreciate your employees."

Later, the city of Stockton proclaimed March 3, 1952, to be Tillie Lewis Day for her contributions to the agricultural and economic development of San Joaquin County. She was escorted by Governor Goodwin J. Knight to the testimonial dinner that was given in her honor. Governor Knight crowned her the "Tomato Queen of the World."[cxcviii]

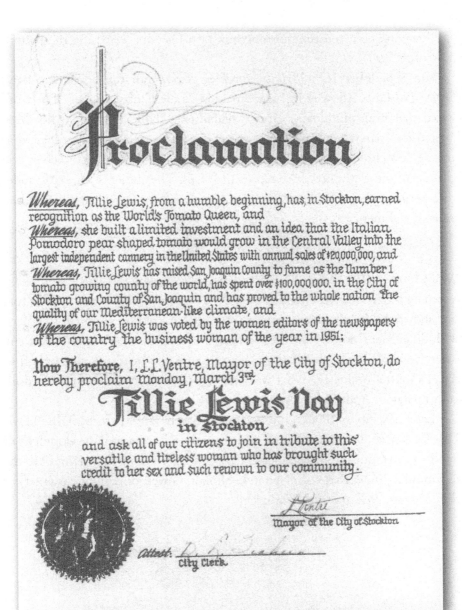

Proclamation

Whereas, Tillie Lewis, from a humble beginning, has, in Stockton, earned recognition as the World's Tomato Queen, and

Whereas, she built a limited investment and an idea that the Italian Pomodoro pear shaped tomato would grow in the Central Valley into the largest independent cannery in the United States with annual sales of $20,000,000, and

Whereas, Tillie Lewis has raised San Joaquin County to fame as the Number 1 tomato growing county of the world, has spent over $100,000,000. in the City of Stockton and County of San Joaquin and has proved to the whole nation The quality of our Mediterranean-like climate, and

Whereas, Tillie Lewis was voted by the women editors of the newspapers of the country the business woman of the year in 1951;

Now Therefore, I, L.L. Ventre, Mayor of the City of Stockton, do hereby proclaim Monday, March 3rd,

Tillie Lewis Day
in Stockton · ·

and ask all of our citizens to join in tribute to this versatile and tireless woman who has brought such credit to her sex and such renown to our community.

Mayor of the City of Stockton

Attest: City Clerk.

On March 3, 1951, the city of Stockton, joined by dignitaries from throughout California, honored the Tomato Queen in style by declaring March 3 "Tillie Lewis Day."

Finally, Tillie cleared her busy schedule to begin the Tasti-Diet tour in earnest. Tillie sold Tasti-Diet around the world to celebrities and politicians. She became the most famous woman in food and a celebrity in her own right. Public speaking—on both local and national forums—became Tillie's full-time second job. Meyer Lewis was her promoter and publicist. As he had done for his college band, Meyer set up entire Tillie tours from transportation to floral arrangements; from accommodations to accolades, Meyer booked everything. On this level, Tillie and Meyer Lewis were a team.

While chatting about using the finest, freshest ingredients from the Flotill product line and the home garden, Tillie appeared on numerous television shows, including NBC's *Mrs. USA*, on September 22, 1952. In a program about home canning, Tillie discussed how she'd gotten out of the kitchen and had become a canning industrialist.[cxcix]

She reminded women to take themselves seriously with any endeavor in life and to take chances. Stick your pretty neck out there, she urged them. "There is one major difference between men and women in business," she said. "When a man makes a mistake, it's accepted. When a woman makes a mistake, it's expected." Tillie spoke on the radio show *Voice of America* numerous times about women in business; sticking to one's ideals to attain any dream, health, and diet; and global hunger and the population explosion.[90]

While at NBC Studios, Tillie ran into the famed comic Milton Berle. Tillie offered "Uncle Miltie"[91] free room and board at her Palm Springs estate and her home in Stockton. Berle mentioned that he was going to Sacramento. Tillie asked if he'd be kind enough to quickly judge a Stockton Flotill chili contest that would be prepared with Flotill tomato products. He agreed. Uncle Miltie clowned around wearing a bright-red fireman's hat and joined in the fun, hamming it up while Tillie beamed along with the ecstatic chili-contest winner.[cc]

---

90 *Voice of America* (VOA) started broadcasting in 1942 and continues to do so today. Starting in 1947, VOA began broadcasting to Russia. Tillie's radio contributions were translated into Russian.

91 Milton Berle (a.k.a. Uncle Miltie) was the most popular man on television at this time.

THE VANDERBILT HOTEL ADDS TASTI-DIET TO THE MENU
The Hotel Vanderbilt's head chef had heard several complaints about Christmas calories adding to the waistlines of his exclusive patrons. After he'd tested the Tasti-Diet on the menu with regular hotel guests, the diet line had proven to be a success. Starting December 17, Vanderbilt guests could select items prepared with Flotill's low-calorie apricots, peaches, plums, figs, gelatins, jellies, puddings, and salad dressings. Vanderbilt general manager Thomas Kelly stated, "Unlike most dietetic foods which are drained of taste, color and shape, these retain color and shape…We feel that the hotel owes it to its patrons to cater to their needs. Dieting, in many cases is necessary. We're adding these items for those folks who watch their weight and for their gourmet quality."[cci] The Vanderbilt menu made Tasti-Diet options a permanent part of the menu starting on February 1, 1953. Other high-end establishments soon followed suit.

The Tasti-Diet lines in Stockton became year-round, instead of seasonal, positions for workers, and off-season employment tripled.[ccii] Tillie created cuter, more impressive, uniforms for the Tasti-Diet workers. It was prestigious to be on the Tasti-Diet team. As long as Tillie was making adorable new Tasti-Diet/Flotill wear for the ladies, Tillie gave every male office staffer, manager, and supervisor the gift of a peachy-tomato-colored, hand-painted silk necktie. Each tie featured a full-color pomodoro tomato and the wearer's name in gaily lettered script. Harry Rosen later recalled of the ties,

> Boy oh boy, those ties were gawd awful. We all kept them on the back of our chairs, or on a nearby hook, to grab and put on if Mrs. Lewis called us in or came strolling by. Mrs. Lewis expected us to wear a shirt and tie in her presence, no matter the temperature, and no one was about to tell Mrs. Lewis these particular horrible ties were, well, horrible. As a lark, I've kept the darn thing. I suspect all the other guys conveniently "lost" theirs.[cciii]

In March, Tillie was featured on the cover of *Food Packer* magazine as one of the "Men of the Month." In homage to her male peers, she wore a black silk man-tailored shirt-dress with an oversize white collar and a "lady cat who ate the canary" grin.

When she returned from the *Food Packer* magazine interview, she breezed past Arthur and Al, who were engaged in a huddle with the cost-analysis group, deep in a debate about repricing fruit cocktail and other products. Tillie said, "Hunt's just put their fruit cocktail on the market shelves for twenty-three cents per can. For goodness sake, price our in-store brand at twenty-one cents and Penthouse superior quality at twenty-four cents, since it is clearly superior. Just watch the market, guys. The market tells you everything." As Al Heiser stated later, "As usual, she was absolutely right."

Clair "Doc" Weast and Tillie Lewis launch more new Tasti-Diet products as the first "available at your grocery store" marketed diet approved by the American Medical Association for maintaining better health and fitness in addition to appearance.

TASTI-DIET LAUNCHED ACROSS THE COUNTRY

On June 24, 1953, memorandums hit the desks of advertisers all over the country with seven-days-per-week newspaper ads, feature stories in business columns, and one-quarter to full-page ads in women's and food sections. Flotill distributed full-color Tasti-Diet grocery store window displays with Tillie's smiling face and four-page color brochures to all stores that carried the Tasti-Diet brand.[cciv]

Meanwhile, Doc Weast had continued to research and write for science journals about specialty foods for healthy diets. He noted a few studies that indicated that diabetes was most aggressive among black communities. Doc cautiously reminded Mrs. Lewis that the diet idea had originated on that train ride he'd enjoyed with the diabetic man, so why not go to where the most diabetics seemed to be, in predominately black communities?

It didn't take any more arm twisting than that. Doc later said, "I never felt I could actually converse with Mrs. Lewis. I presented an idea that she would mull over for rejection or acceptance. If she accepted an idea, the news came to us all 'as her exciting new concept' in memo form and as 'The Property of Tillie Lewis.'"

Tillie hopped on a plane bound for Homer G. Phillip Hospital in Saint Louis with cases of Tasti-Diet to donate to the hospital. Tillie posed with diabetic children of every nationality as well as two black dieticians at the hospital, Mildred Brooks and Bertha Nash.[ccv]

Children being treated for diabetes at Homer G. Philip Hospital in
Saint Louis enjoy a nutritious, and tasty, snack from Tillie Lewis. Photo
courtesy of the San Joaquin County History Society and Museum.

Tillie called in favors to pose with the stars from the stage and screen as well as from the sports world. After providing gifts of Tasti-Diet to the hospital in Saint Louis, Tillie popped into Busch Stadium's dugout to treat the Saint Louis Cardinals to a taste of Tasti-Diet chocolate pudding. Cardinals manager Eddie Stanky and first baseman Steve Bilko took a swing at the new low-calorie treat and deemed that Tillie Lewis had hit a home run with her new diet delight.[92]

Even the Saint Louis Cardinals baseball dugout enjoyed a healthy chocolate pudding. Eddie Stanky (former Brooklyn Dodger) and first baseman Steve Bilko thought Tillie had hit a home run with Tasti-Diet. Photo courtesy of the San Joaquin County Historical Society and Museum.

92 Stanky was a hero in both baseball and society at large. He was the first Brooklyn Dodger to summon the courage to defend his teammate Jackie Robinson. Stanky shouted back at white hecklers who were insulting Robinson, thus changing the color of baseball in America.

A WEEK IN THE LIFE OF THE TOMATO QUEEN'S SCHEDULE
The following is a fairly typical week in the life of Tillie, traveling in Saint Louis during the workweek of June 22 through 26, 1953.

Monday
11:30 a.m.: Pictures with Missouri governor Phil M. Donnelly; press and radio interviews. The next weeks were just as busy, filled with photo ops across the country.

11:50 a.m.: Interview and pictures—*Capitol News* Hotel's Governor Lobby.
12:30 p.m.: Appearance at radio station KWOS.

Tuesday
10:45 a.m.: Hotel newspaper interview with the *Globe Democrat*.
Noon: Radio interview.
1:15 p.m.: Talk before joint advertising clubs, Staler Hotel. Theme: "Woman Invades a Man's World."
4:15 p.m.: WTMV in East Saint Louis: radio interview.
4:25 p.m.: KMOX, "Names in the News" interview.
9:30 p.m.: KWK radio interview.

Wednesday
11:15 a.m.: Saint Louis mayor Raymond Tucker's office for greetings and pictures.
1:30 p.m.: *Playhouse Party* TV show (live audience).
4:00 p.m.: Visit to Homer G. Philips Hospital (black city hospital) for photos with staff and dieticians.
8:00 p.m.: Visit to Saint Louis Cardinals dugout; presentation of Tasti-Diet foods to Eddie Stanky and Steve Bilko.

Thursday
12:30 p.m.: KXOK interview, Martha Lane Shoe.
1:30 p.m.: KSD-TV for interview.

3:30 p.m.: Visit to Municipal Opera Theatre to present the diet to overweight male stars with feminine leads' assistance.

6:00–8:00 p.m.: Cocktail party, Tiara Lounge, Park Plaza Hotel.

Friday

Noon: Talk before the Sales Managers Club, Hotel Staler. Theme: "Selling the Diet Line to Lengthen the Life Line."[ccvi]

In New York, heavyweight champ Rocky Marciano was cornered by tempting Tasti-Diet products. The champ looked up to a grinning Tillie Lewis. She appeared to be explaining the diet system to the handsome boxer.[ccvii] Jimmy Durante stood still as "Doctor" Tillie placed a tape measure around the comic's 24" waistline for his prescription of Tasti-Diet in Hollywood.

IT'S A KNOCKOUT . . . Heavyweight champion Rocky Marciano puts his stamp of approval on the new 14-day diet which is being explained to him by Tillie Lewis, author of the plan to be presented in the N. Y. Journal-American beginning tomorrow. The Tillie Lewis system provides a low calorie diet aided by her personally-developed Tasti-Diet foods which she is demonstrating to the boxer.

Heavyweight boxing champ Rocky Marciano will go a few more rounds while enjoying Tillie Lewis's Tasti-Diet. Photo courtesy of the San Joaquin County Historical Society and Museum.

Back in Hollywood, Jimmy Durante didn't need to lose an inch around his
waist, but Tasti-Diet is low in sugar and salt—*that* was good news for Durante.
Photo courtesy of the San Joaquin County Historical Society and Museum.

Tillie developed a full-page health tip/infomercial ad campaign that ran
in Sunday papers for four consecutive weeks in all major cities. The ads were a
format of the popular "tune in again next week" serial cliffhangers.

In the *Chicago American*, ads ran titled "Calorie Counting No More with
Tasti-Diet," "Double Your Helpings While You Reduce," "Tillie Slims You
Down without Hunger," and "Reducing Fits You into Fall Fashions." Each
installment by Tillie Lewis ended with a personal invitation to write in to
receive your *free* coupon to try Tasti-Diet.

GROUCHO MARX

Tasti-Diet raised even Tillie's self-confidence, so much so that she contacted Groucho Marx and suggested that she appear on his radio and television show, *You Bet Your Life.*

Tillie showed up at NBC studios in Hollywood all set to earn her $340 for the day's taping and loads of publicity for Tasti-Diet. The show was taped on December 11, 1953, for airing on January 6 and 7; Tillie would start 1954 off on national television. She was teamed with a "nobody" who barely spoke English to keep the focus on her. Groucho often paired a "somebody" with a "nobody," where he would showcase the former while ignoring the latter (except as fodder for jokes). Tillie, who was personal friends of the Marx Brothers, had rehearsed witty comebacks as the "hot little tomato" whom Groucho intended for his signature naughty eyebrow-arching and for his off-the-cuff suggestive remarks for good studio-censor-sparring fun.

Groucho Marx and Tillie Lewis on the comedian's popular *You Bet Your Life* television show. Photo courtesy of the San Joaquin County Historical Society and Museum.

Unfortunately for Tillie, her "nobody" was an up-and-coming minor comic from Mexico. Tillie beamed as her old friend Groucho introduced her as the Tomato Queen, with an aside that "[I'll] get right back to squeezing the info out of this little tomato after [I] introduce her slightly sweaty fellow contestant, Mr. Gonzales." Then the sweating began for Tillie. When Groucho asked the man's name, the "nobody" said in very broken English, "Gonzales-Gonzales," followed by a flawlessly rehearsed and hysterical shtick that Pedro Gonzales-Gonzales had perfected in small comedy clubs. Groucho quickly forgot all about the Tomato Queen and bantered well into overtime with the new Mexican comedy star who was being born that very moment, right there on Groucho Marx's show. Tillie was both embarrassed and furious.

Helene Heiser later said, "Tillie stood there with egg on her face—*fried egg*—and it showed. The program aired twice in Stockton for all to see before Tillie's television humiliation was pulled." Tillie received a photo taken with Groucho and a check for $340.

Groucho Marx sent the incensed Mrs. Lewis home and retained Gonzales-Gonzales for another day. Groucho retaped the show with Gonzales-Gonzales as the "somebody" and a Swedish beauty queen as the "nobody" who knew her job was to just hush up and smile prettily.[93]

CAN'T GET ENOUGH

On March 5, according to the Long Island, New York, newspaper headline, "100 Women to Preview Tillie Lewis Diet Fare." The article went on to state, "We ladies of the press shall sample the new diet line and hear secrets of losing weight while still enjoying sweets from the nation's number one lady in food, Tillie Lewis."

Tasti-Diet was such a hit that other companies soon joined the bandwagon, some using the artificial sweetener cyclamate. The Weasts agreed that

---

93 The Gonzales-Gonzales *You Bet Your Life* moment is still one of Groucho's funniest shows. Pedro Gonzales-Gonzales went on to play minor roles in several big American films. The author found that the dates of the Gonzales-Gonzales segment were not a match, but the sources swear their veracity. In any event, Tillie certainly appeared on (and was humiliated during) Groucho's show.

cyclamate tasted even better than their pectin mixture. Tasti-Diet, too, went with cyclamate, and the company's sales skyrocketed when they added diet sodas.

An ad on August 31 stated, "Diet-drinks and cola take a bow in bottles from canner Tillie Lewis's Tasti-Diet. Your first bottle is FREE. Eight flavors of sugar-free, five to ten calories per sixteen-ounce bottle of cola, ginger ale, root beer, lemon-lime, orange, black cherry, black raspberry, and cherry. Mail the bottle crown and your newspaper ad back to your store and receive the fifteen cent cost and three cents postage back, 'on the house,' from Tillie Lewis."

The *New York Post* wrote on September 16, "The nation's soft drink preferences vary in nationality 'ethnic' groups. According to extensive surveys, Italians buy ginger ale and lemon-lime to mix with native wines. Jewish neighborhoods swing toward black cherry and black raspberry while Negroes purchase orange and root beer in a three to one preference over other flavors of the new Tillie Lewis Tasti-Diet beverage line."

DOCTORS PRESCRIBE TASTI-DIET

Newspapers across the nation were bombarded by Tillie's announcement that Tasti-Diet's twenty-one-day diet had won the AMA seal of approval for nutritional health for those in need or desire of a low-calorie, low-sugar diet. Tillie made the official announcement in an address at a canners convention in Chicago.[ccviii] Even today, doctors find the subject of obesity difficult to discuss with patients who are reluctant to address the issue, especially among female patients.

In 1955, Tillie didn't just tell the nation's doctors and hospitals that Tasti-Diet was terrific; she let them taste it. Tillie made the issue of obesity, diabetes, hypertension, and other food-restricted diets easier to swallow in a colossal campaign that targeted doctors and hospitals across the country. She included a case sample of all the products for doctors' and hospital administrators' families to enjoy in addition to unlimited free copies of the menu plan and what were called "Diet Recording Diaries."

The cover of the advertisement, masked as a medical brochure, featured thirteen covers of the major-medical journals of the day as background while the text proclaimed boldly,

40% of your customers are overweight…are you getting your profit from this market? Doctors know the value of the outstanding Tasti-Diet foods thru powerful ads such as these…Every physician has seen the psychological impact on the patient who has been told that he must go on a restricted diet. Whether the diet be carbohydrate limited and exact for diabetes, low-caloric for obesity, or low-sodium for hypertension or other afflictions…the patient immediately visualizes the hardship and inconvenience such a diet will cause. He wonders whether his willpower will prove adequate to bear the deprivation. If the diet is imposed on him for the remainder of his life, as it must be in many instances, he feels he has been given a life sentence.

Today, restricted diets need no longer be a hardship, neither to the patient's psyche nor his palate. Tasti-Diet Foods, Inc. now offers a wide range of Counsel-Accepted, specially prepared tasty foods to fit virtually any diet the physician may prescribe, and which allow the patient the gratifications of "good eating."

The three pages following present a list of these fine foods and their applicability. The three following pages offer doctors, dieters and diabetics "escape from dietary control." Tillie Lewis and Tasti-Diet understands and provides for "the craving for something sweet" through a variety of products from jellies and favorite fruits to asparagus and corn cooked without sugar or salt. Diets will no longer be dull or drab but packed with flavor and freshness.

Doctors are assured that patients will thank their doctors for steering them into health and the first accepted American Medical Association's Council on Foods and Nutrition complete food and diet plan, The Tasti-Diet all available at their local markets.[ccix]

From coast to coast, including in Canada, Tillie offered:

FREE your first can…Sugar-Free Low Calorie Fruits.
Why do we make this astonishing free offer? It's the only
low-calorie fruit ever to win California's Gold Medal…
Yes, Tillie Lewis has no fattening sugar added…Tillie Lewis fruits are
sweetened with Sucaryl—[a] magical discovery that's sweet as sugar
but non-fattening! JUST MAIL COUPON BELOW TODAY.

Customers filled out the coupon, cut it out, and sent it to Stockton; Tillie's
Tasti-Diet staff then had the information on new clients and their favorite
grocery markets.[ccx] They quickly mailed fancy coupons with Tillie's smiling
face to the potential new fans for life.

Throwing luncheon and dinner parties at all the swankiest hotels across
the country introduced Tasti-Diet to the rich, famous, and powerful from
sports figures, politicians, and stars of stage and screen; everybody and their
families wanted to try Tasti-Diet. Tillie's ads promised customers that she'd
ship Tasti-Diet to anyone's favorite grocery store if a customer sent her a letter
and asked her to get them Tasti-Diet in Des Moines or in Tampa Bay.

The famous, like Alabama governor Gordon Pearsons, just sent Tillie a
personal order:

Flotill Products, Box 814, Stockton, California
Gentlemen:
Please send me the following of your Tasti-Diet products:
2 cans (or jars) each…
Unpeeled Apricot halves
Light cherries
Dark cherries
Kadota figs
Peaches
Fruit cocktail
Bartlett pear halves
Also:
2 each…powdered puddings:

Chocolate, Vanilla, French custard
Also:
2 each…grape jelly and apple jelly
Also: 2 each, French type dressing, Chef's dressing, One-calorie dressing, Roquefort-Blue cheese dressing.

Very truly yours,
Gordon Pearsons
Governor of Alabama[ccxi]

Like most of the rich and famous, Minnesota senator Hubert Humphrey just phoned his regular order in directly to Tillie, who shipped his order directly to his residence.

EMBEZZLER RONALD E. MYERS

Tillie prided herself on many things, most of all her ability to choose good, honorable people to trust with her baby, Flotill. She also believed that good people had weak moments and deserved a second chance. That's what she thought about Ronald Myers. Myers, who had been with Flotill nearly since the beginning, had been suspected of borrowing from Flotill accounts in the past. Tillie gently reprimanded Myers, who admitted that he'd been in a financial jam and had indeed foolishly taken funds without asking. He'd meant to repay the accounts.[ccxii]

Tillie forgave him and sent him back to his position as director of the growers' department, but she had an accountant keep an eye on his department's account books.

Arthur Heiser later said, "Tillie was deeply crushed when I told her Ronald Myers had upped the crooked ante by embezzling at least forty thousand dollars in cash and was forging checks to himself. It was one of the only times I'd seen Chips cry." Arthur contacted the police, since Tillie was too distraught to have one of her own arrested. According to the *Stockton Record*, Ronald Myers had "startled authorities by admitting he was convicted of embezzlement in Oklahoma in 1928 and served a two and one-half year prison term. The 57-year-old Myers, who lived in the upscale Tuxedo Street area of Stockton and owned several properties from his 17-year full-time employment at Flotill had stolen at least $70,000. He pled guilty to seven counts of grand theft and [was] sentenced to San Quentin Prison."[ccxiii]

Tillie dried her tears with the satisfaction that she had just the one bad apple in Ronald Myers. She took time off the Tasti-Diet tour to spend the holidays in California with her faithful Flotill family. She signed every Christmas holiday letter herself, wishing each individual employee joy and prosperity. Here is one example, from December 20, 1955:

Dear Ralph,
A Very Merry Christmas and a Happy New Year to you and your loved ones! It is with a great deal of joy that I am able to tell you that Flotill—thanks in no small part to your own efforts—has had a good year...Please accept my personal thanks for the share of Flotill's burden which you have so capably borne...with this kind of teamwork and cooperation we can continue to grow...to the benefit of all.
Sincerely,
Tillie Lewis

Tillie's original signature in blue ink appears to have been wearily penned by the time she got to acknowledging Ralph. Nonetheless, giving her all to the people she felt gave their all was the least she could do. Tillie wanted no repeats of the treachery against her beloved Flotill that had been displayed by Ronald Myers.

To lighten Tillie's mood, Meyer Lewis recorded his own vocal version of the Walt Disney Davy Crocket anthem that was all the rage in 1956. He hoped his revised lyrics and enthusiastic baritone would be the perfect introduction to "Tillie, Tillie Lewis, Queen of Tomato Country."[ccxiv] But Tillie was not amused. The record was relegated to the bottom of Meyer Lewis's desk drawer.

In April of that year, Chico Marx and his band were guests of the Lewises, while the band performed at the United Jewish Welfare Fund to celebrate Israel's eighth anniversary. Tillie was chairwoman and mistress of ceremonies for the event. The principal speaker was Israeli naval hero and commander of the first Israeli warship Yaacov Adam, who was also a guest of Mr. and Mrs. Lewis.[ccxv]

On her TV show, *The Home Show,* the former film star Arlene Francis discussed the success of the city of Stockton and its most famous lady, Tillie Lewis; in 1956, Tillie discussed her rags-to-riches story and urged viewers to rush to their local stores to buy Tasti-Diet.[ccxvi] Bruce Craver of the Stockton chamber of commerce commended Tillie for promoting Stockton as a terrific spot for industry due to its location and superior access to transportation.

TASTI-DIET TOURS NEW YORK

Tillie and Meyer were chauffeured from a luxury liner via Rolls Royce to their suite at the Plaza overlooking Central Park. Their private, white-gloved butler had their theater tickets in hand and their clothes unpacked and freshly pressed. It was standard for her to set her shoes out for a nightly buffing and shine. The restaurants referred to themselves as specialty food purveyors.[ccxvii] Flotill would soon be adding "specialty food purveyors" to their own advertising.

The Associated Press women's editor, Dorothy Roe, said that "the bouncing red-haired Tillie, who introduced pear-shaped tomatoes to the canning business, has embarked on a new enterprise. She breezed into New York the other day, dressed in silver mink and pear-shaped diamonds, to talk about it. It's a diet aimed at cutting 420 million pounds from the United States population over the next few years. Already on sale…the new products include fruits and puddings…which taste sweet without sugar."

Tillie said, "I've been working on the formula for almost ten years.[94] You know how foods with saccharine have a bitter taste? I was determined to find a way to make these foods taste good. Finally—we hit upon the answer, a combination of saccharine and pectin…Now you can go on a diet and not even know it. We have every kind of fruit, pudding and salad dressing."

---

94 As noted earlier, although Doc and Elsie Weast created the formula and diet, Tillie had the legal right to claim the diet as her own.

In New York, Tillie staged a luncheon that added up to only 440 calories. The menu included:

Fruit cocktail
½ lb. broiled chopped steak
Two vegetables
Bread with grape jelly
Chocolate pudding

"Now, if you ate that kind of lunch, you wouldn't feel you were on a diet, would you?" mused Tillie.

Some local men began to notice just how much Tillie had contributed to the area over the years. Just after Thanksgiving, C. J. Pregno from Stockton sent a letter to the editor:

I overheard a man say, "Women are all alike." His inimical voice indicated prejudice…women bear no greater similarity than do men. Years ago Mrs. Tillie Lewis came here looking like a school girl to engage (of all things) in the canning business, an enterprise entirely dominated by men of experience. She seemed so young and out of place. To everyone's surprise her entry was most vigorous and practical. Her presence was everywhere from the sorting tables to the head office. Her success was and is so phenomenal that *Reader's Digest* magazine printed a complete story about it. That degree of achievement could easily give some men a case of megalomania, delusion of grandeur—briefly, [a] swelled head—but not Tillie, as she is often and always respectfully called. She is today, as in the past, a person of dignity and respectability, never too busy for a friendly smile or nod for her many friends…
—C. J. Pregno
402 West Walnut,
Stockton[ccxviii]

Chapter 12

JEWISH PRAISE, BETTER THAN HERSHEY'S, AND FOOTBALL

Still following Luigi Del Gaizo's goal of staying ahead of the competition with state-of-the-art technology, Tillie proudly added Stocktonian inventor Frank Bellato's gigantic tomato, apricot, and peach evaporator. Bellato's company was barely a year old, but his brainchild met Tillie's demand for the highest quality in her products. Bellato's evaporator would preserve the fruits' bright, natural colors and flavors faster, while Mrs. Lewis's use of Bellato's "Thermovac" helped add to the jobs and economy of the Central Valley.[ccxix] Another feather in her cap and a peachier peach.

As long as Tillie was adding innovations, she contracted another local firm, the architects Mayo de Wolf and Associates, to install four-foot square, heat-resistant skylights in the warehouse; these would replace electrical lights and structural columns outside the plant and would remove some lights from the interior to reduce forklift and other large-equipment-related accidents. Keeping local businesses employed and thinking about safety and savings for her people along with Flotill was the Tillie Lewis way of doing business.[ccxx]

JEWISH HIGH PRAISE
The public was used to Tillie's awards for business. A celebration for her kindness was something new. On one night, Mrs. Lewis was thanked for her

charity and for the success of the 1956 launch of the Stockton Jewish Welfare Fund campaign. Tillie had chaired the campaign the past two years. Michael Blankford, author of various Jewish-strife-themed novels and screenwriter of the Jimmy Stewart western *Broken Arrow*, presented Tillie with a scroll of leadership from the United Jewish Appeal. Stockton mayor Fred Bitterman declared that "The community owes Mrs. Lewis a debt beyond the material gifts…but what she has taught of charity and humanitarianism. She has vision, faith, courage, and determination others could well follow." Tillie said,

> This award should go to the Stockton Jewish community and non-Jewish friends [who had generously contributed to the campaign]. Israel has offered to relinquish the recent military gains and is asking only the right to live in peace under the good neighbor policy… There never was a time more important to heed the call of Jewry for the state of Israel and the United Jewish Appeal. I pledge to make this next year the most successful fund raiser Stockton has ever had. The monies collected [will] go to refugees, welfare agencies, hospitals and other charities for the Jewish Community Centers."[ccxxi]

In 1958, Tillie accepted an invitation to join other experts in the California peach industry at their annual growers' convention. Tillie, dressed in a navy-blue skirt suit and a small-brimmed white sailor hat, proved again that she could go peep-toe to wingtip-toe with the men at the debating table.[95] From marketing, financing, and processing, the gentlemen were impressed that the "tomato" who owned Flotill knew her peaches, too.

BETTER THAN HERSHEY'S

During the summer, Flotill set up a "Tasting Center Display" area at the California State Fair in Sacramento. Bill Lewis, Meyer's youngest son, was working the summer at Flotill as an assistant to Harry Rosen. Bill stayed with

---

95 The seventh-annual convention of the California Canning Association (established in 1922) was held in 1958, per Tim Melchiori of the association. "How's the Peach Business Doing?" photo from the San Joaquin County Historical Museum archives.

his father and Tillie at the mansion on Willow, but on weekends he'd see his girlfriend who lived in Berkeley.

On one weekend, the young lady took the bus to see Bill and to attend the State Fair in Sacramento, since Bill had wrecked his car the week before. As the young couple entered the fairgrounds, the food-tasting booths were awaiting them. They sampled the Tasti-Diet Chocolate Pudding, to which the girlfriend made a big fuss and wrote, as a gag, on the comment card in big letters, "BETTER THAN HERSHEY'S."

A few weeks later, Bill heard that Tillie was creating a new ad campaign around the claim by an unbiased fan that "Tasti-Diet chocolate pudding was better than Hershey's." Bill, horrified, confided to his father the little stunt he and his girlfriend had played at the fair. Bill Lewis later said, "Dad's eyes got very big, and he whispered, 'Don't ever tell Chips—she's going to have it framed.'"

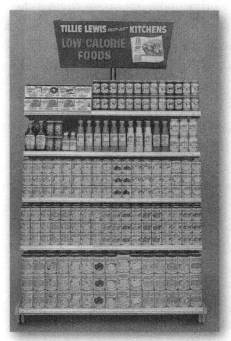

Tasti-Diet display at a grocery store, brimming with
tempting low-calorie and healthy choices.

SHE CERTAINLY CAN CAN-CAN

At the mercy of can prices, availability, and quality, Tillie transformed the former Pacific Can Company into her own can-manufacturing plant across the street from the original Flotill.

From Flotill's beginnings in 1934, even before the building was completed, Tillie had agreed to buy her cans from Pacific Can (later National Can) with a proviso to eventually buy the can company. The Pacific Can Company believed in her enough to back her dreams by financing the building of the original plant and loaning her funds along the way.

Cans are the most expensive portion of the canning process. When the cost of tinplate rises, it also increases the cost of the product. If can makers run out of the size a company needs, then the food company is in trouble. If the cans are dented, the product won't sell. If the can seals are damaged, the food inside could induce illness and even death.

Cans effect the product's quality and the profits for the company. It was time Tillie Lewis took control of the whole process. Besides, she intended to make extra cans to sell to her competitors at a markup.

Again, however, she was met with masculine resistance to the very idea of a woman manufacturing cans. She'd proven that a woman could cook up bunches of fruits and vegetables and fill *manmade* metal cans with food, but ordering and making the cylinders (made of steel, tin, and enamel) was definitely for *men* only.

It is true: can making is a surprisingly complex art that requires highly skilled and well-paid workers. The machines to manufacture a can are complex, sharp, fast, and downright dangerous to those who are not trained and experienced in the heating and precision slicing of metal. Through the can company, Mrs. Lewis would be adding more prime jobs to the San Joaquin Valley.

Within six years, Tillie was making some of the finest cans in the industry, with enough extra containers to sell—at a handsome profit—to other canners. She doubled the size of her can-manufacturing division, which now turned out nearly one million cans a day: approximately three hundred million cans per year.[ccxxii] It was the largest and most modern can-manufacturing fa-cility in California.[96]

At one convention, Tillie bragged about how quickly she could fill can orders. A challenge arose from a customer who was currently suffering an emergency need of a certain odd-size can. He'd pay an undisclosed sum for six million cans if they could be delivered within four days. Tillie took the deal knowing full well that she didn't have even an extra million cans to spare. The gentleman said he would pop in right then and there to inspect the cans to be certain that there would be enough to cover his needs. Tillie made a quick phone call to the warehouse. When Tillie and her doubting customer arrived, the warehouse was stacked nearly wall to wall with shiny cans ready to be filled. Tillie struck the deal.

Tillie's phone call had been to her faithful warehouseman, Ralph Garcia. Mrs. Lewis instructed Ralph and his crew to spread all the cans out as far as they could, leaving a nice, big, empty space in the center that she hoped nobody would notice. Tillie told Ralph that she didn't think she was fibbing, since she believed he could get all her can-makers working around the clock to meet the enormous order. Ralph assured her that they wouldn't let her down. Tillie went back to the convention dinner, while Ralph contacted the rest of the crew, who then worked night and day to meet the order, with cans to spare. Tillie, as usual, remembered her workers with a personal thank-you and an appropriate bonus for all on payday.

FLOTILL FOOTBALL
On October 18, Tillie held her tenth-annual College of the Pacific football party. This year she printed tomato-colored invitations that included head-shots that were cut and pasted in of the main Flotill staff as her personal football team. Tillie "the Toiler" Lewis was head coach.

---

96   This is the state-of-the-art Tillie Lewis Foods can plant that the author's late husband, Richard Williams, was impressed by and began working for in 1978; he suggested writing this biography as a result.

The inside of the invite provides a peek into the actual party goings on. All in cutout clip art, a cocktail glass holds the 4:30 p.m. time at the Lewis residence at 740 Willow Street address. Cocktail hour was extended to one and a half hours. Dinner was at 6:00 p.m., with a formal butler holding a lavish tray. A football receiver ran the 8:30 p.m. game time at Pacific Memorial Stadium with supper-time emblazoned on the cartoon football.

Harder libations were served formally after the game until guests were sliding down a lit lamppost, dead drunk.[ccxxiii] Each year Tillie rented two busses to safely transport the men (and any ladies who wished to watch the game) off to the stadium. The majority of the women stayed at the Lewis mansion with Tillie, who entertained them as if they were welcome guests and not employees.

Tillie joined her formal catering staff in personally serving drinks and hors d'oeuvres to her guests. Mildred Garcia and Rosie Munoz both stated that they felt like royalty being served by the Tomato Queen herself, who insisted on being called "Tillie" at these get-togethers.

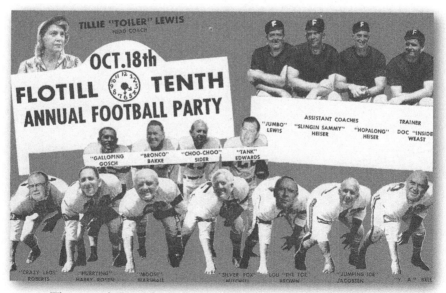

The annual Flotill football party invitation. Tillie and Meyer Lewis hosted many events and festivities throughout the year; this was the most fun and the most-coveted party invitation.

Tillie broke her business protocol to inquire about her lady guests' children and hobbies and engaged in general gal talk. Tillie led them on tours of her home and expansive pool and gardens. Most of the women in attendance were most impressed by the butler's pantry and the professional kitchen with its two huge standing rotisseries, both of which were larger than most refrigerators. One was dedicated to chicken and the other to beef roasts. Tillie bragged that the newspaper and movie mogul William Randolph Hearst's castle in San Simeon only held only one such rotisserie.

There was never a limit on food or drink at the Lewis home, so this football evening became a fairly wild one when the gregarious Meyer Lewis arrived with the rest of the men. His cheeks were always flushed with hot toddies, ready to tend bar and dance the night away.

Chapter 13

QUALITY IN QUANTITY, FAIRY GODMOTHER TILLIE, AND GOOD NIGHT, BEATRICE

Flotill had grown up and grown big by 1961. Tillie decided to go public and to exorcise the spirit of Florindo Del Gaizo, at least from her labels. Tasti-Diet had introduced the Tillie Lewis name to the world, and the world ate it up. She created a full-length promotional movie of herself and Flotill in which she was in full control. This time, no one would edit her out. It is a feature-film-worthy, top-notch product. Tillie produced movie-quality sound with a strong male narrator. It began with Tillie at her desk, holding her very first can of tomatoes manufactured in 1935. Her desk is laden with Tasti-Diet products that Tillie describes, in her nearly British accent, as delicious, "especially the chocolate."

The *Quality in Quantity* film[ccxxiv] focused on the journey of specific fruits and vegetables in Tillie's pristine, antiseptic, top-of-the line equipment, to your very own perfectly labeled can, and onto your dinner table. The film was beyond a vanity piece. Tillie was moving from privately held Flotill to Tillie Lewis Foods (TLF), which traded on the Pacific Coast and on the American Stock Exchange. Along with the film, Tillie had Meyer Lewis pose for the *San Francisco Chronicle*'s June 19 story about Flotill growing into Tillie Lewis Foods.

The *San Francisco Examiner* tried to sink Tillie's ship when the paper got wind of possible tax trouble "bogging down the Tomato Queen's all important first stock issue of 189,016 shares of Tillie Lewis Foods."

The IRS, according to the *Chronicle*, was indicating that it might take all Mrs. Lewis's profit, who was forced to do something she didn't do well—wait out the IRS and hope for a favorable tax ruling.[ccxxv] The IRS gave TLF the green light. Flotill was the past. TLF was the future.

FAIRY GODMOTHER TILLIE

Tillie Lewis, now beloved for tucking a bonus check into employees' pay envelopes for happy life events such as births, weddings, and academic graduations, sometimes went much further in her generosity.

A woman known as Rosa called Tillie at the Flotill office. Rosa, sobbing, told Tillie that she had worked for Flotill about ten years earlier. As many girls did, she'd left Flotill for marriage and a family. Rosa's husband had just passed away, and their baby was afflicted with polio. Rosa cried, "I have no food and no money. I can't take care of my baby." Tillie told her husband, "Meyer, I'm going to go grab some groceries and help this gal." With that, Tillie supplied groceries and cooked and helped with the baby while Rosa recovered from her grief. Meyer suggested that Tillie should hire a cook and a nurse to do the work. Tillie replied, "Hiring kindness is not the same as doing it yourself."[ccxxvi]

Tillie Lewis was credited with helping the child recover from polio. As of 2016, there is still no cure for polio, so perhaps the baby had a less permanent affliction than this. Once she'd grown up, it is likely that Mrs. Lewis would have made a place for such a woman at Flotill/TLF to work.

Bobbie Blair Xenos, a young lady who was recently engaged to be married, worked in the Flotill/TLF Stockton payroll office. Tillie was in a wedding kind of mood when she caught wind of Bobbie's upcoming nuptials. She asked a confused Bobbie to lunch. Bobbie said, "Then off we went to Stockton's bridal boutique, where Tillie sat and instructed me to pick out the perfect dress and accessories for my wedding day." Tillie Lewis purchased the sweet lace gown and all the trimmings for the lucky bride. Tillie never mentioned this bridal gift treat to anyone.

A JAPANESE THANK-YOU IS THE HIGHLIGHT OF 1962

In gratitude for opening her arms to welcome them back in 1946 when few others did, in 1962, the Japanese-American Citizens League honored Tillie Lewis for her unwavering commitment to hiring people on merit, without regard to race, religion, sex, or physical handicap.[ccxxvii] This was one award that truly warmed her heart and brought genuine tears to her eyes; she wished she could have done more for those lovely people during their terrible ordeal.

In October, just in time to ward off the fall chill, Tillie added Anderson Soups[ccxxviii] to the TLF Penthouse lineup.

The Stockton and Modesto newspapers announced, "Always thinking ahead, Tillie expanded, remodeled and redecorated her office inside and out in a modern, sleek and futuristic theme at a cost of $115,000 using local contractors and designers."

NAPLES

In 1963, Tillie was once again taking the grand tour of Europe. She was considering global expansion into the land where it had all started—in the rich Italian soil. Even if she chose not to expand, the press coverage was always nice, and it guaranteed the trip as a legitimate business tax write-off. A gal has to consider a few loopholes when grand hotel suites can cost over eight hundred dollars per night. The Italian columnist Mario Falconi called her *la Regina dei Pomodori*—the Queen of Tomatoes. Falconi continued, "Regal in the setting of the Presidential Suite of the Grand Hotel Vesuvio where before her stayed Princess Grace Kelly and Prince Rainer, Rita Hayworth with Prince Aga Khan, Bogey and Bacall, Enrico Caruso and Luciano Pavarotti, Tillie enthralled the writer."

In fluent Italian, Tillie told Falconi that growing and canning the San Marzano pear-shaped Italian tomato in California was her idea. "But Naples is an integral part. My fortune, the luck of my American establishments[97] started from Naples, or at least what Naples had to inspire me."

Here in the hometown of Florindo Del Gaizo, Tillie altered her "Cinderella meets Prince Charming" storyline and did not heap praise upon the memory of Del Gaizo. She simply stated, "In 1934 I came to Naples and made contact with Del Gaizo and the Napoletana canning industry. I built the company in America. In two years I bought out the company from Del Gaizo."

With the basics of "Why Naples?" covered, Tillie then explained how she had turned the American Del Gaizo experiment from a single little tomato factory into one of the "Big Five" food-canning producers in the world, which earned Tillie more honors than she could count. Falconi raved,

Several periodicals have written about her, such as the *Los Angeles Times* and the *Reader's Digest*. A survey that the Associated Press conducted on large enterprises in which women hold high-ranking positions in the business field and the arts and sciences classified Tillie as the first woman of America.

In her room in the grand hotel overlooking the sea, Tillie Lewis talks with great enthusiasm and easily flowing Italian that I never would have imagined. Here is an American businesswoman like those we read about in books and newspapers. As she speaks and tells her story, her words clearly demonstrate that her intelligence is not limited to the field of business. By herself, little by little, she has learned our language with confidence. Speaking Italian wasn't enough for her, so she studied and was able to read and write Italian with ease. Every once in a while, her husband, Meyer L. Lewis, serves as her lawyer, secretary, or attorney. He recalls an event. He gets up to grab a document or file. Tillie Lewis doesn't talk too much about herself, but she does hold one thing dear: announcing that this business trip will take her first to Rome, Hamburg, and London.

Her main reason for the trip was to build a large canning factory in Naples, based on the same technology that was used in both

---

97   Her Flotill canning plants were the largest producer of tomato products in the world.

Stockton and Modesto.[98] The first contacts have already begun, and the foundation has been started. In two months, Tillie will return, and business will be progressing.

Tomatoes gave her a taste for success, but they have also given her the taste for life: the passion for life in world affairs. Involved in American world affairs is a small, fragile woman who knows how to excel with her intelligence and her willpower: enough to flood the United States with Tillie Lewis Foods, Inc.

The Queen of Tomatoes left Naples with two bags of seeds; just like in the fairy tales, she has returned after almost thirty years. Carrying in her heart the sweet memories of a city where she spent just a few months to perfect a business and where she developed in her mind the idea of a great canned-food factory, this is almost a gift from her success: a factory sprung from the spontaneous germination of those two poor sacks of tomato seeds from the Naples countryside.[99]

Tillie left Naples with no intention of building a thing in Italy. Tillie had already agreed to purchase a canning company in Patterson, California, and was awaiting delivery of the tallest, most grandiose replacement she could find for those seven original copper cookers.

The Patterson Canning Company acquisition placed Tillie into the business of "water-free" or dehydrated foods. With prepared meals, "just add water" was yet another corner of the ever-expanding food market to be conquered. Tillie purchased and installed the new "Hydro-static Sterilizer," which was a King Kong–size, automated, five-story, high-pressure cooker: the first used in an American canning plant. The "Hydro-stat," as they called it, was a huge expense, but it allowed a massive capacity for cooking in a relatively small space. Soon, TLF was packing over one hundred different products, including the original pomodoros.

Next came the punch-out "punch cards." Keeping with her "Thoroughly Modern Tillie" MO, Tillie updated her canning and office equipment to

---

98

99 Translated by Lynn Greeley and Chet Greeley, Manteca, California, December 2010.

maintain her "Quality in Quantity" reputation. Tillie researched the most impressive technologies in computer-business equipment and chose the Honeywell Model 200 over an IBM for its speed. Tillie upgraded the company's software packages.

Tillie herself could happily evaluate most elements of her entire business from her Honeywell-generated "profit impact reports" in the morning and again before she left at the end of every workday.[ccxxix] TLF would always remain at the forefront of technology.

FRUIT COCKTAIL

Tillie's cook spiced up a Christmas dinner party by splashing a little rum into the apricots, along with her favorite holiday spices. She called it her "fruit cocktail." Tillie's great-idea lightbulb blazed in her head.

Tillie called Doc Weast to discuss boozing up Flotill Fruit Cocktail in cans. Cuban rum was Tillie's favorite. Luckily for this new project, Bacardi had left Cuba (and the gorgeous Art Deco building bearing the family name) behind when Fidel Castro took over. The rum and Bacardi were now in the US territory of Puerto Rico.

Doc toted a few cans of what Doc called "rough draft products" in his fancy hand-stitched sample case, with TILLIE LEWIS FOOD, INC. etched in gold lettering upon it— "To impress the big shots," according to Tillie.[100] Doc set up appointments to discuss rum-delicious fruit cocktail approval plans to move forward with the FDA in Washington, DC. The members of the congressional hearing, who thoroughly enjoyed the rough draft Bacardi with apricots, peaches and pears actually used the word "yummy" and smacked their lips at the proposal. Doc Weast won the go-ahead to use an experimental pack of rum-soaked apricots, peaches, and pears only. The name *Fruit cocktail* itself would not be approved at this juncture, since apricots, peaches and pears with alcoholic enhancement was pushing the morality code far enough; but a

---

100 On this first trip, Doc carried product in his fancy case. From then on, he kept his case filled with something nearer and dearer to his heart: a bright-red plastic coffeepot, Styrofoam cups, and a one-pint bottle of Smirnoff vodka.

food admitting that it was actually a canned cocktail was too worrisome for the FDA in 1964.

In any event, the committee was looking forward to sampling more of the new product. The Flotill team knew that not getting the "cocktail" name was a big loss for the marketing that Tillie had planned. They hoped the products would be successful enough to eventually win the "fruit in a cocktail" title.[ccxxx]

BEATRICE

February 28,1964, was the fiftieth wedding anniversary of Tillie's sister, Beatrice, and her husband, Sam Hockheiser. The family held the party a few weeks earlier than the official date, since Bea was desperately ill by this time. Tillie certainly appeared to have ignored both her sister and the cancer that riddled Beatrice's body for more than a year. That cancer might not allow Bea to see her actual wedding anniversary the last day of the month.

Sam and Bea's eldest son, Saul, wrote a beautiful speech that chronicled the lives of his parents, including the end of Mosalina Products[101] in 1955, and his parents' move to California in 1956. Bea and Sam first settled in Stockton before choosing Los Angeles to be closer to Saul and June in 1960.

The family was puzzled and hurt that Tillie was not more vigilant in attending to Beatrice in the final months of her life. Tillie sent her sister no flowers, nor did she make many personal visits that anyone could recall. It was especially hurtful since Beatrice had always been there for Tillie.

Was Tillie just too busy with her business, or was it the abhorrent fear of another dear one being lost to a wasting illness? Their mother Rose had been consumed by tuberculous, and their brother Benjamin had been taken by his own terrible cancer.

The kind and loving Beatrice Ehrlich Hockheiser died a few weeks later, on March 14, 1964, and was buried in Stockton. Bea was seventy-three.

---

101 Mosalina Products was the company Tillie named and helped start in New York with her brother-in-law, sister, and Louis Weisberg in 1918.

Tillie Lewis did nothing remarkable for an entire year. Nothing at all. In a fashion, most un-Tillie-like, Tillie didn't even travel. She even left a tempting trip to Paris for Meyer Lewis to plan on behalf of her great-niece Judy.

Chapter 14

PARIS, ISRAEL, AND THE FIRST WOMAN WITH THE KEYS TO CORPORATE

It was good to have Tillie's connections. On behalf of Tillie and her great-niece Judy Heiser (daughter of nephew Dr. Saul Heiser), Meyer wrote a letter to Florentine Pabst, of the Pabst Blue Ribbon beer fortune, in which he requested that Pabst show "his girl" a good time while she was visiting Paris—but not too good. Florentine lived, worked and played in the tony sections of famous city.

The Pabst family considered Tillie Lewis family; Florentine knew her as "Aunt Tillie." Meyer's letter indicates that he had concern about his sweet, young niece-in-law and her collegiate, good-girl companions. Meyer knew he had reason to worry, since Paris was hosting the crème de la crème of the British Invasion in 1965. The Beatles, the Rolling Stones, and the Kinks were in town.[ccxxxi] Then there was Florentine Pabst, herself.[102]

Florentine was a gorgeous young heiress who wrote for *Paris Match* magazine, the French version of *Rolling Stone*. Florentine was chic and hip—definitely on the A list. Florentine knew everybody famous and infamous.[ccxxxii] Florentine appears to have been involved in some kind of a Turkish bath incident that Meyer mentions but does not explain.

---

102 Jim Morrison [The Doors] and Florentine Pabst were friends.

Meyer followed up in another letter, this time to Judy, in which he offered her "a list of agents throughout Europe to assist her" on her first European adventure, including Florentine Pabst, complete with the heiress's office and home phone numbers. Knowing the lifestyle of Mademoiselle Pabst and wishing Judy and her college-girl companions to feel comfortable, Meyer closed with a little gift.

> I am enclosing a check and if you do get together with [Pabst] you can use whatever is necessary to pick up the tab. If there's any left, spend it as you please.
>
> Have a wonderful trip. Above all, be careful of men of my type who can't be trusted with a pretty girl like yourself…I know from experience!
> Love,
> Uncle Meyer[ccxxxiii]

The Pabst family was known to be generous. Nonetheless, Tillie Lewis would not have the Pabst family thinking she was gauche enough to expect Florentine to pay for anything while "her girl" was in Paris. Paris with Mademoiselle Pabst was to be Tillie's treat.

Paris, London, or Stockton, miniskirts and pantyhose were everywhere and the newest rage. Tillie Lewis was sixty-nine years old when she placed her Lily of France collection of garters and girdles into a white plastic bag and stuffed them into a back closet at 740 Willow Street, where she promptly forgot about them. All women, but especially ladies of business like Tillie, clamored for the new, seamless pantyhose from Glen Raven Mills. Classy and comfortable were no longer an oxymoron: the latest unmentionables had the "panty" built right in. The former twenties flapper fashionista Tillie Lewis was ready to enjoy the freedom of this new development. Miniskirts were in. Tillie raised her lengths to a modern modest and a conservative short.

Tillie had her work and party collection of girdle/garter-free pantyhose that included mesh and gold sparkles.[103]

WHERE THERE'S SMOKE

In August of 1965, five firemen were injured in a blaze at TLF. Stockton fire chief Mitchell Coolures was hailed as a hero after personally hefting a two-hundred-pound firefighter named Robert Payne down a ladder after he'd been overcome by smoke. Literally adding fuel to the fire, the engulfed warehouse was the holding space for the rum-spiced fruit test pack awaiting its day to be tested for taste and alcohol content by the FDA. On that hot summer Stockton afternoon, the test pack of rum-soaked fruit combusted into flames.

The heat was so intense that water boiled and evaporated from the fire hoses before the water could reach the flaming, twenty-foot-high stacks of cans in a rear warehouse. The fire was likely caused by a careless toss of a cigarette, at a cost of $150,000[104] in cans, equipment, and the building, in addition to the health of the firefighters.[ccxxxiv]

Unusual for Tillie and one of her "What next?" great ideas, Tillie lost interest in the Molotov cocktailed fruit, letting Doc Weast's date with the FDA in Washington, DC, go unattended. Tillie turned her interests to the world around her instead.

THE HOLY LAND

Israel wanted to expand its agriculture and grow a thriving tomato variety. Two years before, just before Beatrice died, Tillie had met with famed Israeli general and politician Moshe Dayan when he was Israel's minister of agriculture to discuss a more sustainable agribusiness for his country. The current minister, Haim Gvati, along with Ariel Sharon (prime

---

103 Bridgette Smith, owner of the Willow house formerly owned by Tillie, gifted the huge bag of "Tillie's frillies" to the author.

104 This was $1,150,000 in 2016 dollars.

minister from 2001–2006), Dayan, and the agricultural pioneer Sam Hamburg, toured the Holy Land from the famous Dan Hotel, hosting Tillie and Meyer Lewis.

Sam Hamburg was, according to reporter Helga Dudman (who covered this April 1966 visit), the man "responsible for changing the face of Israel, both agriculturally and economically through new crop development." Meyer said,

> All that we want to do is make our experience available to this country…Briefly, the thinking behind "Operation Tomato" goes something like this:
>
> 1) When not in operation during the citrus-processing season, a good portion of Israel's canning facilities are idle.
> 2) A new tomato strain developed [by] California agronomists with backing from [Tillie Lewis will be] excellent for processing into many products—from catsup, juice, pizza sauce to whole tomatoes.
> 3) This versatile new strain grows well in Israel [and] was planted as an experiment last year with great success.
> 4) With proper market research, export target[s] can be determined since the demand for tomato products in the affluent world is a growing one.

Tillie and Meyer were stunned at the miniscule size of the Israeli tomato cans. Asked about "the little Israeli cans of tomato paste," Tillie diplomatically complimented the taste but couldn't help but mention the size of the tiny can. Tillie said, "Perhaps a housewife might wish to buy [them] in larger quantities."

Told that Israelis eat tomatoes for breakfast, Tillie replied, "We ourselves always have fresh tomatoes on the table in season."

Meyer added, "But not for breakfast."

Left to right: Tillie Lewis, Moshe Dayan, and Ariel Sharon at Dayan's personal residence in Israel. Dayan and Sharon had both been ministers of agriculture in Israel as well as being war heroes and political powerhouses. Israel summoned Tillie Lewis for advice on growing tomatoes in the Holy Land.

The reporter digressed to compliment Tillie's clothes, career, and femininity, as well as her worldwide success. Dudman wrote, "Tillie Lewis's hair is the color of a tomato just ready to ripen and her large eyes are sagaciously wide-spaced." Meyer did not fare as well. The reporter wrote of him, "Mr. Lewis is tall and portly with a military bearing and a pointed moustache."[ccxxxv]

The Lewises stopped to pay their respects at the graves of Tillie's father, and Bilha, in addition to a visit to Dayan's home. Tillie and Meyer posed with Dayan and Sharon in front of Dayan's prized collection of ancient Israeli artifacts.[105]

---

105 Dayan's estate had to return the collection after his death, since it was considered the property of Israel.

BACK TO WORK

Tillie, ever mindful of keeping the Flotill/TLF family happy and as interconnected as possible, sponsored nearly any group event her people suggested in her still-popular suggestion box. She still worried about ways to avoid employee turnover and to maintain comradery. Her company bowling teams were especially popular.

Tillie outfitted her men's and ladies' bowling leagues with the best shirts and shoes she could find. She offered time off and all-expenses-paid hotel stays when her teams began to win state competitions. Tillie was happy to show everybody how content the Flotill/TLF family members were, both in and out of the workplace.[ccxxxvi] The 1966 annual holiday bonus letter included news about "Two major expansions in employee benefit programs: an entirely new sick-leave plan and more liberal program for paid vacations. Both programs will become effective January 1, 1967." Tillie's gift added long-term disability insurance to California-mandated plans plus generous sick-leave days added that credited any unused sick leave while disregarding any use of prior sick leave. She wrote, "It is my sincere hope that our employee-benefit program will contribute to your continued feeling of job satisfaction and security for you and your family." Along with the little holiday check of appreciation, the employees of TLF were having a merry Christmas, indeed.[ccxxxvii]

FIRST WOMAN ON A MAJOR CORPORATE BOARD

The thought process of all large corporations at the time was that women did not belong in the boardroom, unless they were taking notes for dictation or serving coffee. Tillie Lewis's inclusion in the board took careful consideration. Based upon her excellence as a person of business savvy and talent, she was made chairwoman of the newly formed Ogden Food Products Corporation. Two veteran members of Ogden Corp were on her committee. Bert Davi would serve as vice chairman and Lester Ginsburg would be president and CEO.

TLF Inc. and Western California Canners (based in Antioch and Pittsburg, California) were consolidated. Ogden's food acquisitions included

Flavor Pict Inc. of Florida and International Products Corporation (the meat-packing division) in the South American nation of Paraguay.[ccxxxviii] The whole thing sounded far busier than it was. Ogden was phasing Tillie out. Well, she'd just see about that!

Chapter 15

DELEGATE TO ROME, PUBLIC
SPEAKING, MOTIVATING WOMEN,
TV, RADIO, AND RETIREMENT

The years 1967 and 1968 found Tillie in Rome as a US delegate appointed by the US State Department by vice president Hubert H. Humphrey to speak on behalf of the United States at a conference held in Rome on global minimum nutrition standards and the population explosion that had recently become the subject of much discussion. Tillie had befriended the Humphrey family at a charity event, years earlier, when Humphrey (senator at the time) and his wife, Muriel, admitted to being Tasti-Diet fans. Tillie asked where she might send the Humphreys the latest products for them to sample and approve. Muriel, who'd once been a bookkeeper just as Tillie had been, jotted the family address down on the back of Tillie's business card.[ccxxxix]

Long-time Tasti-Diet fan, personal friend, senator, and vice president of the United States Hubert H. Humphrey appointed Tillie Lewis to represent the nation at the Council against Global Hunger summit in Rome in both 1967 and 1968.

Tillie was the only woman at the world conference delegates' table. She was greeted in Rome by the vice president and seated between male delegates from Turkey and the United States. Tillie was photographed with the translation headset that all delegates wore. She smiled for the press cameras while concentrating on the discussion at hand. She told reporters, "Considerable progress was made…The 34 countries participating in the counsel have finalized their determination to promote further collective action to raise levels of nutrition and the standard of living of the people under their respective jurisdictions." She reported to the state department that the increased interest at that year's session would focus on the objectives to better the food conditions of world populations and an expanding world economy.[ccxl] Tillie was being politically correct with her praise, smiling through clenched teeth of worry. She was very concerned with what she knew was a world in which multitudes of children were dying of starvation and suffering from malnutrition. As soon as she was free of the commitment to the delegation, Tillie was planning a public speaking campaign to bring the problem to American awareness. She hoped she could make a difference in feeding the hungry and halting unchecked birthrates in countries that simply could not feed the children who were already here on earth.

Back on American soil, TLF bought Wilson Foods Inc. Peas were the first vegetable to be packed for the 1967 season. Tillie announced that she would be present on day one of the operation for the sake of both morale boosting and for photographs.

Lonell Crosby[106] remembered that day at Wilson Foods, "As Tillie positioned herself for the camera, she noticed only Wilson Company–labeled boxes in the area. She requested that a young man fetch a few boxes from her newly arrived trucks. The young man asked her which boxes he should retrieve; Tillie threw her arms open wide gaily and said, "Son, what's your name? It's lovely to meet you. I'm Tillie Lewis. Get them all. Every box, in every truck, are all mine."

A female employee of the newly acquired Wilson Foods complained to Tillie that her "no-good husband" would pick up her paycheck and gamble it away before she had a chance to even see the check. In those days, a husband could pick up and cash his wife's check, no questions asked, and without her permission. Tillie was enraged. She stopped plant production and called a meeting on the floor for all employees. Tillie told them that from this point forward, "Today, everything changes: only the person whose name is written upon the check will be allowed to remove it from the plant." Mrs. Lewis

---

106 Lonell Crosby was one of Tillie's African-American employees. According to Lonell, he believed himself to be one of her favorite people. I am sure he was correct. Lonell was a charmer.

scolded the men for taking advantage of their wives, and she lectured the ladies to find the backbone to stand up for themselves."

IT'LL SELL FASTER THAN HOTCAKES

Tillie asked the Doc and Elsie Weast team to create a new pancake mix. Tillie mailed free boxes of the mix, with a personal note, along with a jar of Tasti-Diet preserves to everyone she knew, including the wives of her new Ogden family. The pancake mix contained her latest diet product, the cholesterol-free egg substitute Ovocomp. The name Ovocomp was changed to Eggstra after the word Ovocomp proved to be the only distasteful thing about the product.

On December 6, 1967, Tillie's public-relations gal, Mary Brown, wrote to remind Tillie to prepare for the new year's speaking tour, beginning in January, at the Georgia meeting of the ladies' Pilot Club. The club sponsored the hospital ship *Hope* that Tillie and her friend, television star Art Linkletter, were supporters of. Mary Brown suggested that Tillie's speech should focus on "How Women Get to the Top and Stay There." Ms. Brown closed with, "PS Tillie: The pancakes are divine!"[ccxli]

Tillie's speech shocked the Pilot Club and made the papers across the country. Tillie began strongly with, "Women have been brainwashed!"

THE "PILLARS OF STRENGTH" TOUR

Less than a year after becoming the first woman on the board of the Ogden Corporation, Tillie decided that the Ogden boys' club needed to see her flex her muscles but with finesse. As the first woman in the boys' club, she knew she'd have to tread lightly on male egos to keep moving up a ladder that had never had a rung intended for a player in a dress.

Team Tillie publicists contacted newspapers across the country in which they reprinted a single article written by AP news-feature columnist Vivian Brown, changing the title of the article to from city to city but leaving the message intact. In Pennsylvania, Vivian's article read, "Top Tomato Processor, a Woman, Gives Credit for Success to Men." In Salina, Kansas, the very same article had the headline, "Men Are Pillars of the Strength of Women."[ccxlii]Tillie told a Manhattan audience:

⊲⊞⊳

A woman in business must be five times as good as a man to get one-fifth the credit for doing a good job...but I couldn't have done it without men. They are the pillars of strength, and women need to cultivate the art of getting along with men if they want a successful business.

If a woman is put in the position of supervising men, she must be sure she can communicate so that they understand what it is she wants done...Women shouldn't give orders to men. They should make suggestions and let the suggestions become the man's idea. I always figured the better job done by the men, the bigger my company would grow. There is only so much a woman can do, so I've kept [the men] happy...It really boils down to faith in any undertaking, knowing what you want and being satisfied with the price you have to pay to get it.[ccxliii]

TLF (VIA OGDEN) BUYS WESTERN CALIFORNIA CANNERS

The Western California Canners Company belonged to Burt Davi, the Ogden board's vice chairman of food. Davi had begun his plant in 1933, the year prior to Tillie starting Flotill. This was another Ogden family business. What could go wrong?

The plant occupied the waterfront on the west side of Antioch, where it canned asparagus, tomatoes, and sweet corn. The company planned to expand into the neighboring town of Pittsburg, but the plans were challenged in lawsuits that extended into 1975. Pittsburg had a passionate lobby of people who were defending the rights of 179 registered voters currently residing in the El Pueblo subdivision, along with fourteen other people who lived at the Betty Ray Motel, to retain unincorporated property rights rather than incorporate; the expansion would have created good jobs in the community and would have allowed more food canning for the nation.

Tillie was officially weary of the legal battles, price wars, and union problems; the weather affecting crop productions with glut product years and lean products years; and the grinding and ever-growing rules and regulations of the food industry.[ccxliv] Traveling and lecturing about becoming successful was her latest interest.[ccxlv]

Tillie confessed to her fellow Ogden officers that she was tired and needed to travel; she was concerned that "the boys"—her beloved nephews, Arthur and Albert Heiser— "just don't know how to run the business." With that statement, Ogden's troubleshooter, George Visgilio, was assigned to sort out the issues that were plaguing the newly formed food division.

Selling to Ogden did have some unexpected inconveniences for the Tomato Queen and her empire—Ogden now had control of TLF for real. Tillie's massive private office in Stockton was divided into two offices and a conference room. Tillie had an unwelcome roommate in young Mr. Visgilio.[ccxlvi]

TILLIE HITS THE ROAD

Touring, radio, and television was what Tillie decided to do rather than share a space with anyone. Good gracious, she hadn't shared an office even with her husband, Meyer. Tillie rattled some cages when she declared at the Pilot's Club meeting, "So here's my first counsel on getting ahead: *to move up, be able to move out.*"[ccxlvii] This statement inferred that Tillie was advising women to leave their marriages, which was not the case. In a speech that was over sixteen typewritten pages long, Tillie spoke to working women who were stuck in jobs where they were clearly carrying their male superiors. Her exact words were:

> I am talking about that unsung heroine who has become invaluable as an assistant manager, assistant buyer or assistant something-or-other…Top management puts in a succession of rising young [male] executive trainees over her. She does the work, carries the department,

makes sure things go right for the young man. Upper management knows she'll get the job done...How does a woman break the cycle? I say, before she has grown roots.

The solution may be that she should uproot herself and go elsewhere...I am not encouraging employees to be disloyal, but I do say that where merit and loyalty and executive talent are not rewarded with the tangible and physiological incentives of advancement, then the employer is not living up to his side of the arrangement...So there's my first counsel on getting ahead: *to move up, be able to move out*...Professionally we are the equal sex. Let's believe that. Let's have the confidence that our talents and experience are marketable.

When you believe in yourself, in your ability to locate and flourish in another firm, you become bolder in your present job. You are able to make a better case for your well-earned promotion.

My second word of advice is: Show your boss that because women are only number two, they try harder. It might not be fair, but as a woman you *do* have to work harder and *produce more* to equal a man...

Axiom number three is: *don't be afraid to tackle a man's work.* I don't mean working with a pick shovel, lifting bales or toting barges. Physical strength is something most men have over most women... But, in scientific research, medicine, accounting and corporation law...lots of women are math wizards...they should rise to the top of auditing firms...There's no reason why women can't rise to the top of Madison Avenue like Mary Wells Lawrence, advertising head of Brannif Airlines.

She reminded her audience that women ought to be a natural in the food industry, since women buy the food, prepare it, and usually design the menu and purchasing plan in their homes. Why not expand this talent into the work force? Tillie shared with the audience, "No, business is not fun. It's too serious...Some women have said to me [that] it must be fun to be the only woman among a dozen successful men. I'm afraid not. I'm [now on boards of] food companies, shipbuilding [companies], water pollution filtration, steel mills, chemical and paper plants...None of this can be classified as fun for a woman—or even for a man—but, it's certainly invigorating."

Tillie added commentary about her upcoming product lines, which made the speech a TLF commercial to buy her new lines, which she said were "important food products for our families." She restated that she'd taught herself high finance through books and by listening to others: "I wasn't a *dropout!* Economic conditions made me a *force out*." She went on to use her old partially true story of leaving her unhappy marriage in the 1920s to go to night school, eventually becoming a stock-securities broker on Wall Street who was making four times the money as most men before the 1929 crash sent her into the food industry. She continued, "Look around for a need. In good times or bad times, people need to eat. I literally made a career for myself...If women will courageously accept the challenges of a business and professional career, along with the responsibilities that go with them...and contribute their abilities to the problems that confront us...they will find the reward most worthwhile."ccxlviii

FAME

Now that Tillie had created a fortune, her new goal was fame. She and Meyer had done an admirable job as amateurs who were able to market her face and figure along with her products. Tillie wanted immortality in the form of a real biography and a movie about her life, and Tillie wanted to win the Horatio Alger Award.[107] For public relations, it was time to go pro. Tillie hired Hill and Knowlton Inc. of New York as her public-relations counselors. A letter from the firm's vice president, the aforementioned Mary Brown, stated, "Dear Tillie: You must be the most written-about women since Betsy Ross."

A few days later, Tillie was interviewed in Los Angeles for "The Fast Gourmet." Reporter Poppy Cannon noted, "Discreetly decked in diamonds and emeralds, Tillie has become an international figure commuting to Europe [five times last year] and was President [Lyndon] Johnson's US

---

107   The Horatio Alger is the coveted award for Americans who really went from rags to riches.

emissary to the Food Conference in Rome. While Tillie has two fully staffed homes in Stockton and Palm Springs she does the cooking for her husband Thursdays and Sundays." Ms. Cannon described Tillie's "Sunday Supper in Palm Springs" menu and preparation technique in painstaking detail, from washing and drying the "fresh young spinach leaves" for the salad to rubbing dried rosemary between her bejeweled hands to hand-infuse the chilled TLF apricots for dessert. The main course, naturally, was TLF spaghetti with pomodoro sauce.[ccxlix]

CONTEMPT

Stockton community activists were back to complaining that Tillie Lewis was not providing enough for the local workers on a full-time basis. Local groups had gone so far as to state that Tillie Lewis was personally responsible for the severe welfare problem in the area. Arthur Heiser addressed their complaints in a two-page letter to the Stockton city council and the local papers. Arthur reminded the readers that Tillie had begun during the Great Depression; at the time, she hired as many full-time (but mostly seasonal) employees as she could while still allowing her fledging plant to survive. Most of these seasonal workers had been seasonal long before Tillie set foot in California, traveling with the crops, working in the fields or on the railroad, or selling vegetables at the side of the road—whatever work they could find or invent. Tillie gave them dignified, inside work, often at twice their previous wages. Opportunity for growth was open to all.

Once a worker was seasonally employed, he or she could be almost certain to expect a call back. In some cases, an exceptional seasonal worker like Ralph Garcia's father was kept on as Tillie's handyman, gardener, and friend during the off-season. Actual workers knew that Tillie had always rewarded their loyalty.

Heiser pointed out that being accepted by many people in the community had never been easy. In the thirty-three years that Tillie Lewis had been creating wealth for the community, she'd had to deal with the pressure of still being an unaccepted outsider for various reasons.[108]

Tillie's "baby," Flotill, had matured into the largest canner of tomato products in America, with 750 full-time employees expected in 1968—employees who earned wages and benefits great enough to buy their own homes and to send their children to college. Stockton could expect TLF to keep on growing, thus adding more jobs to the area.[ccl]

Chips drove Arthur hard with her demands, but he loved her for her work ethic. It crushed him to see the never-ending anti-Semitism that had always been an issue in Stockton. Arthur could barely tolerate it himself. He had no idea how the very public Tillie Lewis smiled her way through the social events and country clubs[109] knowing full well that many of the people who were happily asking her for contributions to their causes wrinkled their noses at the "Jew broad" behind her back.[ccli]

CYCLAMATES BANNED: TASTI-DIET IN TROUBLE

A TLF ad for Ovocomp from May 27, 1968, that ran in newspapers and magazines across the country touted that "An egg-based product [was] announced today by 'Tillie Lewis, America's foremost producer of Low-Calorie Foods.' Two tablespoons of a new product by TLF and Ogden Corporation made scrambled eggs, cakes and breads. Ovocomp made all recipes that called for whole eggs healthier. It was lower in fat, calories and cholesterol than whole eggs plus guaranteed salmonella-free. Safe, delicious and nutritious."

TLF products were now being sold in all fifty states and fifty-six countries around the world. But after tests on rats suggested that bladder cancer could result in humans who ingested cyclamates, the sweetner in Tasti-Diet, in 1969 the FDA banned cyclamates in the United States. Great Britian followed suit. The Ogden Corporation was not pleased. The rest of the world ignored this

---

108 Arthur Heiser was referring to blatant anti-Semitism within the community. For example, Tillie fought several battles with Stockton's Country Club before being accepted as its first Jewish member. Some clubs and organizations never accepted her.

109 Tillie's great-great nephew, Ricky Barnes, grandson of Albert and Helene Heiser, became a popular professional golfer.

ban, based upon the evidence that the tests indicated that humans would need to drink over three hundred cans of cyclamate products per day to produce a bladder tumor.

But the ban on cyclamates was a bitter pill that halted American sales of Tasti-Diet temporarily. Tillie immediately sold the entire cyclamate version of Tasti-Diet, at a discount, to a very happy Japan. Less than a year later, the original reporting scientific team could not duplicate the negative tests, even on rats. Cyclamates were deemed fine for human consumption, after all.[cclii]

Nonetheless, the damage had been done: America was not buying cyclamates again. However, Doc and Elsie Weast's original pectin-saccharine based formula for Tasti-Diet was added back, nearly overnight, to the popular diet-line, now an American staple and Ogden moneymaker again by the next year. As *Time* reported, "Tasti-Diet had been a winner from the start, and by 1972 posted profits of $6.5 million."[ccliii]

Cyclamates or no, business and connections do go on. Henry Tasca, the US ambassador to Morocco and a diplomatic specialist and author of books on world and US trading policies, brought a group of Moroccan officials by the Stockton plant and the Lewis home for a luncheon that Tillie sponsored in their honor. As recorded in the *Stockton Record*, Meyer wrote that Morocco "wanted to take a look at canning operations in progress, industry trends and coordination of farm systems with canning and frozen food operations… [the Moroccans] are interested in increasing the export of Moroccan goods to Europe."[ccliv]

ADDING TO HER AWARDS

Businesspeople Marion Jacobs and Richard Yoshikawa chose Tillie Lewis as 1969's "Boss of the Year" for the American Business Women's Association. Marion had been Tillie's favorite protégé and was considered a dear friend by both Meyer and Tillie. It was Mrs. Frank Lepape, who worked in TLF's personnel department, who wrote the winning letter in which Mrs. Lewis was nominated for the honor.[cclv]

Photographed wearing a hardhat, Tillie broke ground *again* in 1970 as the first female seaport commissioner in the United States. The position was even more rare since no American seaport had ever had a female even serve on a governing board; Tillie did it as commissioner and chief of the Port of Stockton. This is exactly where she stood as merely an observer for the entrance of the vessel *Daisy Gray* so many years before. She shoveled the first spade of earth for Stockton's new $3.5 million container terminal at port docks ten and eleven. Tillie had taken another first for women.[cclvi]

RETIREMENT?

To discuss various issues, including Tillie's retirement, the full Ogden board met at the Century Plaza Hotel in Los Angeles. When Tillie's limousine arrived, all the men were assembled to greet her at the entrance behind the impressive glass enclosure just inside the hotel. As George Visgilio later recalled, "Tillie swept out of her limo and walked smack into the glass hotel door. Unhurt, she collected herself immediately without the slightest hint of embarrassment. She gave the men of Ogden the impression that *that* was how she always made an entrance. More impressive, the heavily made-up Tomato Queen left a full-faced smear of various cosmetic products' impression of her mug sliding down the glass."[cclvii]

That meeting's agenda included the problems that continued to plague the Antioch plant. George Visgilio was in charge of the water issues and more. He stated that the State of California State Water Resources Control Board order number 71–15 had listed several demands that needed to be corrected in order to comply with the waste-discharge requirements for TLF's Plant W in Antioch.[110]

Arthur Heiser recommended to the board to phase out Antioch altogether and to create a new state-of-the-art TLF tomato-processing plant in Modesto. George Visgilio concurred, and the motion passed. They built Plant H in Modesto. It was efficient and low cost, and it was Ogden/TLF's latest pride

---

110 Antioch posthumously thanked TLF and other canneries by erecting its "Cannery Lady" statue and marker in 1996.

and joy. But Tillie Lewis herself was now just the figurehead of TLF; she was, at best, a consultant. While she was officially limited in her direct duties at TLF and Ogden, Tillie hoped to spit straight into the eye of actual retirement.

December 17, 1971, signaled the first time that Ogden executives sent out the Flotill/TLF holiday letter, sans Tillie. Employees received their first of many TLF form letters addressed, not to individuals, but "To the Members of the Tillie Lewis Foods Profit-Sharing Plan." The brief note informed employees that Ogden was going to boost the pension plan that Mrs. Lewis had already implemented.

All TLF employees saw, for the first time, the future of TLF as a corporate machine and not as the Flotill/TLF family. They were even more sorry that they'd lost the personal touch—the original pen—of their Tomato Queen as much as they missed the annual Tillie bonus checks that were just as absent.[cclviii]

The change in status for Tillie was just as disturbing. She was no longer the essential working cog in the machine that was her company, her baby, her vitality that was tied to Flotill/TLF. She hadn't tossed the baby out with the bath water, but the umbilical cord was officially cut. Tillie felt the loss to her core.

She'd certainly earned the right to retire, relax, and enjoy the money she'd made—but doing what? She'd given up being an actual person to become an entity, a company, a personality. Her physical form had melded with the figurehead of Flotill/TLF. But in fact, Tillie had aged and drastically. Her face had gone from glamorous to garish.

The last time she'd been a regular person, she was a girl—Tillie Ehrlich-Weisberg, at 99 Hudson Street, New York—praying for a fabulous future at any cost. That girl was long gone. She'd become a wealthy old woman. She had financial success, certainly, but with the roller-coaster ride that was her life careening into the final turns, what was she? Who was she now?

Thank goodness Tillie had Meyer Lewis. Meyer made a wonderful traveling companion to the aging Tillie. Now that she was growing older, she could no longer smile and wink her way to a better seat, meal, or social deal.

Tillie had developed no true friends. She'd made the decision after Florindo Del Gaizo died in 1937 that she couldn't afford the time for friends.

Her secretary, Alilea Haywood, was still her secretary. Tillie never shared her personal life with staff before and wasn't about to start now. The old show-biz crew were all long dead. Fanny Brice passed away twenty years before. Worst of all, Beatrice, the only person who'd truly known her, had been gone from this earth for seven years.

Her niece-in-law Lucy Heiser (Arthur's wife) was fifty-four years old. Lucy offered Tillie both her shoulders to cry on numerous occasions over the years. People speak of others who have a "heart of gold"—that most treasured life force lived inside Lucy Heiser. Tillie decided to take Lucy up on at least one of those shoulders now. Lucy and Arthur's daughter, Barbara, twenty-five, was a young lady who was growing up with a soul as giving as her mother's. Both women were there for Tillie as she tried to sort out the latest "What's next?"

Barbara Heiser later said how sad it was to see Auntie Chips coming home defeated instead of elated from Paris now: "Chips went on these fabulous vacations as just another rich, elderly, American tourist. She was no longer the front-page-newspaper headlining 'Tomato Queen.' Chips was suddenly forced to be something she hadn't been: a regular person. A regular person figuring out her true self. Her spiritual self. It wasn't easy for her."[cclix]

Meanwhile, the neighborhood kids, at least, noticed that Mr. Lewis had headed to the airport. After borrowing more money from TLF, he'd decided to try his luck in the food-import business. If Tillie could do it, so could he. Meyer named his company Overseas Marketing Enterprisers.[cclx] Since the Lewises were probably gone for weeks, a few of the neighborhood kids who lived near the mansion on Willow, suffering in the Stockton heat without swimming pools of their own, determined that the coast was clear for a little summer fun. In a plan devised after watching one of the final episodes of the television show *The Beverley Hillbillies*, they hopped the fence of the Lewis estate and went for an illicit swim. "Boy X," who requested that his one and only attempt to enter the world of crime be shared while remaining anonymous, said,

On television, I saw Ellie May Clampett floating around on the lawn chairs in the pool she called the "cement pond" many times. It seemed logical, to my child mind, that Mrs. Lewis's patio furniture ought to float, as well. A couple of us grabbed a few ornate wrought-iron chairs and shoved them into the drink.

We watched in horror as they swiftly, and loudly, sank to the bottom of the pool. At this time, Mrs. Lewis, looking like an angry clown from my nightmares with her makeup and hair way too bright, along with her butler, came running out of the house yelling at us to high heaven. I never ran so fast. This was my one and only criminal offence.

Tillie had devolved into what "Boy X" had said: she had become an overly redheaded, clownish figure from a child's nightmares.

Tillie collided with these youngsters because she stayed behind to accompany Senator George McGovern to an event in Sacramento. This was the second time the senator visited the area. The first was in May where McGovern donned an avocado-colored Tillie Lewis Food baseball cap and sorted through asparagus stalks with the ladies on the TLF line on his first day of campaigning in the California primary.[cclxi] Senator McGovern was the Democratic presidential candidate running against the Republican candidate, Richard M. Nixon.

TRICK OR TREAT

In neighborhoods, nationwide, Halloween gives children the opportunity to mask themselves, waltz right up to the neighbors' doors, and extort a little candy. While some of the houses of Stockton's affluent locked their gates and closed their blinds to this annual invasion of their privacy, the lights were ablaze at 740 Willow Street, welcoming tots with a treat and parents with a peek into the great house of the Tomato Queen herself.

While there was no extravagant Halloween decor, there was Froggert. Appearing to the costumed children more undertaker than servant, the theatrically solemn-faced Froggert, Tillie's British butler, donned his formal uniform of tailored black tuxedo, white bowtie, and kid gloves, greeted each cluster of kids with a deep bow and a droll, "Good evening, young masters and mistresses," and extended a gleaming silver tray of glittering wrapped candies, of which tiny trembling hands gingerly partook and quickly skedaddled.[cclxii]

AUNTIE CHIPS

Tillie did more than just send her great- and great-great nieces and nephews a few dollars or war bonds in envelopes over the years. Chips became Auntie Chips to the newest family members; she paid a little extra attention to the pink and beribboned baby girls. The new little ladies all received pearls, just like Auntie Chips's. Each year, more pearls were added to the growing strands. Tillie's handwritten love note below (from June 8, 1972) is to newborn Sara Beth on linen "*TLE*" stationery.

> Dear Pretty Miss Sara Beth:
> This note is written for the time you learn to read, dear, for I want to tell you that up to [this] date, I've been bragging about your "Mom" [Judy Heiser]—wow—[now] I shall have two girls to brag about. The enclosed is for the beginning of your trousseau. More to come!
> Much love,
> Aunt Chips and Uncle Meyer
>
> PS. When you are 16 months old I shall expect a "present."

Judy believed that the "present" Tillie hoped her baby, Sara Beth, would bestow upon Aunt Chips was a kiss. Tillie was generous with cash for her nephew, Dr. Saul's, family. The check for the baby was enough to buy everything the babe would need for quite some time. On the same stationery, Tillie sent notes and a small fortune to Judy and her husband, Robert:

Dear Robert,
A little late to call this a birthday present, so…This is merely a very, very slight *down* Payment for the new house you will get in Redwood City. With all God's Blessings for the future.
Much love,
Chips

⚜

Dear Judy,
So it's a little late! Birthdays come and go, but buying a new house is a little different…Therefore, you may join your "Bob" and use the little gift for the same purpose if you wish.
A Hug, a Kiss and Much love,
Chips

Judy Heiser respectfully declined to disclose the exact amount that Chips had slipped into the two envelopes. She did state that the total dropped their jaws in surprise. Judy believes they bought all their new furniture and a car with the "little gifts" Chips had sent.[cclxiii] It is unknown how long the Heiser nephews' children and Meyer Lewis's children were each receiving gifts of $3,000 annually, but they were all pleased to receive them.[111]

FRIENDS IN HIGH PLACES
Hubert H. Humphrey, former vice president of the United States and once again senator from Minnesota, sent the following note on his US Senate letterhead dated March 26, 1973.

---

111   This was the maximum allowable yearly gift per giftee to be tax-free; any more than that amount and the giftee would need to pay tax on the overage.

Dear Tillie:

I saw the enclosed article in the *Minneapolis Tribune*, and it reminded me of your loyal support and generous assistance to me. I simply wanted to say hello again. By the way, our mutual friend Norman Sherman[112] would want to be remembered to you.

With all best wishes,

Hubert H.

Tillie sent Herbert and Muriel Humphrey a reply on her latest office memo and stationery that she nicknamed her "Tilliegrams," such as in the following:

Tilliegram April 8, 1973: Mrs. Tillie Lewis interview by radio station KUOP (91.3), "Community Profiles" at 7:00 p.m.

Tilliegram April 10, 1973: Mrs. Tillie Lewis interviewed on "Successful Women" on KVIE channel 6 at 6:30 p.m.[113]

THE *READER'S DIGEST* VERSION

In November, during an interview for *Reader's Digest* and *New Woman* magazines, Tillie told the same old story of Florindo Del Gaizo and his gift of seeds, cash, and blind faith. Mrs. Lewis was dressed in a flowing, floral caftan—a style popularized by Ava and Zsa Zsa Gabor on all the talk shows. From business to fashion, Tillie always was ahead of the trends. Tillie was standing in the daylily section of her garden near an inviting gazebo for the interview; her makeup and hair were perfect. Tillie shared that she had gone from poverty as a housewife to having her own day of honor. She noted that the city of Stockton had proclaimed a "Tillie Lewis Day," the climax of which was a gala testimonial dinner attended by nine hundred people. She recalled that as she was being driven to the city auditorium, the streets were thronged with cheering people. When she entered on the arm of the lieutenant governor, the crowd gave her a standing ovation.[cclxiv]

---

112 Vice President Humphrey's Washington press secretary and friend.

113 Tillie designed her in-house company "Tilliegrams" to look like Western Union telegrams.

Chapter 16

DR. TILLIE LEWIS AND TILLIE LEWIS DRIVE

Meyer and Tillie interrupted a world tour for Tillie to accept her honorary doctorate in business administration from the University of the Pacific on May 25, 1973. To the sound of "Pomp and Circumstance," the eighth-grade dropout who had always proclaimed that "one key to my success is I was unfettered by a formal education" accepted her diploma from UOP president Dr. Stanley McCaffrey with exultant, genuine tears in her eyes and a heart bursting with gratitude.

Being honored with this degree was one of the most cherished moments in her life. The celebration after her "graduation" was filled with cheers and champagne in addition to trinkets engraved with "Dr. Tillie Lewis," including a teal photo album with her new title written in gold leaf.[cclxv]

The still-gushing and newly feted Dr. Tillie Lewis told Rosie Munoz that she believed Rosie was clever enough to teach laboratory skills at UOP. Rosie reminded Tillie that she, too, would need a degree of some kind to move ahead in life. Within the week, Tillie Lewis Foods had assigned Rosie Munoz time off, with pay, to take the required laboratory-microscope courses at the University of California at Berkeley. Rosie easily passed the exams in both food chemistry and hematology[114] Rosie continued with a few Berkeley

---

114 Hematology is the branch of medicine concerned with the study, diagnosis, treatment, and prevention of diseases related to blood.

classes to become certified in microorganisms and solid consistencies in food products at Berkeley's Food Processors Institute. The collegiate fees were paid for by Tillie Lewis. Rosie continued to work her shifts for TLF and became Professor Rosie Munoz in her off hours, where she taught microscopy as an adjunct professor at various colleges in the area.

Rosie was tempted by the local hospitals to teach and work in hematology/microbiology at a substantially higher wage, but she would never formally leave Mrs. Lewis after all her boss had done for her. Mrs. Lewis had contributed enormously to the prosperity of the entire Munoz family and to numerous others. They now owned proper homes and lived decent lives from the opportunities that Tillie Lewis had provided—so much so that Mrs. Lewis was mentioned daily in family prayers. Such was the love for Mrs. Lewis.

TOP-TEN LADIES MUST PROVE IT

Describing Tillie as the "Mite with Seven-League Boots" and the "Queen of Success," *Fortune* magazine declared Tillie to be one of the ten-highest-ranking women in big business. The magazine had three criteria for placing a woman in the top ten: (1) she must work at or own a *Forbes* directory company; (2) she must be active in the company's day-to-day affairs; and (3) she must earn more than $30,000 in personal income. Every woman in the running for the top ten of 1973 was a multimillionaire in her own right. That didn't matter. *Forbes* magazine knew that even women executives earned less money than their male peers, so the personal income bar was lowered to $30,000 and up for those of the fairer sex. This was a hot topic of Mrs. Lewis's speaking tours. The $30,000 and up was based upon the fallacy that "few women could actually be an independent millionaire earning huge sums of money in 1973."

Gentlemen, the superwomen were already there and at the top of several major organizations, businesses, and governments around the world. Several ladies—Tillie Lewis of Tillie Lewis Foods and Ogden Corporation; Mary Wells Lawrence, advertising chair (America's highest-paid woman at the time); Mala Rubinstein of Helena Rubinstein Cosmetics; Katherine

Graham, president of the *Washington Post*; and Olive Ann Beech, chair of Beech Aircraft, to name a few—were the bar-raising, glass-ceiling-breaking movers and shakers of their day.

A DAY IN THE LIFE OF RETIRED TILLIE

On September 13, the sort-of-retired Tillie had to get to work. She told the newspapers, "I guess I'm retired. I am no longer at work between five and six a.m. I don't need to get to work until seven or eight a.m." This day was another jam-packed Ogden tour of the TLF Cannery Operations Division and the Ogden Corporation board meeting.

The point that Mrs. Lewis was stressing in this meeting was that she was still making top-quality products at the lowest possible costs with ongoing increases in production. Tillie paid attention to what variety of tomato yielded the most fruit and was the simplest to peel. Since day one, Tillie and her company had been on the alert for new equipment and technologies. Nothing had changed for Tillie since she'd begun the business in 1934/1935 with her "everything should be ready to change, advance, improve" philosophy.

Tillie wrote in her notes for the meeting agenda that her plans, both on the drawing board and at the conceptual stage, indicated no leveling off of TLF's productivity; the company would continue to increase productivity (and thus profits) for the immediate future.

Tillie's agenda for the day was a booklet that covered every movement of all the people involved in the busy day. She allowed fifteen minutes to de-board guests from the airplanes, fifteen minutes to arrive at each stop, except for the fifty minutes for luncheon. Once delivered back to the airplanes, at the day's end, the guests were each gifted with TLF products and local wines to enjoy on the plane with engraved note cards indicating their handsome TLF gift baskets had already been delivered to their wives at home. Tillie's message to Ogden Corporation was clear. She was not to be overlooked. Tillie Lewis, the Tomato Queen, was still alive and well.

TILLIE OF THE VALLEY

On January 6, Ruth Winter of the *San Francisco Examiner* interviewed Tillie. Winter wrote the following snippets:

* They call her Tillie of the Valley. She is probably one of the most successful business women America has produced in this century and she gave me some advice for woman with their eye on their own executive suite.

* It has [already] been done. It can be done. It's easier to do today than it was yesterday...

* A woman has to be five times as good as a man to get one-fifth the recognition, but it can be done.

* Don't compete [with any man]; work with [everyone],

* Don't give [a man] orders. Discuss a point. Ask for his opinion. Never ask a man "Do you understand [a vital point you are making]?

* Ask if you spoke too fast. Repeat it politely.

* If a man makes a pass, don't recognize it [i.e., don't react]. Never accept an inappropriate romantic invitation in the workplace.

* Be a good listener but a short answerer. Don't small talk during your business day.

* Never handle the same piece of paper twice. Make a decision to act or discard a decision the first time you see it.

* Admit when you are wrong.

* Finger pointing, finding blame, is a waste of time.

The public relations person, Sandy Black, advised various television, radio, and speaking boards to choose Mrs. Lewis as a personality for public appearances. She said,

Since her service to the country and appointment by US Vice-President Hubert H. Humphrey as first female representative on behalf of the United States to a summit on global hunger in Rome, Tillie has been campaigning on television and radio on behalf of something aside from her own company and self-interest. The new and improved Tillie Lewis would maintain a "thematic approach" to her speeches and interviews. The theme was: 1) encourage farmers to increase their crop supplies; 2) [ensure] that such supplies are managed and distributed properly.

Sandy Black and Colleen Dorfman of PRB Public Relations felt that Tillie "was already versed and rehearsed in other ideas and solutions to the world food crisis. Tillie Lewis now cared about saving the world from hunger was a new story that needed to be told."[cclxvi] On April 2, 1974, Tillie's *Los Angeles Herald Examiner* article, "America's Fabulous Self-Made Women," explained some of her business tenets:

> One principle is that if you want your business to grow, you must help your people grow, too. Kindness begets kindness. Two, call me a square, or is it a prude? I never let a man see me as anything more or less than a woman. Men would sometimes come [into my] office and pass a light joke of a sexual nature, [and] I wouldn't move a muscle. Men would ask me for a drink after work and I'd always [pretend to] have something else to do. I may have missed a little fun, but I surely missed a lot more problems by keeping business just business.

On May 28, Tillie delivered a speech at Stockton's Outstanding Student Award Luncheon with the theme "Common Sense Citizens Needed." She said that it was 100 percent their responsibility "to achieve your dreams. Minimize your risks by doing the work, the research, and asking questions toward getting what you want out of life." She took her own advice by requesting at least a street to be named after her in Stockton. She made that request call to Arthur Heiser from her car on her newly installed Motorola car phone. It was black and massive, and it had a normal handset, which pleased Mrs. Lewis, since others could clearly see the Tomato Queen using a telephone from the backseat of her chauffeured limousine.

Children from the streets of South Stockton awaiting the ice cream man were some of the first to catch a glimpse of the latest thing in technology. As one bystander recalled,

> "Just a white lady in a fancy car would have caught our attention, but we nearly forgot about our frozen malted-milk cups and orange push-up ice-creams seeing Tillie Lewis talking on a telephone and waving at us, slowly driving by on that hot August day. No, we'd never seen anything like it!"[cclxvii]

Albert Heiser put in the request to the city of Stockton to change the name of Kern Street to Tillie Lewis Drive as a tribute to his aunt, but the city denied the honorary name change. The city of Stockton was not interested in renaming any street as an honor on behalf of the woman who not only employed much of the citizenry, at one time or another, but who also owned most of the land and the buildings in the area. Heiser was given the appropriate forms and fee charts to petition for a paid name change. He complied with the requests, and fees, but he requested that reporters not be informed that the change of name was anything other than an honor that was long overdue to Mrs. Lewis.

Tillie hired professional photographers for the unveiling and dedication of the street, invited the appropriate dignitaries, hosted her own reception, and created and distributed the copies for official publication: "Tillie Lewis, Food Leader, Honored by Street Name Change in Stockton, California." The publication continued by saying that by May of 1975, Tillie Lewis would have opened a $3.3 million, sixty-three-thousand-square-foot labeling and distributing center for bottles and cans, which would be the largest one-story structure in Stockton and would employ about two hundred local people.[cclxvii]

Tillie feigned a blush when the city of Stockton did show up with the proper fanfare and at least made the pretense of a genuine fuss. The city officials performed a proper unveiling and changed the street name in front of the first Flotill plant to "Tillie Lewis Drive." She wore an enormous orchid corsage she'd given herself, which she'd carefully pinned to her stunning new leopard coat.[115]

The TLF-sponsored event later served a sumptuous buffet at the Lewis mansion, complete with a cake that Tillie had designed that replicated the signage on the new Tillie Lewis Drive—further proof that if you really want a thing done, do it yourself.

An interview in the *Cosmopolitan* article "36 Women with Real Power Who Can Help You" discussed Tillie (with the title of "Consultant"). The issue featured Farrah Fawcett on the cover. The article reminded readers that Tillie's name on a label signified taste and quality, but to those who knew her best, her success was the reward for her daring and perseverance and had made her a millionaire. The article then quoted Tillie at length:

> "Nobody thought the Italian Pomodoro tomato could be grown in this country," the married 71-year-old executive says today. "I had very little money then, but I wrote to universities in Naples, Rome and California to get the studies of soil, wind and rain. I practically lived in the library before going to Europe to investigate the Pomodoro firsthand. Then I brought [it] back home…Back then, it was next to impossible for a woman to get a bank loan. Today you can get a lot of help—both financial and research—if you are dedicated…Self-discipline is the secret of success with your own company. College isn't essential…It is [100 percent your] responsibility. You've got to really want it, but [any] field is wide open for all."

---

115 Tillie was informed that leopard was officially on the endangered species list. She never wore the coat in public again.

Chapter 17

MERV GRIFFIN, VAN CLIBURN, INTERNATIONAL WOMAN OF THE YEAR, AND MEYER LEWIS IS GONE

Tillie joined Merv Griffin on his nationally broadcasted television show; her appearance was shown on local stations on September 2, 1975, at 6:30 p.m. Tillie spoke to Merv and his vast television audience about her campaign against world hunger.[cclxix]

Tillie Lewis—a tireless spokeswoman and the foremost expert of meticulous preparation of diet-oriented foods, appears with Merv Griffin in your market...Mrs. Lewis [is] considered by *Fortune* magazine [to be] one of the premiere women in industry. She and Mr. Griffin, daytime's number one attraction, are the perfect choice to get the story [of world hunger] across. Mrs. Lewis's deep concern for the world's hungry and her determination to do something about it finds a ready listener and another helping hand with the compassionate side of Merv...The show ranges from peeled Italian-style tomato production to diet-food engineering in the delightful free-flowing style of Merv Griffin at his best. Mrs. Lewis keeps Merv down to earth and right on track. Together, they tell the story of Tillie Lewis Foods. Tune in. You'll profit by it.[cclxx]

VAN CLIBURN

Tillie actively supported the arts in the Stockton area. She helped to bring local theater and music to life with regular contributions to art exhibits, concerts, and community theatre. When local committees set their sights a little higher—first with the hope of bringing the world-famous pianist Van Cliburn (Harvey Lavan "Van" Cliburn Jr.) to play and later to bring the opera star Beverly Sills to sing for the citizens of Stockton—they turned their hopes to Tillie Lewis. If she could add a "spark of community enthusiasm," Van Cliburn would be performing with the Stockton Symphony, thanks to Tillie.

The "spark" they refer to was the $8,000 needed to pay the pianist. Popular rumor was that Tillie, standing in public at another charity event in February, had demurely deferred to her husband, asking him to be kind enough to give the Stockton Symphony a few dollars for the fund.[cclxxi] Meyer reportedly reached into his pocket and dramatically pulled out a money clip with exactly the $8,000 needed to put on the performance, much to the surprise of the elite ladies' clubs of Stockton. The actual $8,000 check from TLF arrived on Valentine's Day, addressed to Beverly Fitch McCarthy, president of the SSA.

Fitch McCarthy states in a letter dated that same day, "The Stockton Symphony is most grateful for your generous donation of $8,000 to sponsor Van Cliburn...There is no question that this event will mark one of the greatest contributions to our community's musical history."[cclxxii]

The truth was that Meyer was often in financial need of loans from his wife for this or that, including various gin rummy debts. That $8,000 was Tillie's. On October 12, 1975, Fitch McCarthy sent Tillie and Meyer a letter informing them that the SSA had unanimously voted to make the Lewises honorary members of their board of directors for their contributions to the symphony. Ms. Fitch McCarthy stated, "Your names will be added to the four-other people ever to receive such [a] designation in the orchestra's history."[cclxxiii]

INTERNATIONAL WOMAN OF THE YEAR

San Joaquin County voted Tillie the "International Woman of the Year [1975]." As such, San Joaquin Delta College thanked Tillie for being its keynote speaker for the "In Celebration of Women" banquet. Fitch McCarthy, joined by two of her colleagues, wrote, "There is little doubt in our minds that your name, and all the wonderful things that you are, filled the banquet room to generous proportions...You represent a fine role model for women who are interested in executive positions. One does not need to be told that she thinks like a man when there are fine executive women such as yourself to emulate."

Settled in at her suite at the Waldorf Astoria, Tillie spoke to *Guideposts* magazine's Richard Schneider about her faith in God and about God's guidance. A year later, the magazine sent her the story for approval, a self-addressed stamped envelope, and a one-hundred-dollar check.[cclxxiv] As far as she was concerned, Tillie was scraping the bottom of her connections barrel to keep some attention upon her. She'd grown addicted to it.

Whenever she was in town, Tillie frequented the local synagogue, Temple Israel. In the old days, all eyes were always on her. What was she wearing? Look at her hair! Now, fellow worshippers complained that Tillie would arrive more than fashionably late and feign some form of distress to announce her arrival. As Helene Heiser recalled, "Tillie would huff and puff in a struggle to remove a massive fur coat or tap loudly with her shoe on the pew, as if she was knocking mud off her custom-designer high heels. Anything to get the congregation to acknowledge that she'd arrived."[cclxxv]

LET'S DO LUNCH

One day, Tillie was schmoozing with Sylvia Ablon at the Ablon family's Park Avenue address in New York. Sylvia's husband, Ralph, was the CEO of Ogden Corporation and had technically been Tillie's first boss in a very long time. Showing off, in case the Ablons didn't get the Van Cliburn and Merv Griffin memo, Tillie promised "to get the information about the bracelets, just for fun" while she enclosed information about the Van Cliburn concert she'd just provided for the citizens of San Joaquin in addition to an article about the Merv Griffin show starring Tillie from a few weeks before. Kowtowing at this juncture of her life had to have made Tillie Lewis slightly ill.

On December 3, Tillie jotted a brief note to UOP president, Dr. McCaffrey, to inform him of a party she was throwing herself as an official Ogden board member to celebrate her fortieth anniversary in the food business. She lamented that she couldn't send McCaffrey the official resolution of her board status in its "lovely framed copy." Tillie wanted McCaffrey to save the date, since she and Meyer were "leaving on Saturday for the Orient and perhaps all around [the globe]."cclxxvi Tillie Lewis was running out of people, and newspapers, to brag to. This would be their grand finale. Meyer Lewis arranged all the special accommodations to make it as special a tour as he could for his ego-deflated wife. If the United States was weary of the "Tales of Tillie," then he'd have her on the front pages in Asia and Europe.

Written in Chinese, a copy arrived of the Taiwan version of the Tillie Lewis "rags to riches" story. Sun Wave and Trading Company, importer/exporter of Taipei, Taiwan, Republic of China, sent a letter of congratulations to Tillie. The story had been published in the largest business magazine/paper in Taiwan. Tillie attached a thank-you note to Elaine Dun of the Stockton Public Library for kindly translating the Chinese story for her. Tillie Lewis was not about to have articles in the world unapproved by her just because they weren't written in English.cclxxvii The same went for front-page articles in the papers of Denmark, Germany, and Japan that thanked Tillie for being an inspiration to men and women by refusing to submit to the circumstances of her childhood misfortunes and for reaching her dreams.[116]

Meyer and Tillie were months into the "all around" the world tour when Meyer fell ill. Seriously ill.

Tillie flew her failing husband on the Ogden Corporation private plane, with a nurse in attendance, to New York, where he lay for three weeks. His doctors misdiagnosed meningitis as a stroke. By the time the true nature of the illness was discovered, Meyer's nervous system was fried—he was comatose. They tried a few desperate measures, such as steroids. The family was summoned.

---

[116] The translations, in Chinese and Danish, are both "Thank you. You are an inspiration, Tillie."

Tillie was sitting with her unconscious husband, noticeably upset. Both of Meyer's sons, Bob and Bill, flew to New York. Bill left a few days after the doctors gave up hope. Bob had a lot of emotional unfinished business to do with his father, however, and remained stead-fast until the seventy-two-year-old Meyer Lewis died, on July 31, 1976.[cclxxviii]

Dr. Fred Plum treated Meyer at New York Hospital's Cornell Medical Center. He wrote Tillie after reviewing Meyer's autopsy.

A synopsis of the detailed, gory, report confirmed a terrible meningitis and that it was certainly a blessing, for Meyer, that he did not suffer...Let me tell you again what a pleasure it was knowing you here in New York. I was only sorry that the circumstances were so unhappy for you and your family.
Sincerely,
Fred Plum, MD[cclxxix]

Bob Lewis flew back on the Ogden Corporation private jet with his father's body for burial in Stockton. Stockton's Rabbi Rosenberg's eulogy correctly summed up Meyer Lewis, saying that "Meyer enjoyed life and contributed that joy of life to all around him."[cclxxx] Bill Lewis later wrote to say, "At the funeral, Tillie walked up to the coffin and slumped on it, saying what sounded like, 'Why? Why?' She wasn't sobbing. She might have been angry that he left her—or maybe it was for show. There was a reception back at 740 Willow Street. Albert Heiser was cracking jokes. Everyone was drinking and loud."[cclxxxi]

Bill approached Tillie privately to discuss an Israeli stamp collection his father had been amassing for years that he'd promised to Bill. Tillie said she knew nothing about such a collection. Meyer's sons asked Tillie what had been left to them. Her curt answer was, "Enough for a bottle of champagne."

Tillie was aware that Meyer had not left anything to her, and that was fine. Her will didn't leave anything to him, either. What was not fine was the way the will was worded. Tillie had expected the will to state, "I leave nothing to my *dear* wife, Tillie." Instead it said only, "I leave nothing to my wife, Tillie."

According to Bill Lewis, the perceived insult of leaving out the "dear" led the Tomato Queen to lash out at Meyer after his death by "calling all of Meyer's outstanding loans and gin rummy debts." The Lewises, led by a relation of Meyer's, began groundwork toward a lawsuit against Tillie Lewis on behalf of the heirs of Meyer Lewis.

This was kept secret, however, and was intended for implementation after the death of Tillie herself, since some of Meyer's relations were still on Tillie's payroll. It wouldn't pay to cross the Tomato Queen during life.[cclxxxii] Meyer's estate was valued at $460,000. Tillie was firm in her belief that her late husband had been in debt to Tillie Lewis Foods since the 1947 Tucker car deal and that he still owed the company $233,000 at the time of his death. Meyer's two sons never enjoyed Tillie's promised bottle of champagne. She welched on the deal. The boys did split the remaining monies.

As a human being, Meyer was a joy to be around. He was fun, clever, spontaneous, and a terrific public-relations man. Meyer fell short at every personal business venture he tried. Between the Tucker cars, the date farm, and the import-export company he'd started near the end of his life, Meyer lost every dime he ever invested, but he had a wonderful time.[cclxxxiii]

Chapter 18

LEAVING A LEGACY, GLOBAL HUNGER,
MAGAZINES, AND BEVERLY SILLS

In a confessional note to Tillie's secretary from the *Modesto Bee* colum-
nist Margaret Kreiss for a lengthy interview assignment about the Tomato
Queen to be released five days later, Ms. Kreiss admitted that she "enjoyed
meeting with Mrs. Lewis very much...I was petrified when I got the assign-
ment, and tried to get out of it. I don't know anything about the industry...
Tell TL she has been voted 'Mogul of the year' around here...If I ever get to
Palm Springs, I'll collect the martini [Tillie offered] or settle for coffee in
Stockton."cclxxxiv

The nervousness at meeting the Tomato Queen and lack of subject knowledge showed in Ms. Kreiss's piece. The article appeared on Sunday, February
8, 1976, in the *Modesto Bee* and was titled "A Tycoon's Grim View: Tillie
Lewis Fears Hunger in a World She Has Helped Feed." A portion of it read,
"Tillie Lewis is not one of your garden-variety tycoons. She sits in the office
of her 350-acre establishment and worries about world hunger. Mrs. Lewis
pointed her finger like an inquisitor [and asked], 'Do you realize that while
we are sitting here in this room, thousands of people are starving to death all
over the world? We in this country, along with other responsible nations, have

made a great effort in the past, but we're going to have to do a lot more [to feed the starving].'"

It was a two-page photo article that Tillie strove to hit home with advice, statistics and plans for global food production and population control. Ms. Kreiss began and ended the interview with, "Can you tell us all how do you peel a tomato?" Tillie tried to evade the silly question throughout the interview. Tillie had grown passionate about the global hunger situation since her tenure at the Rome Conferences on behalf of the the US. However, at the interviews end the Tomato Queen reluctantly relented, "How do I peel a tomato? I peel them just like you do. Just plunge the tomato into scalding water for a second or two, start at the top, and peel it down. No problem."

TILLIE LEWIS WAS STILL GROWING

The *Stockton Record* proclaimed that Tillie Lewis had two processing plants in Stockton, one in Modesto, and one in Antioch, but Tillie Lewis, the little tomato that could, was still chugging along and had completed a $3.3 million distribution center off Kern Street in Stockton. At three-blocks long by three-blocks wide, the behemoth was the Central Valley's largest single-story structure.

Tillie began to reflect seriously upon her legacy. It seemed impossible, but there was a chance she might not live forever either. She had Arthur Heiser petition the district to christen a building at San Joaquin Delta College the "Tillie Lewis Theatre."

On March 31, Tillie officially applied to win the, aforementioned, 1977 Horatio Alger Award. Norman Vincent Peale was the chairman of that year's committee. She'd met the Reverend Peale—the famous author of *The Power of Positive Thinking*—several times in the past. They shared the same circle of optimistic entrepreneurs, speakers, and associates. Since the Horatio Alger Award honored self-made Americans who came from rags to riches;

established excellence in their endeavors; and held a belief in hard work, honesty, self-reliance, and perseverance over obstacles,[cclxxxv] Tillie felt she should be a shoo-in.

Tillie's secretary, Alilea Martin, went diligently to work obtaining the requirements. She began with the top two:

1. Send a biography of the applicant's struggle from childhood to success to the individual's professional publicity/PR contact for additional information.

2. Public relations. Team Tillie was trying hard to convince the city of Stockton to voluntarily name a building after her. Despite the financial contributions she'd made to music and theater, having the new San Joaquin Delta College theater named in her honor was a steep hill to climb.

LIFE MAGAZINE SPECIAL REPORT

Before Tillie and Meyer set off for what was to be his farewell holiday in April of 1976, Tillie had been nominated for an amazing honor: the United States was celebrating its bicentennial, and *Time* magazine selected Tillie to be part of the magazine's special report on "Remarkable American Women 1776–1976." Tillie approved the article and photograph prior to the trip. It was published while they were on vacation and hit the newsstands on July 4, Meyer's seventy-second birthday. Tillie was glad Meyer enjoyed this special birthday gift along with all the favorite treats he knew she'd "surprise" him with. For the bicentennial issue of *Life*, the editors saluted 166 American women "as independent spirits who broke free from passive, home-hugging stereotypes and made a difference in American life." Alongside Susan B. Anthony, Abigail Adams, Eleanor Roosevelt, Janis Joplin, Angela Davis, Barbara Walters, and 160 other American women both famous and infamous was Tillie Lewis.[cclxxxvi]

She got ahead
by knowing
her tomatoes

Tillie Lewis

Tillie Lewis dropped out of high
school at 15 to marry a Brooklyn grocer. The marriage soon failed, but
not before she had learned her
tomatoes—namely, that the pear-
shaped variety which gives good spaghetti sauce its tang had to be
imported from Italy. Tillie kept wondering why this tomato couldn't
be grown in the U.S. In 1934, at age
30, she went to Italy and persuaded
a prominent Italian tomato packer
to provide her with $10,000 in
financing, four bags of seed and six
used vacuum kettles to process the re-
sulting tomatoes. After convincing
skeptical California farmers
that the seeds would grow, she installed the kettles at Stockton
(left). Her tomatoes thrived, and her
kettles became the nucleus of a
food-processing enterprise with annual sales of $145 million.

*Holding a miniature model of one of her 1935 tomato-processing
kettles, Tillie Lewis posed in front of the original in 1975.* 1964 STEVE SCHAPIRO

Tillie Lewis was selected by *Life* magazine for a list of remarkable American women from 1776 to 1976 for America's bicentennial birthday celebration on July 4, 1976. Tillie was featured alongside Susan B. Anthony, Abigail Adams, Eleanor Roosevelt, Janis Joplin, Angela Davis, Barbara Walters, and 160 others.

Now that she had the attention of the country, Tillie still did not tell the world how she was the first woman president of a new food-processing industry she'd begun during the Great Depression, that she'd developed the first diet-product line, that she was the nation's first female port commissioner, that she'd worked to fight world hunger as a US delegate in Rome, or that she'd been the first woman on the board of a major conglomerate. Instead, she told readers her tired old tale, including the usual fib about her age. *Life* reported on July 4, 1976:

> She got ahead by knowing her tomatoes…Tillie Lewis dropped out of high school at fifteen to marry a Brooklyn grocer. The marriage soon failed, but not before she had learned her tomatoes—namely, that the pear-shaped variety which gives good spaghetti sauce its

tang had to be imported from Italy. In 1934, at age 30, she went to Italy and persuaded a prominent Italian tomato packer to provide her with $10,000 in financing, four bags of seed and six used vacuum kettles to process the resulting tomatoes…After convincing skeptical California farmers that the seeds would grow, she installed the kettles at Stockton. Her tomatoes thrived and her kettles became the nucleus of a food processing enterprise with [annual sales] of $145 million.

As one byproduct of her Horatio Alger Award campaign, *Who's Who of American Women* interviewed Tillie on May 3, 1976. Her familiar story of Florindo Del Gaizo gifting her the *pomodoro* business, no strings attached, included few revisions. Tillie was running out of fresh material, and still the awards continued to pile up.

BEVERLY SILLS—OPERA IN STOCKTON

Tillie sat front and center. The seat next to her was for Meyer. She left it empty to remind Stockton of her recent loss. Rosie Munoz later said,

> I made so many good friends at Tillie Lewis Foods, I felt bad that Mrs. Lewis seemed so alone. Right after Mr. Lewis died, Beverly Sills, the opera star, was singing here in Stockton, paid for by the Lewises, and Mrs. Lewis was sitting in the front row with her late husband's empty seat next to her. It was so sad that Mrs. Lewis had so much here in Stockton, but not any friends. During intermission, I went and sat with her. Tillie was seething after the third round of prolonged applause. For goodness sake, she'd footed most of the bill to bring Ms. Sills to Stockton. Where was Tillie's applause? Tillie grumbled to me, "What was making music one night in a lifetime compared to putting food on their tables and roofs over their heads seven days a week?"
>
> I patted her hand and told her she looked beautiful. Then I nodded toward Mr. Lewis's vacant seat and said how sorry I was.
>
> Mrs. Lewis had tears in her eyes as she thanked me for my thoughtfulness."

One observer named Vince Perrin (of the *Stockton Record*) did not notice the empty seat front and center. As he remembered the event,

> The great American diva Beverly Sills once delighted an audience during a Stockton Symphony concert at the old Stockton Junior High School auditorium. Not a seat was empty that night.
>
> The orchestra, conducted by Kyung-Soo Won, reveled in an evening of opera overtures and arias sung by Sills, then in her prime and here at the behest of her Stockton friends, Henry and Judy Brewster… Capping the concert was a duet between the famed coloratura and Caryl May Scott, the symphony's first-chair flute player who retired recently. Their instruments, a voice and a flute, sang incandescently as one. Afterward in the lobby, Sills greeted fans with kindly chosen words, a joking remark, her hearty laugh…[cclxxxvii]

NATIONAL GEOGRAPHIC MAGAZINE

Gazing as if lost in happy memories, Tillie Lewis was featured in *National Geographic* in her sumptuous Stockton mansion's music room at her ornate and antique French marquetry Steinway piano laden with Tiffany treasures, including a photo of the recently deceased Meyer Lewis. Tillie wore a silk brocade dress that complemented the color of the Steinway, her triple-strand pearl necklace against the background of olive-green draperies and wallpaper that made her auburn hair glisten. Her hands rested lightly on top of the piano that she had no idea how to play.

Wrapping up her self-promotional year, Tillie had proven just how determined she was to be on the "Inquiring Minds" of all Americans when she chatted with the infamous and sensationalist checkout-line paper the *National Inquirer*. On the same pages that promise, "Your Neighbor Is from Outer Space" and "Half-Fish Man Fired for Shedding Scales," Tillie is one of the only actual humans in the December 7, 1976, issue. Some of the quotes in the article included the following:

* "Common sense and dedication can propel a woman to the top in business… [along with] hard work, dedication and patience."
* "In 1930, people were dubious about success for a woman."
* "I knew what I wanted to do and I made it work."
* "I didn't sit around waiting for opportunity. I made my own opportunities, and they paid off."

The article went on to report:

Today the company has 5,500 employees with 1976 sales expected to hit $145 million. Mrs. Lewis is mostly retired, [and] her nephew, Arthur Heiser, is president of Tillie Lewis Foods. She now sleeps in, no longer arriving at the plant before 6:00 a.m. She usually strolls in an hour later, at 7:00, to oversee business affairs at TLF and the Ogden Corporation, speaking engagements and charity events she is deeply involved with…Mrs. Lewis joined the multibillion dollar New York Ogden Corporation conglomerate in 1966 as the lone woman on the fifteen-member board…Ogden vice-president, Stanley Frankel said, "We have nothing but praise for Mrs. Lewis as a person and proficient businesswoman."

Chapter 19

FADE TO BLACK: THE FINAL BOW

Vince Perrin of the *Stockton Record* wrote the "Critic's Choice" column for the paper. On January 3, 1977, Mr. Perrin commented, "A year ago last fall [Tillie] paid the bill that brought pianist Van Cliburn to Stockton. Last fall her check helped bring soprano Beverly Sills here. Last week she gave a $500 grant to the Stockton Arts Commission. Is there no way to repay the generosity of Tillie Lewis?"[cclxxxviii] A few weeks later, on January 26, Tillie became the first woman to be inducted into the Canners League Hall of Fame. Tillie dictated her first-draft introduction to Alilea Martin:

> I have always said that common sense is the key to success in business. I believe that you must listen and obtain all of the facts before reaching any business decision; then, whatever your decision, limit your risk. In addition, you should treat all those with whom you come in contact, whether employees or business associates, with courtesy and consideration. With regard to life, I would say first, is my love of God—love of my fellow man—love of service to my fellow man—and above all, give love and help to all children.

NATIONAL SECRETARY'S DAY

On Wednesday, April 27, Mrs. Lewis's secretary, Alilea Martin, was preparing information for Tillie's afternoon meeting with author Caroline Bird's husband; the author intended to include Tillie in her compilation book entitled *Enterprising Women*. Tillie and Caroline Bird had crisscrossed the nation since August of 1974, always missing each other. Carolyn and Tillie were corresponding with questions and answers through the mail. In 1975, Tillie thanked Carolyn for a copy of a rough draft that Tillie "corrected because the facts were incorrect."[cclxxxix] Tillie extended an invitation to Mrs. Bird to stop in at Tillie's suite at the Waldorf Astoria while Tillie had business in New York. Tillie hoped that this would be an important, extensive interview for the "Tillie fame" project. Tillie discovered that, as in other compilations of accomplished women, Tillie would merely be mentioned, along with fifty other women. More disappointing, Tillie's story was relegated to a short chapter about the women of World War II. For over two years of book discussion to devolve into a few pages about a brief period in her career, Tillie agreed to speak to the author's husband, Mr. Bird since this wasn't the press Tillie was hoping for.

Before meeting with Mr. Bird, Tillie was already booked. Normally, Alilea Martin would have driven Tillie to her 6:30 a.m. speaking engagement at Stockton's Holiday Inn. Instead, local businesswoman, Marion Jacobs[ccxc] was playing chauffer du jour. Marion was a woman who had deeply admired Mrs. Lewis when Marion was a teenager. Marion wasn't a teenager anymore; she was a prominent entrepreneur herself. And she had a multitude of other things to do besides drive Tillie Lewis around. While Marion navigated, Tillie Lewis rechecked her teeth for traces of errant lipstick in her fourteen-karat, gold-engraved compact. Satisfied, Tillie snapped the monogrammed case closed, placed it into her handbag, and straightened both her dress and her posture. She mouthed the first few lines of her well-rehearsed speech.

It was National Secretaries Day. Marion made a mental bet that Tillie would rehash her "women have been brainwashed by men" lecture. Marion mused that she could give the darn speech herself, she had heard it so often—as had most of the ladies who lunched in Stockton.

Marion escorted the beaming Mrs. Lewis to the center of the head table, ushered in by polite applause, before Marion selected a seat near the back of the room; there Marion greeted the ladies she knew while sipping coffee and picking at a raspberry-cheese Danish. It would likely be a long, dull morning for Marion Jacobs.

At the dais, without further ado, Tillie began her usual prattle about her brush with fate and a pear-shaped tomato that was, according to Tillie, pre-ordained by God himself. Meanwhile, Marion was enjoying eavesdropping in on a catty commentary about "so and so being in the company of what's-his-name, while you-know-what was going on."

Tillie verbally faltered, saying "…and ladies, ladies, um…" Marion heard the normally unflappable Tillie Lewis fumble her familiar tale. Noticing Tillie's features darken, Marion was certain Tillie had grimaced, then stammered, while pointing directly at the side of her head and motioning distress.

Marion scurried to Tillie's side as the industrialist mewed a thank-you to the audience and leaned into Marion with a barely audible, "Get me out of here—I have a horrible headache." Holding her head in her hands, Tillie cried that her head was pounding like she'd never felt in her life. Marion raced Tillie to the limousine and rushed to Dameron Hospital and the emergency entrance.

Mrs. Lewis was slumped face-first, neck bent and contorted, against the passenger door. Marion began to honk the horn and shout for help yards before she braked to a stop. Marion extracted the keys from the ignition and rounded the car, feeling less than helpless as the emergency staff expeditiously placed Mrs. Lewis onto a gurney and sped her inside. Marion breathlessly caught up with them.

Weakened and vulnerable for the first time in her adult life the empress of agribusiness humbly beseeched Marion, "Please stay with me." With her eyes fluttering in pain and despair, Tillie offered a frail grasp of her bejeweled hand. Tillie Lewis fell silent. Marion was destined to stand guard until somebody—anybody—else would arrive. Desperately, Marion beseeched in alarm, "Somebody come remove Mrs. Lewis's jewelry!"[ccxci]

A bystander named Helen Thomas noticed the commotion of an incoming emergency. She scurried to the ER to catch the action. She heard someone say, "It's Tillie Lewis!" She strained her neck over whispering gawkers to see that it was indeed Tillie Lewis, lying motionless on a gurney. Marion Jacobs, stood patting Tillie's hand while semihysterically shouting for somebody to do something about her jewelry. Anybody who remotely knew Tillie Lewis could only imagine what hell one would have to pay when Mrs. Lewis recovered if something sparkly had gone missing.

Helen, a member of the theatre and art's associations of Stockton, would busy herself planning the perfect get-well bouquet to deliver to Tillie during visiting hours. Tillie Lewis would surely expect a hospital suite with floral tributes floor to ceiling, each gaudier than the next. Tillie Lewis was the antithesis of a lady, in Helen's mind. Most of the staff and volunteers figured that Tillie Lewis had finally fainted from the exertion that resulted from climbing some always-lengthening ladder of success.[117]

It truly wasn't unkindness that permeated the emergency room; Tillie Lewis actually being at death's door had simply not occurred to anyone.

Meanwhile, Alilea Martin picked up her phone at Tillie Lewis Foods, anticipating the boss's fastidious list of reminders to ready herself for the afternoon's meeting with the husband of Caroline Bird. Alilea had Mrs. Lewis's life story organized into dozens of files. She was well aware of the importance of the "variation slants" necessary for each circumstance and publication. She knew that a Jewish version and a Christian version would require revisions that Mrs. Lewis would wish to review. Alilea had had her proverbial hand slapped before and was not likely to send anything Tillie-related out for publication without Mrs. Lewis's personal approval *with* signature.

"Tillie Lewis's office, Mrs. Martin speaking," Alilea brightly chirped.

"Thank God, Mrs. Martin...this is Marion Jacobs. I'm at Dameron Hospital...Mrs. Lewis has had a stroke, and there's no one coming!"

---

117 Phone interview with anonymous source. An amalgam of names is used in place of the actual sources.

Alilea stood frozen and pressed the phone closer to her ear, as if pushing the instrument into her head would somehow transform this surreal message. Surely she must have misheard the statement. Nearly shouting at Jacobs, she said, "Miss Jacobs, did you say Mrs. Lewis is in the hospital?"

"Yes, they've taken her away, nobody's come, and I need to leave. The emergency staff has her jewelry; I was very careful to watch them; they have all her things. Please come and get them as soon as you can. I'm sorry. Dameron Hospital—please come." The line went dead.

Struck dumb as if she'd been sucker punched, Alilea had no idea how long she held the silent phone. Competent, capable, and loyal, Alilea collected herself, placed the receiver into its cradle, and ran, giving no thought to what the rest of the office staff might be thinking.

Alilea Martin would have no knowledge of how long she had been at the hospital and how many phone calls she made or to whom. She loved Mrs. Lewis and would do whatever was required or necessary. She efficiently placed the bulky envelope full of valuables into Mrs. Lewis's crocodile handbag and sat waiting for somebody to tell her that Mrs. Lewis was awake and ready to receive visitors.

Alilea stopped at the nurse's station to let the staff know that she'd be in the gift shop for a few moments selecting a bouquet and a get-well card, or grabbing a quick coffee in the cafeteria when Mrs. Lewis's family arrived.[118]

Meanwhile, Arthur and Albert Heiser were out of town attending a canner's convention in Santa Barbara with their wives when Tillie fell ill. They would not know of Tillie's condition until late Thursday evening, when they received Alilea Martin's urgent message. Since it was commonplace to be disturbed on a pleasure trip or a vacation by a host of their aunt's major to minor emergencies, it was glorious to have distance as a reason to ignore Chips and her minions. Chips had not actually been "the boss" for quite some time, but it wouldn't be prudent to remind her of that fact.[ccxcii]

Mrs. Martin's repeated phone calls to the Santa Barbara hotel went unanswered. The Dameron staff was polite but unyielding regarding hospital

---

118 Anonymous interview with the author, as well as a phone interview with the sister of Alilea Martin.

policy that ICU patients could be visited only by immediate family. Weary and reluctant, Alilea finally just went home.

On April 30, 1977, Tillie was expected at 9:45 a.m. to chair a panel discussion designed with the older female worker in mind for Stockton's American Association of University Women. Tillie's group discussion for the audience was to be "How to Look for a Job." Other panel members included Toni Magers of Kelly Services, George Ernst of the Bank of Stockton, Aleta Marshall of the San Joaquin Employment and Training Department, and Edith Diamond of SCAN. Senator John Garamendi would speak at the noon session on the topic of "The Work Ethic." A costumed historical dramatization highlighting twenty important local women was to close the program, with a local actress portraying Tillie serving as the finale. The presentation script read,

> And it is fitting that we end with a modern-day pioneer,
> Tillie Lewis. To many Americans, Tillie Lewis exemplifies the fact that America's frontiers have not yet been reached. To countries who heard her broadcasts on "Voice of America," she symbolizes the American way of life and the free enterprise system. To the dieting public she is a God-send…From 1952 when six hundred members of the Associated Press voted her "Woman of the Year in Business," to the present, the eyes of the world have been upon her.[ccxciii]

The program was presented as planned without Mrs. Lewis on the panel, of course; everyone had read in the papers that Tillie Lewis was in the hospital, gravely ill.

On Saturday, Dameron Hospital called Arthur Heiser. Always the rock, Arthur took the news with little outward emotion. Tillie's doctor stated that Mrs. Lewis was brain-dead. It was up to the family whether or not to leave her on life support. Arthur, fearing a severe reprimand, told the doctor to wait while he contacted the rest of the family. He had always run the big stuff by Tillie, and it wasn't going to get any bigger than this. He wanted this call to be on the heads, hands, and hearts of all.

The nephews and their wives congregated at Arthur and Lucy's home, blocks from the hospital. Arthur Heiser reminded everyone that Tillie would not wish to live like the vegetable the doctor said she would remain. Arthur had never met this doctor, nor had any of his other family members. Nobody from the family had gone to the hospital at all. Arthur said, "The doctor had a good solid voice on the telephone. He seemed to know what he was talking about…Saul, himself a physician, spoke to this doctor and [said] he seemed like a good egg. The medical tests and staff had concurred that this stroke was a doozy and that Chips was surely done for. From a business standpoint, the decision to let her go was simple."

With everyone in place and listening, Arthur called the doctor back and queried aloud to all, "Let her go?" Their faces were solemn, nodding in affirmation yet staring at the floor. Arthur let out a deep sigh before saying to the doctor, "This is what she would have wanted." That simple business-like call to the doctor completed Tillie's final transaction.

Tillie had lain attached to the bleeping, beeping, puff and wheeze of life-support devices, her only companions from Wednesday morning, April 27, until that phone call. There was no satin pillow to prop up her head. No silken dressing gown to complement her complexion. There were no flowers on display. No cards of hope or encouragement. No hairdresser, perfume, or makeup to prepare her for a proper exit. Tillie was forgotten in this stark, cheerless room of tubes and disinfectant. No one came to hold her hand, say a prayer, or kiss her a last good night.

Unknown staff members silenced the contraptions on Saturday, April 30, 1977. The diminutive, drained, and ashen Tillie, with rippling shudders toward her final struggle, died. The Tomato Queen was gone.

The hospital staff called the Heiser home, again, with confirmation and consolation. To the assembled family, Arthur bowed his head and said simply, "That's it," followed by a solemn, pregnant pause before slapping his thighs to punctuate the moment in his mind. The group sat for several more minutes in silence. The thought of their world without the orchestration of Tillie Lewis was at once both too terrible and too good to be true.

Helene Heiser poignantly reflected later, "I was too stunned to move. I was looking at my feet, feeling numb. I think the saddest, strangest thing was that nobody cried." Arthur suggested that they should get started planning the funeral at Tillie's place on Willow and that they should tell Froggert and Nora, the butler and maid, in person. Nobody wanted to accompany him, so another tough task fell to Arthur. Upon arrival, Arthur informed Froggert of his mistress's passing. The butler politely excused himself and made his way toward the kitchen. Arthur quietly let himself out.

THE FINAL "WHAT'S NEXT"?

On May 2, George Visgilio posted a memo stating, "In memory of the passing of the founder of our company, all TLF activities will be closed on Tuesday May 3, 1977...Minimum essential services to maintain safety, security, handle perishable commodities and provide outbound shipments of customer trucks."

Everyone able would attend the funeral.

The end had come to a life that was triumphant. The funeral on May 3, 1977, began at 11:00 a.m. at Stockton's Temple Israel, conducted by Rabbis Bernard Rosenberg and Steven Chester. The family requested memorials to be made to Temple Israel, Boys Town of Israel, or to the Tillie Lewis Scholarship Fund at the University of the Pacific. The following were murmurs of the assemblage heard by reporter Marjorie Flaherty of the *Stockton Record*; as Rabbi Bernard Rosenberg eulogized, "Tillie Lewis has left memorials written not in stone, not in words, but in the lives of people." The Rabbi's continued,

"There is a whole economy, a whole industry that is different because of her. People are working, people have jobs because of a young woman who dared, a young woman who refused to take 'no,' a young woman who plunged on and on."

"The end has come to a life that was triumphant...driven by a dream, goaded by a goal. She saw what she wanted to do, she had the strength to achieve it at an age when she could enjoy it, and she lived long enough for family, friends and associates to know what she had achieved."

Various comments were made by the large assembly after the service,

"She was quite a gal."

"She worked hard."

"She was wonderful."

"She was inspirational."[ccxciv]

People vied for the opportunity to be a pallbearer. Those who were selected received a separate listing in a *Stockton Record* column: "Pallbearers were announced today for Tillie Lewis, industrialist, who died Saturday at a local hospital. They are Robert Lewis, William Lewis, Matthew Lewis, Ralph Ablon, Jefferson Peyser, Bernard Simons and Oscar Budd Kleinfeld. Honorary pallbearers will be Dr. Stanley McCaffrey, Llewellyn Brown, Walter Orr, Al Sider, George Froehlich, Joseph Quinn, Dr. Clair Weast, Harry Rosen and Leonard Mandel."

With one exception, Tillie's family remained stoic at her funeral service. Grief is very personal. Her eldest nephew, Dr. Saul Heiser, was bereft. Saul spoke to no one. He wept throughout his aunt's service and remained visibly upset after the funeral, when others began to joke, drink, and share stories. Saul was clearly heartbroken.[ccxcv] As Helene Heiser reflected later,

If you weren't family, you just loved her [anyway]. She made her workers happy to know her; happy to help her. Yes, she was always the center of attention, but she should have been. She did things, in those days, no woman had ever done. *For some of us, employees and family, she saved us.* [Emphatically stated.] She started hiring in Stockton during the Great Depression. She hired Jews, deaf people, Mexicans, Japanese, women—everybody who wanted a job, she was willing to give us all a chance.

THE QUEEN IS DEAD

The press had a field day. At first the newspapers were polite and respectful. Then the bashing began. In their defense, the papers didn't create this news; they just reported it. Some of the headlines included "Tillie Lewis Leaves Imprint on Stockton," "Eulogy for Tillie Lewis: A Realization of Success," "Tillie Lewis Wills $100,000 to UOP and $100,000 to Temple Israel," "The $11.5 Million Tillie Lewis Left," "Battle Underway for Tillie Lewis's Huge Estate," and "The Battle over the Tomato Queen's Estate." Somebody even wanted to name the San Joaquin Delta College Theatre after Tillie Lewis!

Tillie's historical burial—the campaign to ignore her contributions and accomplishments—began two months after her physical death with the *Stockton Record*, dated July 12, 1977, in the article "Summer Mail and Other Souvenirs" by Vince Perrin.

> Jim Hammond, former manager of [the] Stockton Civic Auditorium, wrote from his Santa Cruz home, responding to my column on the naming of Delta College's new concert hall and theater. "The Tillie Lewis Theater! Better be the Tillie Lewis Memorial Warehouse," he suggests...Dollars were the name of Tillie's game, and whatever her gifts, they were tax dollar deductible; you can count on it...Who, in discussing theatre, would even think of Tillie Lewis? Who? Leo Burke, that's who. Burke is the Delta [San Joaquin Delta College] board chairman who broke the tie vote dividing trustees; their action, depressing in its finality, has cantilevered the arts community. For what it's worth, these views are shared by many.

That view was not shared by all. Ever loyal, Alilea Martin sent a letter to the editor objecting to the ungrateful cruelty of this article less than two and a half months after her boss's death. Alilea's letter was never printed and was returned with a "check this box" form letter stapled to it.

Her anger at the Perrin article was palpable. She typed her letter to the editor. Her elegant signature was corrupted by rage and loss. She copied over her first name twice in an attempt to straighten the angry script.

Dear Sir:

The Critic's column which appeared several weeks ago concerning the naming of the theatre and concert hall at San Joaquin Delta College was, in my opinion, in very poor taste; but his column which appeared in last week's paper was positively vindictive.

All contributions made to educational, religious, and charitable institutions are tax deductible and, without thousands of such contributions made each year by individuals, Corporations, etc., most of these institutions could not exist...We should be grateful to those who do contribute...But of more importance to the community— Warren Atherton for his GI Bill of Rights and Tillie Lewis for founding a company here and providing thousands of jobs for people in this community.

In closing I should simply like to say that [it] should not be necessary to ridicule those for whom the buildings have been named, in order to pay tribute to others who were also worthy of having buildings named for them.

Very truly yours,
Alilea Haywood Martin

PS. It is my hope that you will print this letter in your "Letters to the Editor" section.

The *Stockton Record* did not comply. Instead, Mrs. Martin's plea was returned with this form letter stapled to it:

Dear Letters Contributor:

Thanks for writing to the *Record*. I am returning your recent letter, however, as unsuitable for publication because it is: Repetitious of published letters.

Cordially yours,
Stockton Record
Avery L. Kizer
Editor, Opinion Page

THE TILLIE LEWIS THEATRE

The Tillie Lewis Theatre officially opened with the musical *The Music Man* on July 14, 1977, with a brief ceremony honoring Mrs. Lewis just before the curtain rose for the first time. The date was one day after Tillie's birthday, July 13—that serendipitous day that Tillie had maneuvered to officially do everything positive she could throughout her lifetime. The theater program, by Lou Nardi[119], read,

Mrs. Lewis was a grand lady in every sense of the word and her remarkable achievements in business and government made her an international figure. She was living proof of the innovative talents of women and she actively engaged in helping women to see themselves in leadership roles. Her contributions and her interests were wide, varied and far reaching. She was deeply concerned with culture and the arts. As a result of her generosity, such organizations as the Stockton Symphony, The Stockton Opera Association and the Stockton Civic Theatre will long remember her. We are proud

---

119 Musical Theatre Director.

that our theatre has been named for such a distinguished lady and we hope our endeavors in the Tillie Lewis Theatre will always be a tribute to her memory.

Tillie would have approved.

AND THE WINNER WAS

She didn't sew ladies' hats or whip up facial creams or cosmetics. It began with a pear-shaped tomato, but it could have been anything. Tillie was on the lookout for potential ways to escape misfortune from the day she determined that living in a tenement slum was *not* going to work for her. With not one day wasted on self-pity, Tillie thought her way up and out of poverty and into a life of abundance. Her words of advice were to "find a need. Fill it to the best of your ability and to the highest of standards. Expect that need to change and be three steps ahead of the competition." She shaped her own world in which she could remain a feminine woman who was as strong as any mythical god or goddess without breaking a manicured fingernail or putting a run in her stockings. She told her audiences at various times,

> *Have as many irons in the fire as you can handle plus one…*
>
> *Accept that success and failure are conjoined and do not be stopped in your growth forward by either…*
>
> *Success may create false security resulting in stagnation. Failure happens in every venture. Shrug it off as the price of education, a hiccup on the riches road…*
>
> *It is 100 percent your responsibility to achieve your dreams. Minimize your risks by doing the work, the research, and asking questions toward getting what you want out of life…*
>
> *And above all, never ever give up.*

Tillie Lewis (born July 13, 1896; died April 30, 1977). She was eighty-one years old. True to Tillie style, her age and year of birth are incorrect on her tombstone.

EPILOGUE

The *Stockton Record* reported in an article with the headline "Tillie Lewis Will Leaves $100,000 to UOP":

> Temple Israel will each receive $100,000 from the estate of Tillie Lewis. The bulk of the estate is left equally to three nephews, Arthur, Albert and Dr. Saul Heiser.
>
> Tillie further gifted a $10,000 bequest to Saint Mary's Catholic Church (for religious and educational purposes),[120] $15,000 to "my loyal and devoted secretary Alilea Haywood Martin and $25,000 each to the Hebrew Free Loan Association of San Francisco and Boys Town of Jerusalem, Israel.[ccxcvi]

The battle over the Tomato Queen's estate hit the *Stockton Record* at the end of July but had actually begun just after Meyer Lewis's death almost a year before Tillie's. The legal skirmish between the Meyer Lewis estate and the Tillie Lewis estate was pretty big news. The public took sides. The case was fodder for local jokes. The water cooler, beauty parlor, and barbershop anti-Tillie commentary was colossal.

---

120 Saint Mary's was the Catholic church that had loaned Tillie $1,000 in 1939; it had been repaid tenfold over the years. Nevertheless, Tillie wished to leave one last gift of gratitude.

An anonymous family member of Meyer's led a lawsuit to regain the other half of Meyer's original estate that Tillie retained as loan indebtedness, plus a share of the Tillie Lewis empire in its entirety, claiming "all assets as community property." The *Stockton Record* printed that the law firm would receive "10% of the first $65,000 recovered from the Tillie Lewis estate and 25% of any amount over $65,000."

Tillie's nephew Arthur Heiser[121] said, "In my opinion, the claim for extended family members to profit from community property is ridiculous. Number one, Meyer died first. In a dispute, whatever he had *should* have gone to the widow, Tillie. The community aspect of the estate died with Meyer. That Meyer's certain family members wanted a claim was understandable, but Tillie clearly left the sum of $1.00 to any person, other than her nephews, who might have a claim to her estate, in her will."

Tillie's estate was estimated at over $10 million,[122] although probate judge James P. Darrah determined the figure to be closer to $11.5 million. Judge Darrah ruled that Meyer Lewis's heirs were entitled to a jury trial on the subject. The questions posed were: Did Tillie withhold assets, including stock, from her husband during their marriage?[ccxcvii] Had Tillie ever commingled her business, or personal, property with Meyer's? Was there any reasonable proof of an agreement between Meyer and Tillie Lewis regarding ownership?[ccxcviii]

Meyer enjoyed the luxuries of marriage to a wealthy, accomplished woman. His financial status was as a paid employee from 1941 until his death. Meyer had a record of loans from the company for his investment ventures, and never from Tillie directly. Was Tillie Lewis Foods community property? Even so, would Meyer's *heirs* be entitled to those funds when Meyer died before Tillie?

To halt the courtroom drama and expenses, Arthur Heiser settled with the Meyer Lewis heirs for an undisclosed amount of money.

---

121 Arthur Heiser held his degree in law from Cornell, though he did not act in a legal capacity.
122 This was approximately $42 million in 2016 dollars.

EVERYTHING GOES

Days before the auctions to the public, the family-only version of an auction took place. This was a special time of grieving and memories. No one celebrated the loss of Tillie. But she was gone. Truly gone. Some of the personal items that Chips left that had long been admired, or had special meaning for someone, were withheld from the auction and simply given as gifts to the family member who prized it the most.

Each piece held a history of its own. Someone got the heavy wrought-iron patio furniture that had gone for that "cement pond" dive to the bottom of Chips's pool. Someone else wanted one of Tillie's massive desks that she had ordered from a wood craftsman from an amazing display at the 1939/1940 World's Fair in New York. The crystal bird salt-and-pepper shakers stayed in Stockton, reminders of special dinners when each of the guests had their very own waitstaff to serve them. And so on—memories that Chips, a.k.a. the Tomato Queen, had lived her life in grand style.

Her bedroom still smelled of her signature perfume. The lingering scent caused everyone to pause. Part of Tillie Lewis was still in residence.

They divided up the fur collection between the nieces-in-laws: the same lovely girls whom Chips had entertained on a meal of pasta pomodoro that she'd prepared herself in New York all those years before. Her nephews had chosen their wives well. But these ladies were not Tillie Lewis. The nieces were women of a quiet, casual sophistication. They were exceptional wives, mothers, and helpmates. Being the center of attention was not their style.

These pelts were infused with elegant events all over the world. But the delightful memories were strictly Tillie's, and she was gone. Lucy, June, and Helene might never actually wear the coats. Nonetheless, they had been precious to Tillie. Some things were simply for the family. Strangers shouldn't prance about in Chips's minks, sables, ermines, chinchillas, and leopard swing coat. These would be saved for great-greater-greatest nieces to thrill in pretend, wear to the prom, or stroll through Paris connected to the long-gone Auntie Chips—Tillie's "girls" catching a glimpse of their images in the windows and mirrors of a fabulous future, taking a bit of Tillie along the way.

THE OTHER STUFF

Butterfield and Butterfield auctioneers of San Francisco included Tillie's items in sale lot number 2969, including the important XVIII Century English Furniture, French Marquetry Steinway and other grand pianos, Persian and Chinese rugs, porcelain, silver, crystal, and objects d'art from the estate of Tillie Lewis removed from the Palm Springs and Stockton, California residences.

The personal belongings of the woman who'd built a corporate power-house on the pear-shaped tomato were sold in two days of rapid-fire bidding. Mrs. Lewis had an eccletic taste. There was no set theme to her treasured collections except that they were of exceptional condition and value. She had silver settings from Germany, ornate clocks from France, and chairs from eighteenth-century England. Mrs. Lewis "bought what she liked," said a friend.

Two paintings by Heywood Hardy depicted a fox hunt and sold for $4,250 each. The ornate Steinway piano sold for an underbid of a mere $12,000, much to the joy of the squealing woman who won it and the groans of the dealers who passed on it. A losing dealer, shaking his head in disappointment, congratulated the lucky winner with a handshake.

The auction catalogue contained 692 items, including several sets of items. From Steinway to Louis Comfort Tiffany, the items included sterling-silver dinner services, 292-piece sterling-silver flatware, various tea sets, French linen cloths, several important paintings, and numerous ornate, Oriental carpets. Tillie's things were sold to the highest bidder.[ccxcix] Her jewelry was sold through a separate auction house. The $21,000 that one Oriental, Kashan carpet fetched could have bought a modest house. The three "important" carpets all went to private parties. The carpet dealers were visibly annoyed that their agents had been outbid by regular folks. One carpet dealer was heard crying, "Who? Who?" in an attempt to discover the identity of the buyer of the century-old rug in perfect condition. Within forty-eight hours, at 3:00 p.m., the collections of Tillie Lewis had been cashed in and bid farewell.[ccc]

The jewelry went next, from a fourteen-karat-gold tape measure and $18,000 sapphire clip earrings to a $60,000 emerald-and-diamond bracelet. There was no accounting for the Lord Harry Clifton canary-diamond ring or the triple strands of pearls in the estimated $400,000; they were likely sold separately and the proceeds divided appropriately.

Tillie's stock portfolio included sixty-four thousand shares of stock from the Ogden Corporation. She'd also held stock from Pan-American, Aloha, and American Airlines; Southern Pacific Railroad; and Norton Simon.[123][ccci]

Her 7,420-square-foot 1928 house at 740 Willow Street in Stockton—with four bedrooms and five bathrooms on .75 acres with a pool—was sold to Harley and Brigitte Smith for $250,000.[124] Her 1931 estate at 657 North Via Miraleste in Palm Springs—covering 7,517 square feet, with nine bedrooms and seven and a quarter baths on 1.79 manicured acres with interior and exterior gardens, fountains, and a pool—was sold on May 1, 1978, for $350,000.[125]

FAREWELL

On January 22, 1978, not long into the new year, the layoffs and cutbacks began. The original plant in Stockton would no longer be needing six to nine hundred seasonal employees.[cccii]

In May of 1979, Richard Glass Williams accepted a position at the can-making division of Tillie Lewis Foods. The can making plant was the only strong division left. Mrs. Lewis had been gone only two years. Richard marveled at the quality of the equipment throughout the plant, along with the level of sophistication the layout had. He knew the darn place held the opportunity for growth in every square inch. The building whispered of possibility, future, and "What's next?" Richard thought the "man" who built this place sure knew what "he" was doing.[126]

---

123 Norton Simon owned Hunts, Max Factor, Avis Rental Cars, and more.

124 The Smiths graciously allowed the author access to the house and grounds and a bag of Tillie's forgotten corsets from the 1940s, referred to as "Tillie's frillies."

125 Palm Springs house worth between roughly $3 million and $4.8 million in August of 2016, according to Zillow.

126 While not a chauvinist, it just did not occur to Richard Williams that a woman could have built this can manufacturing plant.

What intrigued him most was that along with the sharp-edged, state-of-the-art equipment was a strange (for a can plant) sense of the feminine. From the color palate, carpeting choices, and furnishings to the numerous massive portraits of a redheaded woman of wealth with haunting eyes, this was a warm and welcoming space—not the usual strictly steel-and-tinplate can plant.

Richard asked his new supervisor who the lady was. "Oh, that's Tillie Lewis. She was supposed to have been some housewife who invented a recipe to cook a tomato." Richard whistled long and low under his breath while he surveyed the buildings and acreage that this majestic lady had commanded. "A housewife? A recipe? No! Not this woman. She had to be much more than that…"

The Modesto canneries closed at the end of the season in 1979, two and a half years after Tillie's death, which left no place for thousands of seasonal workers to go. One by one, the other canneries were sold off in what former workers called a slow and painful death. The last cannery plant standing was the original Flotill, from 1935. The final pomodoro was packed in 1984.[ccciii]

Flotill/Tillie Lewis Foods took its last gasp on February 27, 1987. TLF couldn't survive without Tillie pushing the company to bigger and better ideas. Ten years after her death, the Ogden Corporation sold the last of the multimillion-dollar Tillie Lewis processing plants, canneries, and distribution center. Over the years, at least 3,150 seasonal and full-time employees received their closure letters.

The company Tillie had founded was gone, and its assets were sold to PET Inc., located in Hannibal, Missouri. These assets included the last of the seven copper cookers sent by Tillie's partner, Florindo Del Gaizo, from Italy in 1934 to begin Flotill. The state-of-the-art cannery plant that had paid a living wage for local citizens for over fifty years now sat locked in chains and decay, forgotten like the Tomato Queen herself.

The following are excerpts from a series of articles written in April of 1987 for the *Stockton Record* when the new owners at PET Inc. went too far in their redistribution of one particular asset.

"For more than 50 years, the copper kettle in front of the Tillie Lewis Foods plant on Fresno Avenue stood as a corporate symbol of the empire founded by the gutsy industrialist Tillie Weisberg Lewis in 1934."

"Mayor Barbara Fass commented on the sale of the copper kettle 'This is called the rape and plunder of the city of Stockton and San Joaquin County...this is stealing one of Stockton's important historic relics.'"

"The people of Stockton are outraged at the kettle-napping...the storm of angry letters from citizens forced an injunction filed by The San Joaquin County Board of Supervisors to retrieve the pot."

"The removal of Tillie's copper kettle spurred the city and county into an uproar...Supervisor George Barber was jubilant about the county's luck in retrieving the old kettle."

"Maybe we ought to go out and welcome it back," said Mayor Barbara Fass.[127]

In 2003, a letter to the *Stockton Record* was written about Latina news-article contributor Elena Caceres's essay attack on Stockton's canneries. Ethnic dissatisfaction had been on a steady rise in the community that had once proudly claimed it was "Stockton: Someplace Special." Those words had been emblazoned brightly on the water tank and signage that welcomed newcomers (and reminded locals) of how good they had it near the rivers, fertile soil, and friendly communities of the Central Valley. That sentiment of positive specialty had been fading away—just like the words on the water tank—from neglect, more than from the hot summer sun. Vanishing was the strength of character that those of every ethnicity had brought to the Central Valley throughout the Great Depression. In the glory days of Tillie Lewis, Stockton

---

127   The copper kettle now shines brightly at Stockton's Haggin Museum.

truly was someplace special. Joe C. Garcia penned an eloquent objection to Elena Caceres's words:

> Until her May 16 column on canneries and cannery workers, Elena Caceres' thought/memory-jogging essays have been something I looked forward to each week.
>
> I am compelled to respond to her description of life in the canneries by sharing the experiences of the Garcia family and their associates.
>
> My Mexico-born father worked at Flotill as a label machine operator for many years. Eldest brother Ralph began working there in 1935 and was warehouse manager at their Modesto and Stockton plants. Another brother, Frank, was a Flotill shift supervisor for several years. A third brother, Manuel, retired as warehouse superintendent at Flotill.
>
> My first full-time seasonal job began when I left Edison High after completing my sophomore year. Yes, a dropout at 16, but I walked down that aisle to receive my diploma at age 39. I worked at Stockton Foods (now Del Monte) in 1944 that first season; worked the 1945 season at Frank Wilson Cannery; and next season began my career at Flotill. At all three canneries, opportunity to learn and advance was open to anyone who wished to take it; witness my [family's] employment history. We all reached positions of responsibility and authority through cannery work. Other families did the same; [the] Vargas, Bejerano and Espinoza families come to mind.
>
> Because of the canneries and their hard-working employees of Mexican, African, Chinese, Italian, Filipino, Japanese, Portuguese, Anglo and other descents, Stockton thrived and prospered, both materially and socially. Please, Ms. Caceres, don't bite the hand that has fed, taught and nurtured the Garcia family, most of our friends and thousands of our neighbors.

Somewhere in the ether, Tillie Lewis whispered, "Thank you, Joe."

RICHARD GLASS WILLIAMS

Richard Glass Williams pondered that "Tillie Lewis must have been someone very special" for a long time. He carried that thought with him over the years until his wife decided to get her college degree as soon as the kids were grown. She wondered, "What subject could I write about and build upon over the next four years of college that would connect local, California, national, women's, religious, and business history that hasn't already been done to death?"

Richard knew the answer. He said, "Let me introduce you to the acres and acres and the buildings and landmarks that were once Tillie Lewis." Tillie Lewis, the woman, was the only product Tillie Lewis ever undersold. She was never the naive, innocent Cinderella who was swept along by fate that she portrayed herself to be. Tillie was an original story, an ethereally striking spitfire who steered her own fate and was determined to find fame and fortune, no matter how she had to do it and no matter what the cost.

The spirit of Tillie Lewis was strong enough to defy death. The containers of her past were dusted off, polished, and began to be shined up that very day. The questions were asked, the stories recorded, and Tillie Lewis, though these pages, is once again glistening like one of her seven beautiful Italian copper cookers; she is retaking her place, front and center, at the table of history, just like a good plate of pasta pomodoro.

ACKNOWLEDGMENTS

F ar too many organizations and people deserve acknowledgment for this book, so I have listed them all categorically and in no particular order. You were all precious to the telling of *Tillie*.

Tillie's family: Barbara Heiser, Nancy Heiser, Judy Heiser, William "Bill" Lewis, Helene Heiser, Albert Heiser, Arthur Heiser, Rosalee Lewis, and Jerry Hochheiser.

Flotill/TLF family: Clair "Doc" Weast, Harry and Ken Rosen, Rosie Munoz, Serafino "Ralph" and Mildred Garcia, Pat Stanco, John Dunivan, Lonell Crosby Sr., Bobbie Blair Xenos, Shirley Lubin, Jennie Panelli, Angelina "Angie" Gomez, Jose Cruz Garcia Jr., Peter Froehlich, and George Visgilio.

The cities and people of Stockton, Modesto, and Turlock, California: The Haggin Museum and staff, Kimberly Bowden, Tod Ruhstaller, Susan Obert, Lisa Cooperman, the San Joaquin County Historical Society and Museum, Leigh Johnson, the Bank of Stockton archives, William "Bill" Maxwell, the Stockton Police Department archives, Ron Chapman, Patti Gotelli, Marion Jacobs, David Lindsey, Elizabeth Herenick, Sheldon Barr, Harley and Brigitte Smith, Georgia Gene Herring, Yolanda Roscelli, Clifford Stevens, the *Stockton Record*, the *Record*, the *Modesto Bee*, San Joaquin County Delta College, Steve Schermerhorn, Lynn Hawley, the University of the Pacific, Ken Albala, Edith Sparks, California State University at Turlock's amazing history department, and my mentor Nancy Taniguchi.

New York: Heirloom tomato queen and author Dr. Amy Goldman, Miriam Weiner: Routes to Roots. Utah: Ancestry.com of Lehi, Utah 1997-2006. A source invaluable to this author and recommended to all readers to explore the past.

My family: Elizabeth "Lise" Talbott, Kian Tobin, Max Ching, Richard Glass Williams, and Wayne Charles Wood, who put up with a tremendous amount of grief while I made time for *Tillie*.

NOTES

i. Goldman, Herbert G., *Fanny Brice: The Original Funny Girl*, New York: Oxford University Press, 1992.

ii. Ibid.

iii. Albert Heiser, Fanny Brice sings "Lovie Joe," interview with the author at Heiser's home.

iv. Goldman, Herbert G., *Fanny Brice: The Original Funny Girl*, New York: Oxford University Press, 1992, pp. 176–80.

v. Ibid.

vi. NBC Radio, "Good News of 1938," aired November 25, 1937; *Fanny Brice*, by Herbert G. Goldman.

vii. Jose Iturbi, property for sale.

viii. "Villa Madama: Case Study," RIBA architecture.com, http://www.architecture.com/LibraryDrawingsAndPhotographs/Palladio/ExhibitingPalladio.

ix. Albert Heiser memories.

x. Ralph and Mildred Garcia, interview with the author.

xi. Charles A. Wills, "Destination America," www.pbs.org/destinationameican/wn_noflash_5.html.

xii. De Ianni, N. *Dizionario Biografico Treccani*, "Luigi Del Gaizo," translated from the Italian, Googleusercontent.com.

xiii. White Studios, photography of New York, Broadway, and Ziegfeld stage; original gift from Barbara Heiser.

xiv. Douglas Martin, "Former Ziegfeld Follies Girl Recalls the Glory Days," *New York Times*, October 18, 1996.

xv. Ibid. Tillie was with Ziegfeld long enough to obtain an original of that photograph.

xvi. White Studios, "Ziegfeld 1911," Fanny Brice photograph.

xvii. Douglas Martin, "Former Ziegfeld Follies Girl Recalls the Glory Days," *New York Times*, October 18, 1996.

xviii. *La Pubblicita a una Science Sociologica*, http://contnet.lib.sfu.ca/cgi-bin/ get image.exe? CISOROOT.

xix. Douglas Martin, "Former Ziegfeld Follies Girl Recalls the Glory Days," *New York Times*, October 18, 1996.

xx. Conlin, Joseph R., *The American Past: A Survey of American History*, 9th ed., vol. 2., Boston, Wadsworth/Cengage Learning, 2009, 2010.

xxi. New York Times. 1905. Killer Heat Wave, Storm, Death Toll Rises.

xxii. Saul Heiser speech for Beatrice and Sam Hockheiser's fiftieth wedding anniversary.

xxiii. Ancestry.com.

xxiv. In telling the author this story, Arthur Heiser bristled at the idea that people assumed Tillie's father, Jacob Ehrlich, had been impoverished.

xxv.   Michael Zadeh, "Jewish Wealth Secrets. A True Man Is One Who…" Jewishwealthsecrets.com.

xxvi.   Michael Wilkerson. *Eastern District High School*. Brooklyn, New York, 2000.

xxvii. Ibid.

xxviii. Deeptha Thattai. *A History of Public Education in the United States*. Journal of Literacy and Education in Developing Societies. Chicago. 2001.

xxix.   Barbara Heiser, interview with the author, December 2, 2005.

xxx.   Albert Heiser, Arthur Heiser, Barbara Heiser multiple interviews to the author.

xxxi.   Jerry Hochheiser, rough draft, "The Italian Grocery Business," three-page letter mailed to the author for use in this book, January 23, 2010.

xxxii. Reva Clar, *Western States Jewish Historical Quarterly*, January 1984, vol. XVI, no. 2, p. 139.

xxxiii. "Girls and Glitter in 'Follies of 1911,'" *New York Times*, June 27, 1911.

xxxiv. "'Follies of 1912' Is a Beauty Show," *New York Times*, October 22, 1912.

xxxv.   N. De Ianni. *Bibliography Dictionary-Treccani*, "Luigi Del Gaizo."

xxxvi. Carnegie, Dale, *Public Speaking and Influencing Men in Business*, 2007 [1912], BN Publishing.

xxxvii. Oral accounts from Albert Heiser, Arthur Heiser and Barbara Heiser to the author.

xxxviii. Saul Heiser, fiftieth wedding anniversary of Samuel and Beatrice Hochheiser, speech and notes, February 1964, gift from Barbara Heiser to the author.

xxxix. Arthur Heiser, multiple interviews with the author.

xl. Saul Heiser, fiftieth wedding anniversary of Sam and Beatrice Hockheiser, speech, February 1964.

xli. Ancestry.com, "US WWII Draft Card. Louis Weisberg. Born November 4, 1892. Austria. Age 49."

xlii. *Encyclopedia of Cleveland*, "Wholesale Grocery History," http://ech.cwru.edu/ech-cgi/article.pl?id+WG.

xliii. https://jovinacooksitalian.com/2015/01/20/the-old-italian-american-grocery-stores/.

xliv. Albert Heiser, phone interview with the author, March 24, 2006.

xlv. Ancestry.com, "1920 United States Federal Census."

xlvi. Albert Heiser, interview with the author.

xlvii. De Ianni, N., *Bibliography Dictionary—Treccani*, "Luigi Del Gaizo," six pages translated from the Italian.

xlviii. "Clifton Village. Welcome to Clifton Village," www.clifton-village.org.uk/home.htm.

xlix.   Albert Heiser, interview with the author, February 12, 2003.

l.   Arthur Heiser, interview with the author.

li.   Weisberg, Tillie, original photo album, 1926, gift to the author from Barbara Heiser; on loan to Haggin Museum, property of the author.

lii.   Ibid.

liii.   Ibid.

liv.   People's History, "1926: The Attempted Assassination of Mussolini in Rome," libcom.org/history.

lv.   Tillie Lewis, multiple articles in the *Stockton Record, Modesto Bee*, various papers from San Francisco and all over the world.

lvi.   Photos of Brooklyn Botanical Garden, women and children gardening tomatoes, http://www.bbg.org/collections/historicimages.

lvii.   Brooklyn Botanical Garden, Historic Image Collection, "Banana in Economic House—1916 Bunch"; "Tomato 'Leaf Roll'"; "Brooklyn Training School for Girls, 1920"; photos by Louis Buhle, www.bbg.org/cgi/hic/hic_detail.cgi?03481 and www.bbg.org/cgi/hic/hic_detail.cgi?02126.

lviii. Muriel Fisher, "Big Business Built on Book Larnin,'" *New York Telegram*, November 8, 1951, Haggin Museum archives.

lix.   Miriam Weiner. *Routes to Roots.* Ancestry and genealogy research for another client provided insight and documentation to birthdates and deaths of Tillie's early days.

lx. Ibid.

lxi. Miriam Weiner, e-mails from Ms. Weiner's research to the author, November 2009.

lxii. Barbara Heiser, phone interview with the author, June 30, 2016.

lxiii. Original black-and-white photographs, c. 1931, of Jacob Ehrlich, L. Weisberg, S. Hochheiser, and their grandsons; Jacob and Bessie; and Jacob, Bessie/Bilha, and an unknown woman; gift of Barbara Heiser to the author.

lxiv. Umbach, Kenneth W., *A Statistical Treaty of the Great Central Valley.*

lxv. Martin Kelly, About.com, "American History Expert: What Is the Smoot-Hawley Tariff?"

lxvi. Sidney Fields, "Only Human. Tillie Lewis: Tomatoes Wouldn't Wait," *Sunday Mirror*, November 11, 1951, Micke Grove archives.

lxvii. Herbert Stoy, "People at Work," *The Record*, July 18, 1960, article gift of Harry Rosen to the author.

lxviii. Flotill Food Products Division Statement of Incorporation—History, CD #98-33-52, April 9, 1941, Haggin Museum archives.

lxix. Michael Fitzgerald, "Busy Port Deserves Recognition," February 6, 2008.

lxx. Sean O'Hara, "A Map of the World's Mediterranean Climates," *The Mediterranean Garden Society*, April 2, 2006.

lxxi.   Reva Clar. *Western States Jewish History Quarterly*. January 1984, vol. XVI, no. 2, p. 142.

lxxii. De Ianni, N., *Biographical Dictionary—Treccani*, "Luigi Del Gaizo," translation in the author's archives.

lxxiii. *Western Canner and Packer*, September 1935, original in collection of the author.

lxxiv. John Dunivan, phone and e-mail interview, with photographs of Tillie and Lloyd.

lxxv.   Ralph Garcia, letters and papers given as a gift to the author.

lxxvi. Ralph and Mildred Garcia, video interview with the author (August 10, 2006) at the Garcia home in Modesto, California.

lxxvii. From Ralph Garcia, Harry Rosen, Doc Weast, Rosie Munoz, and Lonell Crosby, separate interviews with the author with multiple subjects.

lxxviii. Lusha Nelson, original photograph of Tillie in diamond tiara and gilt gown, author's collection.

lxxix. Presenting the House of Flotill catalog of 1946, produced by Tillie Weisberg.

lxxx.   Tillie Weisberg. Stockton Record, Modesto Bee, September 1945.

lxxxi. Judith Morgan and Neil Morgan, "California's Surprising Inland Delta," *National Geographic*, vol. 150, no. 3, September 1976, pp. 412–429.

lxxxii. Wikipedia. "Stockton Cannery Strike of 1937." Wikipedia.org/wiki/Stockton_cannery_strike_of_1937.

lxxxiii. Rosie Munoz and Clair Doc Weast, interviews with the author, 2003–2005.

lxxxiv. Such covenants were upheld by the court in the 1926 ruling of *Corrigan v. Buckley*, only to be declared later legal but "unenforceable" in the 1948 decision of *Shelley v. Kraemer*.

lxxxv. Numerous residents of the area who prefer to remain unnamed, July 2006–September 2009.

lxxxvi. Delso invitation, June 1937, Haggin Museum archives.

lxxxvii. "Cannery Season Suffers 40% in Production," *Stockton Record*, November 24, 1938, Micke Grove archives.

lxxxviii. The Campbell Funeral Church held funerals for John Lennon, Ed Sullivan, Jacqueline Kennedy Onassis, and the Notorious BIG as well as Rudolph Valentino.

lxxxix. Ancestry.com, "Historical Newspapers, Birth, Marriage, Death Announcements," 1851–2003.

xc. Naples Cathedral history and photographs, July 28, 2011, www.duomodinapoli.it.

xci. A. Sala, letter to E. J. Wait, April 14, 1939, Haggin Museum archives, Tillie Lewis.

xcii. A.W.G., P. Pastene & Co. Inc., October 1, 1937, letter to Mrs. Weisberg, Haggin Museum archives.

xciii. Ancestry.com, "1938. Arrival, New York. 1820–1957," record for Luigi Del Gaizo.

xciv. Helene Heiser, Ralph Garcia, Harry Rosen, and Doc Weast, separate interviews with the author.

xcv. Barbara Heiser, Doc Weast, Harry Rosen, and Ralph Garcia, interviews with the author.

xcvi. W. R. Hearst (1863–1951), newspapers, films, ranches, Hearst Castle in San Simeon, California, available to tour; Hearst had many different companies that thrive today.

xcvii. S. Kilroy, interoffice communication, retirement speech of Harry Rosen, January 11, 1979, gift of Doc Weast to the author.

xcviii. Harry Rosen, interview with the author from O'Conner Woods, Stockton. 2004.

xcix. Patrick Stanco, interview with the author.

c. Tillie Weisberg, Flotill "Quality in Quantity" catalog, Haggin Museum archives, 1947.

ci. Helene Heiser. Interview to author with Barbara Heiser present.

cii. Merced Historical Society, 1938 records from phone call to the author, December 9, 2015.

ciii. Gillian Jones, Levinsky & Jones letter dated December 16, 1938, Haggin Museum archives.

civ. E. F. Euphrat, letter, March 7, 1939, Haggin Museum archive / Tillie Lewis collection.

cv. Tillie Weisberg-Lewis. Tillie made this statement numerous times in papers and magazines.

cvi. Eugene Singer, Star Corrugated Box Co., Inc., Argyle Ave., Los Angeles, and Maspeth, Long Island, New York; April 17, 1939; Haggin Museum, Stockton Collection archives, Heiser Gift Box 11.

cvii. Eugene Singer to William Crouse, April 17, 1939, Haggin Museum archives.

cviii. Tillie Lewis, letter to Pacific Can controller loan for $4110.29, June 2, 1939, Haggin Museum archives.

cix. "High School Dropout Makes Good," *Reader's Digest*, 1960, Haggin Museum archives.

cx. Barbara Heiser, numerous video and oral interviews with the author.

cxi. Arthur Heiser, phone interview with the author, March 24, 2006.

cxii. http://www.kvie.org/programs/kvie/viewfinder/little_manila/transcript.htm.

cxiii. Rosie Munoz, Patrick Stanco, Albert Heiser, and Ralph Garcia, separate interviews with the author, 2003–2009.

cxiv. Lonell Crosby and Jennie Panelli, separate oral interviews with the author.

cxv. Patrick Stanco, oral interview, June, 2004, interview with the author at Stanko's home in Stockton.

cxvi. Margaret Kreiss, "Living," *Modesto Bee*, Sunday, February 8, 1976; copy in Harry Rosen collection, gift to the author.

cxvii. IMDB, William Morris Bioff, www.williammorrisbioff imdb.com.

cxviii. "Daily News of the Show World," *Variety*, Monday, November 27, 1939, vol. 25, no. 70, Micke Grove, Lodi archives.

cxix. Bill Lewis, Meyer Lewis bio written by Bill Lewis to the author and phone interviews, 2009.

cxx. Ibid.

cxxi. Source: *Japantown Atlas*: "Northern California—Stockton." http://japantownatlas.com/map-stockton.html.

cxxii. FBI declassified report, June 19, 1941, file #100-1432.

cxxiii. United States Trademarks, "Conquista," serial #71401210, December 24, 1937.

cxxiv. Clar, *Western States Jewish History*, p. 151.

cxxv. Lytham Town Trust, description of the grand hall, interiors, lands, and brief history of the Clintons, Lythamtontrust.org.

cxxvi. Multiple family members and ladies of Flotill; Tillie's clothes and shoes were legendary in their unique style and beauty.

cxxvii. Man unnamed; author owns original short film, and the Haggin Museum often plays a copy. Filmmaker's name may be obtained at the Haggin Museum.

cxxviii. "Flotill Products, Incorporation History," April 9, 1941, Haggin Museum archives.

cxxix. Tillie Weisberg, letter and questionnaire to Flotill family, September 1941, original gift of Doc Weast to the author.

cxxx. Jennie Panelli, interview with the author in the presence of Panelli's niece, Julie Stephens, April 12, 2010.

cxxxi. William Green, American Federation of Labor letter commending Tillie's war-bond bonus, July 9, 1942, Micke Grove archives.

cxxxii. Arthur Heiser, video interview with the author.

cxxxiii. John C. Dunivan (son of Lloyd Dunivan), along with Barbara Heiser and Angie Gomez, interview with the author, March 20, 2011.

cxxxiv. Barbara Heiser, interview with the author at the home of Arthur Heiser and Barbara Heiser (great-niece).

cxxxv. Rosie Munoz, interview with the author.

cxxxvi. William Lewis, written interview, December 5, 2009.

cxxxvii. Clifford Stevens, interview with the author, May 12, 2008, at his home at 444 Birchwood, Manteca, California.

cxxxviii. Ralph Garcia, interview with the author.

cxxxix. Sidney Fields, "Tillie Lewis: Tomatoes Wouldn't Wait," *Sunday Mirror*, November 11, 1951, Micke Grove archives.

cxl. Ralph Garcia, interviews with the author.

cxli. Albala, Ken, "The Tomato Queen of San Joaquin," *Gastronomica Journal*, Spring 2010.

cxlii.   "Local Cannery Sued by OPA on Sales," *Stockton Record*, 1942.

cxliii. Reva Clar. *Western States Jewish History*, p. 144.

cxliv.   *Ibid.*

cxlv.   1945 *Flotill* newsletter, Haggin Museum archives.

cxlvi.   Arthur Heiser, Barbara Heiser, Helene Heiser, and Judith Heiser, various interviews with the author.

cxlvii. Heiser, Helene, interview with the author with Barbara Heiser present.

cxlviii. Michael Wurst, interview with C. A. Weast, February 2, 2005, copy gift to the author from Doc Weast, UOP archives.

cxlix.   Ibid., UOP archives, February 2, 2005; Doc Weast, typed notes to the author, pp. 1–14, 2004.

cl.   Doc Weast, interview with the author.

cli.   *Stockton Record* and *Modesto Bee*, June 1945.

clii.   Tillie and Meyer Lewis's 1948 wedding album; Fanny Brice is on the invitation guest list as well as numerous family stories of Fanny and Tillie's friendship.

cliii.   Paul Tritenbach landscape designs for the Baker/Willow house, San Joaquin Historical Society archives at Micke Grove.

cliv.   William Lewis, e-mail to the author, November 22, 2009.

clv. Jimmy Smothers, memories of soldier A. C. Boyd, www.Scrapbookpages. com/Ohrdruf/index.

clvi. On December 17, 1944, Major General Henry C. Pratt announced that beginning January 2, 1945, the federal government would officially end the exclusion order that prevented Japanese and Japanese-Americans from returning to the West Coast following their release from World War II internment camps.

clvii. "Allied Aerial Bombings of Italy," www.metapedia.org/wiki/aerial bombings of Italy.

clviii. De Ianni, N., *Dizionario Biografico Treccani*, "Luigi Del Gaizo," author archives.

clix. Rosie Munoz, interview at convalescent hospital, July 2004, with the author and Doc Weast.

clx. Harry Rosen, oral interview with the author.

clxi. Tillie Weisberg, original holiday letter to Harry Rosen, December 14, 1946, gift from Doc Weast to the author.

clxii. Shirley Lubin of Stockton, oral interview with the author.

clxiii. Ancestry.com, "Cruise Passengers. Havana," November 29, 1929, http:// imageservice.ancestry.com/iexec/image.x?f=getimage&dbid.

clxiv. Gaffron, Mike, "Minnesota, Hats Off to Thee—A History of the University of Minnesota Bands 1892–1992," University of Minnesota Band Alumni Society, 1992.

clxv. LuRoy Krumweid, "The Concert Band," http://sz0098.evmail.comcast.net/service/home/~Lefowitz%20-%201930%20Gopher, author's collection.

clxvi. P. M. Francoeur, letter of apricot compliment to Flotill, March 18, 1947, Haggin Museum archives.

clxvii. Israel Ehrlich family tree, gift of Barbara Heiser to the author.

clxviii. Doc Weast, interview with the author.

clxix. Ibid. Doc Weast added handwritten notes for the author "just to get it right"; some of this material is from pp. 1–76 of legal-pad notes to the author in her collection.

clxx. Toni Nettie Galluzzo, letter to Tillie Lewis from American Graphics Corp., Chicago, May 24, 1974, Micke Grove archives.

clxxi. Helene Heiser, oral interviews with the author.

clxxii. William Lewis, biography of Meyer Lewis given to the author, 2009.

clxxiii. Jeannette Brownlee chauffeured by Tillie photo, gift from Barbara Heiser to the author.

clxxiv. Barbara Heiser, interview with the author.

clxxv. Tillie Lewis, bridal memories wedding album, November 7, 1948, copy gift to the author from Helene Heiser, 2007.

clxxvi. "California Dates and Date Production," www.seecalifornia.com/farms/california-dates.html.

clxxvii.   Undisclosed contributor, phone interview with the author, September 6, 2006.

clxxviii.   FBI file #49-11618-8, April 4, 1949.

clxxix.   Harry Rosen, memo to Banks Miller, May 24, 1948, gift from Doc Weast to the author.

c.   Paul Cotter, Reconstruction Finance Corp., letter to J. Edgar Hoover, January 24, 1949, copy from FBI report, 1950.

clxxxi.   Harry Rosen, interview with Kyle Williams, 2004.

clxxxii.   William Lewis, notes, December 6, 2009.

clxxxiii.   William Lewis, bits and pieces of an e-mail to the author, December 5, 2009.

clxxxiv.   William Lewis, e-mail about Tillie and Meyer Lewis dated December 4, 2009, and interview with Arthur Heiser, 2009.

clxxxv.   "Stockton Can Rations for US Troops," *Stockton Record*, April 11, 1951, Haggin Museum archives.

clxxxvi.   "GIs in Korea Tell Tillie They Like the Chow She Sends," *Stockton Record*, Haggin Museum archives.

clxxxvii.   "Corporal Needham and Senator Sample Flotill," *Stockton Record*.

clxxxviii.   Reva Clar. *Western States Jewish History*, p. 144.

clxxxix.   "Tillie's Unpunctured Romance," *Time* archive, 1951, www.time-proxy.yaga.com/time/archive/printout/0,23657,857087-0,00.html.

cxc.   Muriel Fisher, "Big Business Built on Book Larnin'," *New York Telegram*, November 8, 1951, Haggin Museum archives.

cxci.   Ancestry.com, "Source Information," www.ancestry.com database, multiple news articles.

cxcii. Women's Advertising Club admission ticket, "A Woman's Adventures in a Man's World," Saint Louis, Missouri, June 23, 1953, Haggin Museum archives.

cxciii. Doc Weast; Doc retold this story numerous times through many interviews with the author, 2006–2009.

cxciv. Ancestry.com, "Oshkosh Daily Northwestern Wisconsin," record for an ancestor, "She is Too Fat for Me: One Husband's Grounds for Divorce," August 10, 1955.

cxcv.   Ancestry.com database, *Stars and Stripes* newspapers; Europe, Mediterranean, and North Africa editions, 1942–1964.

cxcvi. Harry Rosen, Doc Weast, and Arthur Heiser, various stories told to the author, 2004–2009.

cxcvii. "New Stockton Trade Club Has Successful Launching," *Stockton Record*, September 18, 1951, author's collection.

cxcviii. *Stockton Record*, March 5, 1977.

cxcix. Josie Walters-Johnston, reference librarian at the Library of Congress, e-mail to the author, January 20, 2006.

cc.   Phyllis Battelle, "America's Fabulous Women: A Tomato Made Tillie's Fortune," *Chicago Today*, May 23, 1974, Micke Grove archives.

cci.   Thomas Kelly, "New York Vanderbilt Release," December 15, 1952; "First Hotel to Feature Low-Calorie Items," Micke Grove archives.

ccii.   *Stockton Record*, February 12, 1953.

cciii.   Harry Rosen, interview; necktie in the author's collection.

cciv.   Justin L. Faherty, memorandum to Robert A. Willier, June 24, 1954, "Tillie Lewis Diet Promotion."

ccv.   Tillie Lewis, unpublished photos, Wednesday, June 24, 1953, Saint Louis; Haggin Museum archives.

ccvi.   Schedule of Tillie Lewis's visit to Saint Louis, June 22–26, 1953, Haggin Museum archives.

ccvii.   "It's A Knockout..." *New York Journal*, August 8, 1953, Haggin Museum archives.

ccviii. "21-Day Diet Wins Approval of AMA," *Chicago American*, February 18, 1955, Micke Grove archives.

ccix.   Flotill, Tasti-Diet. 1955. "Doctors Know," San Joaquin County Historical Society archives at Micke Grove.

ccx.   Ancestry.com, "Marion Star. Marion, Ohio," October 9, 1962, record for an ancestor.

ccxi.   Gordon Persons, letter or Tasti-Diet order, April 2, 1953, Haggin Museum archives.

ccxii.   Arthur Heiser, interview with the author.

ccxiii. "Embezzler Gets Terms in Prison," *Stockton Record*, Vallcjo (California) *Times Herald*, December 15, 17, and 29, 1955; January 4 and 13, 1956.

ccxiv. Williams Lewis, interview with the author.

ccxv. "Fund Drive Entertainer—Chico Marx," *Stockton Record*, April 27, 1956, Jewish World Fund Drive, April 14, 1956.

ccxvi. "Arlen Francis to Extol City of TV, November 2," *Stockton Record*, October 16, 1956, Harry Rosen collection.

ccxvii. Ancestry.com and additional facts from the Plaza, New York.

ccxviii. C. J. Pregno, editorial pages: letters, *Stockton Record*, December 6, 1956, Micke Grove Museum archives.

ccxix. "Preserving Natural Taste and Color of Food Products Brings Success," *Stockton Record*, April 6, 1957, Harry Rosen collection to the author.

ccxx. "Warehouse at Cannery Has Unique Design," *Stockton Record*, May 18, 1957, author's collection, gift of Doc Weast.

ccxxi. "Tillie Lewis Paid High Honor by Local Jewish Community," *Stockton Record*, March 4, 1957, Micke Grove archives.

ccxxii. Dorothy Walworth, "The Girl Who Parlayed Pomodoros into Prosperity," *Spectrum*, 1968, Micke Grove archives.

ccxxiii. Flotill football invitation, original card in collection of the author, gift of Doc Weast.

ccxxiv.   Quality in Quantity. Film produced for Flotill starring Tillie Lewis. Original film at San Joaquin Delta College Library.

ccxxv.   Donald K. White, "Tax Men Delay Stockton's Tillie," *San Francisco Examiner*, September 22, 1961, gift from Doc Weast to the author.

ccxxvi.   Crane, Carolyn, "A Person in Time: Tillie Lewis," 1995, used by permission of San Joaquin County Schools, Haggin Museum archives.

ccxxvii.   Cynthia Teremura, "One Nice Tomato," *Guideposts*, 1976, New York.

ccxxviii. Val Alstyne and Noel Corporation, "Preliminary Prospectus," prepared for Tillie Lewis Foods, 1962, pp. 17 and 31.

ccxxix.   Honeywell Computer Application Profile for TLF, 1968, delivered at convention from the Beverly Hilton, Beverly Hills, California, to Mrs. A. Haywood; "For your file!" written in Tillie Lewis's hand, Micke Grove archives.

ccxxx.   Doc Weast, notes, discussion with author of fire at plant and the creation of fruit with rum, July, 2005.

ccxxxi.   www.Paris1965, Beatles, Stones, Kinks, Mini-skirts.

ccxxxii.   Florentine Pabst and Jim Morrison https://www.facebook.com/jim-morrisonfriendsgatheredtogether/photos/a.547746348635774.10737 41827.547740101969732/557292621014480/?type=1&theater

ccxxxiii. Meyer Lewis, letter to Judy Hockheiser about Paris plan, July 1, 1965, Haggin Museum archives.

ccxxxiv. "Five Fireman Injured Battling $150,000 Tillie Lewis Co. Blaze," *Stockton Record*, August 5, 1965, Harry Rosen gift, author's collection.

ccxxxv. Helga Dudman, "Tillie's Tomato Know-How Coming to Israel," *Jerusalem Post*, April 5, 1966, Micke Grove archives.

ccxxxvi. Shirley Lubin, interview with the author and personal photographs, 1967–1969, TLF bowling team women's winners at San Fernando Valley and Lake Tahoe at Harrah's.

ccxxxvii. Tillie Lewis, letter to Ralph Garcia, December 15, 1966, gift of Ralph Garcia to the author.

ccxxxviii. Ogden Corporation newsletter, "For immediate release," 1968, Haggin Museum archives.

ccxxxix. *Stockton Record*, September 1967, October 1968.

ccxl. "Tillie Lewis Attends Food Conclave," *Modesto Bee*, November 10, 1968, Micke Grove archives.

ccxli. Mary T. Brown; Hill and Knowlton, Inc., December 6, 1967, Haggin Museum archives.

ccxlii. *Salina Journal*, Friday, December 15, 1967, p. 10; the *Derrick*, Oil City–Franklin–Claron, Pennsylvania, Tuesday, December 12, 1967.

ccxliii. Vivian Brown, "Women in Business Must Do 5 Times as Good as the Man," *Modesto Bee*, November 10, 1968.

ccxliv. Arthur Heiser, phone interview with the author, March 24, 2006.

ccxlv.   *Tillie Lewis Foods, Inc. v. City of Pittsburg* [Civ. No. 30324. Court of Appeals of California, First Appellate District, Division Four, October 7, 1975]; *Tillie Lewis Foods, Inc. et al., Plaintiffs and Respondents, v. City of Pittsburg et al., Defendants and Appellants; El Pueblo Tenants Council et al., Interveners and Appellants.*

ccxlvi.   George Visgilio, interview online (e-mail & LinkedIn) with the author, May 25–27, 2016.

ccxlvii. Pilot Club speech, New York City, January 1968, Micke Grove archives.

ccxlviii. Ibid.

ccxlix.   Poppy Cannon, General Features Corp. Times Mirror Square, Los Angeles, February 5–10, 1968, Haggin Museum archives.

ccl.   Arthur Heiser, letter to city council of Stockton, March 4, 1968, stamped to FLDR: "Not Added to War Detail Papers but added to Info. Re. T. Lewis"; Tillie was still being watched and kept on file by authorities.

ccli.   Arthur Heiser, interview with the author at Heiser's Stockton home.

cclii.   www.newworldencyclopedia.org/entry/cyclamtes, December 27, 2015.

ccliii.   "Winning Wallflower," *Time*, April 2, 1973, http://time-proxy.yaga.com/time/archive/printout.

ccliv.   Meyer Lewis, letter to Mel Bennet, *Stockton Record*, June 10, 1969, Micke Grove archives.

cclv. "Tillie Lewis Is Boss of Year for Local ABWA Chapter," *Stockton Record*, November 1969, Haggin Museum archives.

cclvi. California Inland World Port," *Tideways*, 1970. Port of Stockton, vol. 19, no. 1, pp. 4–5.

cclvii. George Visgilio, e-mail interview with the author, May 27, 2016.

cclviii. Lester Ginsburg, Tillie Lewis Foods, holiday form letter received by Ralph Garcia, December 17, 1971, gift from Garcia to the author.

cclix. Barbara Heiser, phone call to the author, June 30, 2016.

cclx. Tillie Lewis Foods newsletter, "Meyer L. Lewis 7/4/04–7/31/76," August 1976, Doc Weast, gift to the author.

cclxi. "Advice over Asparagus," *Stockton Record*, May 25, 1972. Haggin Museum archives.

cclxii. Based upon a memory of Halloween at the Lewis household shared by David Lindsey with the author, February 7, 2011.

cclxiii. Judith Heiser, interview at her home with the author; copies of notes and letters.

cclxiv. Dorothy Walworth, "How a Female High School Dropout Built a Business...$150 Million a Year," *Reader's Digest*, reprinted by *New Woman*, November–December 1973, Haggin Museum Archive.

cclxv. Dr. Tillie Lewis, album in private collection of the author, gift from the Heiser family.

cclxvi. Sandy Black, Public Relations Board, Inc., 545 Madison Ave., New York, June 24, 1974, letter in the Micke Grove archive collection.

cclxvii. African American Stockton historian who prefers to remain unnamed, told to the author April 2006.

cclxviii. Tillie Lewis Foods, flyer with photo to publishers, January 1975, gift from Doc Weast to the author.

cclxix. Tillie Lewis Foods, Ogden Corporation notification, August 1975, Haggin Museum.

cclxx. Tillie Lewis Foods, "Two Great Names Get Together," August 23, 1975, Haggin Museum archives.

cclxxi. "Offer Assures Van Cliburn Concert," *Stockton Record*, February 6, 1975, Haggin Museum archives.

cclxxii. Beverly Fitch McCarty, letter, "Stockton Symphony Assoc. Thanking Meyer and Tillie Lewis for $8,000 for Van Cliburn," Haggin Museum archives.

cclxxiii. Beverly Fitch McCarthy, letter, October 12, 1975, Haggin Museum archives.

cclxxiv. Richard Schneider, letter to Tillie Lewis, September 21, 1976.

cclxxv. Helene Heiser, interview with the author.

cclxxvi. Tillie Lewis, letter to Dr. McCaffrey, December 3, 1975, author's collection.

cclxxvii.   George Conley, Sunwave & Trading Co., Taipei, Taiwan, letter to Mr. and Mrs. Lewis, November 5, 1975, Haggin Museum archives.

cclxxviii. Bill Lewis, written interview with the author, November 29, 2009.

cclxxix.   Fred Plum, letter from New York Hospital's Cornell Medical Center, August 5, 1976, Micke Grove archives.

cclxxx.   Tillie Lewis Foods, management newsletter, August 1976, gift from Doc Weast to the author.

cclxxxi.   Bill Lewis, written interview with the author, November 22, 2009.

cclxxxii.   Ibid.

cclxxxiii. "Fight over Tomato Queen Estate," *San Francisco Examiner*, July 24, 1977, gift from Doc Weast to the author.

cclxxxiv.   Margaret Kreiss, "Thank You Letter to Mrs. Alilea Martin," *Sacramento Bee*, February 3, 1976, Haggin Museum archives.

cclxxxv.   Horatio Alger Award Association, "An Investment in America's Future," http://www.horatioaler.org/aboutus.cfm.

cclxxxvi.   *Life* special report, "Winners in a Man's World," April 1976, p. 21.

cclxxxvii. Vince Perrin, letters to the *Stockton Record*, July 6, 2007, www.recordnet.com/article/20070706.

cclxxxviii. Vince Perrin, "Critic's Choice," *Stockton Record*, Monday, January 3, 1977, Haggin Museum archives.

cclxxxix. Tillie Lewis, letter to Carolyn Bird (author of then pending book, *Enterprising Women*), June 17, 1975, copy in author's collection.

ccxc. Marion Jacobs. Oral written interview to author at Ms. Jacobs home in 2003. Ms. Jacobs was gracious and recommended I contact others, including Patti Gotelli for information.

ccxci. Marion Jacobs interview with Kyle Williams at the home of Marion Jacobs June 11, 2004.

ccxcii. Barbara Heiser, phone interview with the author, July 2016.

ccxciii. Program for American Association of University Women. April 30, 1977. Stockton, California.

ccxciv. Marjorie Flaherty, *Stockton Record*, May 3, 1977, article in Doc Weast papers.

ccxcv. Bill Lewis, written interview with the author, November 23, 2009.

ccxcvi. Helen Flynn, *Stockton Record* staff, June 1977, article in Harry Rosen collection, gift to the author.

ccxcvii. "Battle Underway for Tillie Lewis' Huge Estate," *Stockton Record*, July 17, 1977, Haggin Museum archives.

ccxcviii. Helen Flynn, *Record* staff, "Who Gets What? The $11.5 Million Tillie Lewis Left," July 1978, Haggin Museum archives.

ccxcix. Butterfield & Butterfield catalogue, November 7–9, 1977, gift to the author from Barbara and Arthur Heiser, 2008.

ccc.   Dick Clever and *Stockton Record* staff, "Tillie Lewis Auction; Rug Brings $21,000," *Stockton Record*, October 9, 1977, Haggin Museum archives.

ccci.   Helen Flynn, "Who Gets What? The $11.5 Million Tillie Lewis Left," *Stockton Record*, July 1978, Haggin Museum archives.

cccii.   "Tillie Lewis Plant Cutback to Affect 900 Employees," *Stockton Record*, January 22, 1978, gift from Doc Weast to the author.

ccciii. Tim Moran, "End of an Era for Tillie Lewis: Stockton Cannery's Closing Ends Firm's 52 Years in Business," *Modesto Bee*, February 1987.

BIBLIOGRAPHY

Albala, Ken. "The Tomato Queen of San Joaquin." *Gastronomica Journal*, Spring 2010.

Bird, Carolyn. *Enterprising Women.* 1976. McLeod: Canada.

Cannistraro, Philip V. *Historical Dictionary of Fascist Italy.* 1982. Greenwood Press: Connecticut.

Clar, Reva. January 1984. "Tillie Lewis: California's Agricultural Industrialist." *Western States Jewish History*, pp. 139–154.

Epstein, Lawrence J. 2007. *The Edge of a Dream: The Story of Jewish Immigrants on New York's Lower East Side 1880–1920.* Jossey-Bas: San Francisco.

Goldman, Amy. 2008. *The Heirloom Tomato.* New York: Bloomsbury

Goldman, Herbert G. 1992. *Fanny Brice.* New York: Oxford University Press.

Guisepi, R. A. (n.d.) Korean War. http://history-world.org/korean_war.htm.

Hopkinson, Deborah. *Shutting Out the Sky: Tenements of New York 1880–1924.* Orchard Books: New York.

Manekin, Rachel. 2010. "Galacia: The Rise of Anti-Semitism." *Yivo Encyclopedia of Jews in Eastern Europe.* http//www.YivoencyclopediaofjewsinEasternEurope.

Marlow, Joan. *The Great Women.* 1979. Galahad Books: New York

NYU Stern. (n.d.) "History of NYU Stern. Timeline." New York: NYU Stern. http://www.stern.nyu.edu/AboutStern/History/.

Packard, Alice. 1968–1969. "She Made a Million Plus." *Women Who Do*, pp. 117–118.

Riis, Jacob A. *How the Other Half Lives.* 1890. Reprint 1997. Penguin Books: New York.

Thattai, Deeptha. 2001. *A History of Public Education in the United States.* November. http:www.servntfree.net/~aidmn-ejournal/publications/2001-11/PublicEducationInTheUnitedStates.html.

US Department of Labor. 2009. Bureau of Labor Statistics CPI Calculator. February 11. http://www.bls.gov/cpi/cpifact8.htm.

Vogelsang, H. A. 1940. "Preliminary Report on Tillie Weisberg. File No. 100–1432." Police Report: Stockton Police Department, Stockton, CA.

Wilkerson, Michael. (n.d.) Eastern District High School. http://maxweber.hunter.cuny.edu/histo/salzman/schools/Wilkerson.html.